THE JEZEBEL EFFECT

Also by Kyra Cornelius Kramer
Blood Will Tell: A Medical Explanation of the Tyranny of Henry VIII

THE JEZEBEL EFFECT:

WHY THE SLUT SHAMING OF FAMOUS QUEENS STILL MATTERS

KYRA CORNELIUS KRAMER

Original text copyright © 2015 by Kyra C. Kramer

First United States Edition

All rights reserved. No part of this book may be reproduced in any form or by any electronic or mechanical means, including information storage and retrieval systems, without permission in writing from the publisher, except by a reviewer who may quote brief passages in a review.

Ash Wood Press
Bloomington, Indiana

DEDICATION

This book is dedicated to all the women who have been called Jezebels for staying true to what they believe in.

Keep on rocking that boat.

TABLE OF CONTENTS

DEDICATION	5
CHAPTER ONE	8
CHAPTER TWO	23
CHAPTER THREE	34
CHAPTER FOUR	48
CHAPTER FIVE	63
CHAPTER SIX	79
CHAPTER SEVEN	92
CHAPTER EIGHT	114
CHAPTER NINE	125
CHAPTER TEN	135
CHAPTER ELEVEN	145
CHAPTER TWELVE	159
CHAPTER THIRTEEN	174
CHAPTER FOURTEEN	185
CHAPTER FIFTEEN	198
CHAPTER SIXTEEN	214

CONTENTS

CHAPTER SEVENTEEN	232
CHAPTER EIGHTEEN	247
CHAPTER NINETEEN	258
CHAPTER TWENTY	265
CHAPTER TWENTY-ONE	280
CHAPTER TWENTY-TWO	294
CHAPTER TWENTY THREE	308
CHAPTER TWENTY-FOUR	323
CHAPTER TWENTY-FIVE	334
CHAPTER TWENTY-SIX	349
BIBLIOGRAPHY	358
A LOOK INSIDE: BLOOD WILL TELL	389

CHAPTER ONE

"She is such a slut!"

The label of "slut" was feared above all others when I was a teenage girl in the late 80's. Some of the messages were direct; to wit the religious figures assuring me that my virginity was the only thing keeping me from the bowels of hell when I died. Some of the messages were more subtle and coded. My mom warned me not to have premarital sex because, "Why buy the cow when the milk is free?" My sexuality (or lack thereof) was the main reason a farmer would pick me rather than any other cows out there in the dating pasture. Nice boys never married women of easy virtue, so I mustn't be a trollop if I didn't want to die alone and childless. My cherry would not only get me a spot in heaven, it would get me a big rock on my ring finger.

The popular media also chipped in to solidify this ideology. Television and movies showed me that naughty non-virginal women did not ride off into the sunset with the hero. On the contrary, a woman who had sex was either the villainous foil for the heroine and/or a natural target for serial killers, preferably after gratuitous nudity. I learned early and well that the sight of breasts spelled doom for any character in a movie. Books, especially the romance novels I enjoyed, made it clear that a man's emotional compass was his rampant manroot and by golly he had better be the first and only man to dock his turgid ship of love in a woman's throbbing velvet port or she would lose him forever. Not only were romance novelists saddled with an expectation and demand for purple prose, the main way a heroine had sex was via "forced seduction", which the modern reader would recognize as "acquaintance rape". Non-consensual intercourse was just about the only way the heroine was allowed to have sex that would prevent her from being labeled a cheap floozy.

Ah, but things are different now, are they not? A person can comb the shelves for a romance novel with forced seduction and find nary a one. Moreover, the hero of the story is much less likely to expect or encounter a virginal heroine -- especially in a contemporary romance. On both the silver screen and the small screen, the female protagonist can now have sex without necessarily jeopardizing her life or future happiness. If women under the age of 30 run into the old adage about milk and the cow, they are more likely to laugh uproariously than to take it to heart. Mainstream culture has learned to acknowledge that women can like sex. We're all good to go now, right?

Wrong.

In spite of the positive strides toward women's equality that have been taken in the last few decades, the term slut is still alive and roaming freely in the cultural matrix. The odds are high that you have heard about a particular woman being a bimbo. The odds are also high that you've aimed that slur in the direction of a woman who had pissed you off. If you are a woman reading this sentence, there is a strong likelihood that you have been called the equivalent of a rancid doxy by someone who was angry at you.

But what *is* a slut, really? How do you know who is slutty and who isn't? In this enlightened age, why does the word slut continue to stalk women like an overdone specter in an overwrought gothic novel?

Conversationally the word slut conjures up the image of a promiscuous woman, but what determines when a woman is promiscuous? How many sex partners does it take to make her a strumpet? Two? Twenty-two? Two hundred and two? What is the magic number of sex partners that crosses a woman over from being a "good girl" to a "bad girl"? One sexual partner prior to marriage would be unlikely to get a woman labeled a bawdy broad in Belgium, but a single premarital lover could get a woman punished as a prostitute in Pakistan. One culture's puta is another culture's prude.

Although sex is commonly thought to be the main factor in sluttiness, sexual activity alone isn't enough to get you called a minx. When a girl or woman is singled out as a skank it often has little to do with her *actual* sexual history or proclivities. A lot of the time the so-called drossel has not been promiscuous even by the strictest cultural definition. She may have had *less* sexual experience than her peers or colleagues.

So what is the difference between the girl next door and a slammerkin? What does a girl or woman have to do to demonstrate that she is a hussy?

Sad to say, there are MANY things a girl or woman can do that will get her accused of being easy. Instead of bed-hopping, the presumed jade may have developed "too" soon or looked "too" provocative by wearing clothes that were "too" revealing. (Wear a top that looks "too" tight because your sweater bunnies are bigger than average? You slut!) Even if she dresses demurely, she may have gotten "too" much male attention. (Guys think you are hot? You slut!) A woman may have 'stolen' someone's boyfriend or simply been the object of his affection. (My crush asked you out? You slut!)

Then there are the slutty things a woman can do that have nothing to do with her body or physical appearance. The woman may get maligned as being loosey-goosey for having made a man feel rejected, upset, or subordinated by her authority. (Give your opinions "too" freely? You slut!) She may have done something that is typically considered a masculine prerogative and her sexuality becomes suspect because of it. (Have a ribald sense of humor and a crass approach to reproduction? You slut!) She may just be a girl who talked back when she was supposed to shut up. (Have a smart mouth? You slut!)

    Sometimes the inescapable fact a woman has a vagina is enough to get her labeled as a hoochiemama. This kind of misogyny runs rampant, especially in groups of Men's Rights Activists (MRAs). This kind of man deeply resents what he perceives as a woman's "pussy power". (You have something I want and thus I feel as though you have power over me. You slut!) Anonymously and online, MRAs complain that feminism has taught "women to have unbridled sex through lowered moral standards and birth control, [which] has reduced the vagina to a commodity product" and now "it is impossible to tell "the sluts" apart from any other woman" because all women are would-be courtesans who will "open their legs for dinner these days" (Thomas, 2010). Simultaneously and with a complete lack of awareness for the irony, MRAs also complain that women make men "dance for the pussy" but then don't give them any of it as a ploy to control men's behavior (Marcotte, 2011). According to the sophisticated logic of the MRAs, all women are total whores who don't put out enough.

    There is almost no way for a woman or girl to guarantee no one will call her a slut. The use of the word is so vast and varied that a woman can be a virgin and yet still gain the reputation of being Tarty McHo, Mayor of Skeeveyburg. If you are a woman then accusations of sluttiness "can be applied to any activity that doesn't include knitting, praying, or sitting perfectly still lest any sudden movements be deemed whorish" (Valenti, 2009).

The slut label can be hurled in a woman's direction under almost any circumstances. Beyoncé Knowles was called a "whore" and "trashy" because she danced provocatively with her own husband on stage at the Grammys (Harmsworth, 2014). As a woman, Knowles was not supposed to be openly and actively sexual even with the man she has society's theoretical blessing to sleep with. According to Focus on the Family -- a far-right conservative organization that both decries feminism and yet assures women that being married is a feminist thing to do because it empowers women -- a husband's sex drive is "God's gift" to his wife and "it is right and godly to claim your husband's sexual desire as a potent source of influence in your marriage" (Slattery, 2009). Okay, so Beyoncé was right and godly like a boss, right? Nope. She was *too* sexy. Apparently women must be sexy enough to please their husbands but not *too* sexy. There is a line that Nice Young Ladies do not cross but they will never be told explicitly where this invisible line is prior to their attempts to be sexy. A woman will know she has crossed it only after she is called a scarlet woman.

You can also be accused of being a two-bit whore even when you are talking about the avoidance of sex. In 2012 a law student named Sandra Fluke was reviled when she testified to congress about the medical necessity of birth control pills *unconnected to sexual activity* (Bassett and Benderly, 2012). She explained that even women who do not have sex may need birth control pills wholly for medical reasons unrelated to intercourse. For this atrocity Fluke was called a slut by shock-jock Rush Limbaugh, who also demanded she make him a sex tape (Reeve, 2012). Other conservative pundits called Fluke a "skank" and a "shiftless rent-a-cooch from East Whoreville". In Fluke's case, it was simply the act of speaking out in contradiction of the status quo instead of shutting up and keeping her proper place as a woman that made her a slut.

Calling a woman who has the audacity to disagree with you a slut isn't something reserved for conservatives, of course. Conservative pundit Michelle Malkin reports that she has been called a "Manila whore" and worse by leftist opponents (Malkin, 2012). Ed Shultz called Laura Ingraham a "right-wing slut" (*The Washington Post*, 2011). Political comedian Bill Maher called female politicians Michelle Bachmann and Sarah Palin "two bimbos" (Joyella, 2011) and much worse. A commenter on the website for news magazine *Liberals Unite* called Anne Coulter a "slut puppet" (Fischer, 2014). These left-wing attacks on right-wing women make two things crystal clear. The first is that misogyny still runs amok on both sides of the political aisle, and the second is that being called a slut obviously has little to do with sexual activity.

Sluthood poses quite the conundrum. If being slutty isn't based on sexual activity -- if a woman can be a called a mattressback both when having sex and when not having sex -- then what is the real definition of a jezebel? What makes a woman a floozy, and when?

In a nutshell, a slut is a girl or woman who broke a gender based cultural taboo; she did something women aren't *supposed* to do. She was a bad woman.

Once a woman is labeled a tramp her worth, her very value as a human being, is called into question by the smear. Nothing vilifies a woman faster than being called a slut, and the use of the word as a means of discrediting or controlling a woman is called slut shaming. Slut shaming is the go-to method of punishing woman for her perceived sociocultural transgression, sexual or otherwise. In spite of our supposedly post-feminist society, slut shaming is as prevalent today as it was for the Victorians. The margins of the page might have changed but the words are still written in stone and women who don't stay between the lines will learn that they will be made to pay for it.

Any woman can be slut shamed, but what happens when a woman gets real power and/or prestige in her community? Does the slut shaming increase?

Yes and no.

If they are maintaining the sociocultural status quo, then they are usually the recipients of callous sexism rather than slut shaming. Margaret Thatcher, who was profoundly conservative and enacted multiple policies that anchored patriarchal authority into the bedrock of Britain, got called sexist and misogynistic monikers *even by her own party*. She made The Iron Lady her unofficial motto, but it was just the best of a lot of bad choices. She certainly didn't want Attila the Hen as her nickname. Her left leaning opponents indulged in tirades against the "bitch". When she died, people gleefully played the song "Ding Dong the Witch is Dead" from the *Wizard of Oz* as though this were a really witty thing to do. She was also called a cunt, but since male politicians are just as likely to have that delightful word follow their name I'll admit it is a gender neutral insult in the United Kingdom. Nevertheless, it is a not a gender neutral *word*.

Conservative female leaders may be the target of sexism more often than slut shaming, but it still occurs. A Greek journalist called German chancellor Angela Merkel a "dirty Berlin slut" (Phelan, 2012). While I vehemently disagree with the German policy of austerity and can understand why a Greek would be livid, calling Merkel a slut is beyond politics; his comments planted a flag deep in the heartland of misogyny. There has never been as much as a whiff of sexual impropriety about Angela Merkel during her tenure as chancellor. She was slut shamed solely because someone disagreed with her use of her political power, which is independent of any one man's support.

The sexism faced by Thatcher and Merkel is mild compared to what happens when a progressive woman obtains power that seems to threaten gendered ideologies. That is when the bovine feces really impacts with the windmill blades. Just look at what Hillary Clinton has endured. There has not only been the garden-variety sexism, wherein Clinton's body is mocked as fat and she is called the ball-busting bitchy lesbian spawn of Satan; there has also been slut shaming nearly beyond belief. If you Google her name, you'll see the word slut has been used in tandem with the words "Hillary Clinton" an inordinate amount of times for a woman who was never caught-out in any sort of sexual transgression.

NRA spokesman and washed-up one-hit wonder Ted Nugent said of Hillary Clinton, "This bitch is nothing but a two-bit whore for Fidel Castro" (Gertz, 2012). Considering that Ted Nugent admitted that he defecated in his pants for days in order to avoid the draft for the anti-communism Viet Nam War (Read, 2013), his accusations of Hillary Clinton's communist sympathies ring hollow. Nugent's fellow draft dodger, Rush Limbaugh, declared that Hillary Clinton was the "Sex-retary of State" (Strasser, 2012). It's not just middle-aged male drug abusers clinging desperately to their place in the sun that have slut shamed Hillary Clinton, either. The female Air America radio host Randi Rhodes was suspended for calling Hillary Clinton "a big fucking whore" (Huffington Post, 2008).

Moreover, if one should choose to wade into the far right blogosphere, one will quickly discover that "whore" and "slut" are some of the milder sexualized terms being used to denigrate Clinton. Not her political ideology, mind you, which is fair game. No. Those sexual slurs are slut shaming Hillary Clinton as a *person*, not a politician. The vitriol spewed on Clinton, accusations that include the words "slut" or "whore" in them, surpass the political and go straight into slut shaming attempts to get her to go back to her proper place. The people who claim they want her to shut her legs are actually the ones who want her to shut her mouth.

There is a famous French phrase: *plus ça change, plus c'est la même chose* (the more things change, the more they stay the same). It means that after a revolution of any kind has swept through society, it turns out in the long term that not much has really transformed; only the cultural window dressing has been modified. This saying has become a proverb because it is nearly always correct. The feminist movement may have changed some things that make it seem as though we all now live in a world radically different from the misogynistic past, but those changes are not necessarily profound. It is the equivalent to repainting a room and changing the drapes; it makes the room seem new but a closer look shows that all the furniture is still stuck into the grooves it had previously worn into the carpet. You will still hit your shin on the same coffee table you always hit it on when you walk past the sofa. Women may have the right to vote but those who step out of their place and into the public arena are still being slut shamed in an attempt to pressure them to toe the cultural line.

What can be done to actually move the furniture? One of the ways that the metaphorical coffee table can be pushed aside is by changing the perception of history. History is more than mere facts. History is also a narrative, an account of events as seen through the lens of certain perspectives (Hennessy, 2012). For too long the only viewpoint available was history of that looked at through the presumption that slut shaming was a normal, or even correct, way of assessing women. Using the sexual lives (mythical or not) of famous female historical figures to denigrate their accomplishments presents slut shaming as a natural, socially approved, and even *logical* way of valuing women. It reinforces the idea that a woman's true worth lies between her demurely crossed legs. This is particularly true of renowned women rulers.

Very few queens are prominent historical figures on par with Henry VIII or Peter the Great. For the most part queens are less famous because they were sidelined into the roles of crowned consorts and official heir-bearers rather than given access to actual power. Of the queens whom history remembers vividly, most of them are as infamous as they are famous. The biggest reason for this is that, in the words of Laurel Thatcher Ulrich, well behaved women seldom make history. If a woman has been a good girl, she has almost always kept her lips clamped and her knees tight together and has known her "place" in society. In contrast, queens that made their mark on the world have tended to do it in spite of social assumptions about what women should – or could – do.

Slut shamed queens are women who have challenged social mores and changed the world. They are women like Jezebel, who defended her culture and fought back against usurpers. Or like Cleopatra, who did more to keep her kingdom safe from Roman control than most kings of her era. Famous queens are those like Anne Boleyn, whose moral code would not allow her to be a powerful man's mistress. They are women like Katheryn Howard, who dared to have sex for pleasure, or those like Catherine the Great, who enjoyed ruling men as much as she enjoyed them as lovers. As a result of the strength and/or the defiance of gender norms these women displayed, they have all been roundly abused in history as trollops, tramps, and tarts.

Once a queen was historically designated as a brazen hussy, her deeds were subsequently interpreted as slutty without due skepticism. The actions of many famous queens were reverse engineered so that any historical event offered "evidence" of their lewdness, no matter how seriously facts had to be contorted to fit that narrative.

But that was all so long ago! Why should we care about the slut shaming of queens? How do slanders about queen who died hundreds of years ago affect anything in the present?

It matters because history and gender are actually deeply intertwined.

One of the ways that cultural norms about gender, the understanding of the 'way people should be', is transmitted and solidified in the public mind is by official history (Hennessy, 2012). History depicted as a place where women either did embroidery like good girls or slutted it up like bad girls is not only inaccurate, it harms modern women's sense of themselves and what they can accomplish. History *matters* because it is a lens through which people view the world. How can girls or women think of these strong queens as role models or heroines if to emulate them is to risk being slut shamed?

Some of the most dynamic and influential queens who ever reigned have been thoroughly slut shamed during their lifetimes and via historical tittle-tattle long after their deaths. Queens who became powerful in their own right, or who were impossible for men to control, or who flew in the face of past and present cultural assertions about gendered traits, have been configured as floozies. Strong queens expose the idea that women are inherently meek and passive as the flimflam it is. Therefore, these women were seen as threats to social order in the past, and they are still subconsciously viewed that way today. They are also slut-shamed in order to degrade their accomplishments and to make them appear to be gender *anomalies*. Women cannot be as powerful as men, unless they are freaks of nature.

That's why queens stand out. They are womanly symbols of a culture and/or country. In the past they had dominion over all the men in their kingdom. They are feminized power incarnate. Dominant women were often seen as threats to the current social matrix and were discouraged accordingly. While slut shaming was only one of the myriad ways other women warned away from power, it has often been the most effective and has certainly been the most easily employed.

Nevertheless, not all queens have been slut shamed. Some queens pass into history without accusations of putative sluttiness. Why are some queens singled out for slut shaming, while others are left to enjoy a virtuous reputation? What leaves some women remembered as Good Queen Maude and others as the French She-Wolf?

It can't just be that those who were slut shamed were all "too" strong – women who committed the sin of commanding men rather than submitting to them. Isabella I of Castile, Queen of Spain, was not a cat's paw for her husband, King Ferdinand of Aragon; she was his equal. She rode into battle, she conquered, she slaughtered, and she ruled with a stainless-steel grip on her underlings. Isabella I even paved the way for the Spanish Inquisition, which only lunatics think was a good idea. The Spanish Inquisition drove more than 170,000 Jews from their homes and killed or forcibly converted countless others. Isabella I of Castile was no sweet-tempered creampuff. Why isn't she known as Isabella the Cruel? Why are there no rumors she made the beast with two backs with men other than Ferdinand?

For that matter, why isn't "Bloody" Mary I of England slut shamed? She usurped the throne from the lawful queen, Jane Grey, and then murdered the innocent teenager for political reasons (Ives, 2009). That is, by anyone's standards, a crappy thing to do. Since most women who have done something this transgressive get accusations of sexual misconduct added to their list of sins, why is Mary I given a pass?

The most likely explanation is because neither Isabella nor her granddaughter Mary ever sought equality for any other woman but themselves. In fact, both Isabella and Mary saw themselves as divinely appointed outliers and viewed *other* women as a teeming mass of potential sinners. There was no proto-feminism rocking of the boat, I assure you. Both queens actively defended and strengthened cultural norms in general. Thus, their gender became secondary to their support of the larger system. Furthermore, Mary and Isabella were devoutly religious and did everything in their power to spread the influence and control of the Catholic Church, which defined the existing gender ideologies. The Medieval Church made the beliefs in women's inferiority not only correct, but sacred. Supporting the church was the equivalent of supporting the patriarchy of the times.

In contrast, many slut-shamed queens not only rocked the boat, they launched Grace O'Malley-worthy pirate attacks upon it. Although none of them would describe themselves as feminist (no one had invented the word yet), they all -- either overtly or more subtly through art and literature -- advocated for the enlightenment of at least some members of the female sex. This was, like feminism today, not an attempt to reverse society and create female rule over men. It was, like feminism today, an attempt to give women the same rights and opportunities as those who were born with a penis. As a result it was, like feminism today, seen as threat to the social norm. Culture subsequently pulled out all the slut shaming big guns to repel these piratical women seeking to board to the ship of state.

Proto-feminism isn't the only thing to inspire the slut shaming of a queen. Other slut shamed queens broke the gender mold in a way that their cultures could not forgive; the precedent they set was too dangerous. There are also slut shamed queens who have merely been convenient scapegoats for historical events.

Restoring famous queens to their proper place as exemplars of feminine strength means first giving them the respect they deserve. The myth of sluttiness needs to be removed from these queens and historical facts need to be presented without the presumption of female deviance. In this way the cultural landscape can be transformed in small increments until it has become something radically different. Social change is often the result of people being made aware of an inequality and deciding it sucks. Pointing out the way famous queens have been slut shamed in the past may make the slut shaming of the present be viewed with more skeptical awareness.

If nothing else, the history of harlot queens deserves a more honest approach. They need to be seen in their role as rulers and as human beings, rather than as trashy women who happened to wear a crown. They deserve to be remembered for their bravery and will to survive and their canny political maneuvering, not as round-heeled and manipulative dimwits. If they are to be reviled, let them be reviled for actions they have performed while fully dressed.

Look at some famous queens without slut-tinted glasses and what you see will surprise you.

CHAPTER TWO

No book on slut shamed queens could be complete without the one who started it all, the one to whom all other sluts are compared – Jezebel. The Israelite queen Jezebel is one of the most famous women in history and the one of the most well-known of the biblical bad girls. Her name has been synonymous with "whore" for millennia. She reigns as a symbol of evil women in the Torah of Judaism, the Old Testament of the Christian Bible, and in the Islamic interpretations of the texts of the Quran. Considering that more than half of the planet's population subscribes to one of those three religions, Jezebel is a woman of global ill repute.

Too bad everything most people think they know about her is a pile of steaming malarkey.

The combined evidence provided by archeological digs, biblical scholarship, and epistemological analysis offers ample proof that Jezebel was *not* a slut. In actuality, she was a smart princess, brave ruler, loyal wife and loving mother. Jezebel has been the victim of one of the most slanderous and successful smear campaigns in history.

Without a doubt, scripture paints her in a negative light. According to those accounts, Jezebel was a schemer who murdered a local farmer for his land. She reportedly lured Ahab away from his Jewish beliefs with her sexual prowess and had Yahweh's prophets slaughtered to make way for the worship of the Phonetician god Baal. Sacred texts record that a general named Jehu finally saved Israel from Jezebel's terrors.

Jehu shot the king, who was the son of Jezebel and Ahab, in the back with an arrow and then went on to destroy the wicked queen mother. After she was thrown to her death at Jehu's request, horses trampled the body and dogs ate everything but her head and her hands.

Jezebel is more than just a farmer-killing, husband-enthralling, prophet-persecuting wicked queen, however. She has the dubious distinction of being known as the harlot to end all harlots. Even the murders that have been attributed to her are recounted with less censure than her make-up wearing sluttiness. She has been described as "the epitome of carnality", who "stood for everything that was ungodly and unholy" (Carter, 2010:9), a "wicked and corrupt woman, the godmother of harlots and abomination of the earth" (Domini, 2010:21), and a woman whose "cruelty eats like a cancer through both Hebrew Kingdoms and infects more than her own generation" (Phipps, 1992:76). It is claimed that under Jezebel's rule, "Immorality, temple prostitution, even the sacrifice of children were the order of the day" (Higgs, 2004:177). There is even an interpretation of scripture wherein the queen put on her make-up to greet Jehu when he rode into town as a last ditch effort to enslave him to her womanly wiles and spare her life.

She is so conflated with sexual excess and sin that her very name is an epithet used to describe a woman who is a strumpet or a whore. Not a hooker-with-a-heart-of-gold or Pretty Woman type whore either. Nope. If a woman is a Jezebel then she is a trollop with the addendum of a devious, conniving nature. Women who are called "Jezebels" are not merely "seductive in nature with heavily painted faces", they are also women "who are overly aggressive, controlling and manipulative" (Freed: 2012:10) Like Eve before her,

Jezebel is accused of tempting her man into sins he would have otherwise not committed and she is the symbol of all women who imperil others (especially men) with their womanly wiles. A true Jezebel uses her sexual allure to turn good people (usually men) into bad ones. A Jezebel isn't simply fallen woman; she is a woman determined to make others fall too, even if she has to drag them down herself.

Jezebel's name and reputation are not subject to redemption, either. Even when Jezebel is being "defended" in modern media, the idea that she was a murderous bimbo is the bait to entice readers onto the hook. *US News & World Report* featured an article that trumpeted, "Jezebel was a Killer and a Prostitute, but She had Her Good Side". The article declares:

"After her marriage to King Ahab, Jezebel emerges as the power behind the throne ... an opportunity for Jezebel to foster the spread of her Baal religion with its many gods, ritual sex, and temple prostitutes. She hates the monotheistic Hebrew religion ... Under his wife's malevolent influence King Ahab protects and encourages pagan rituals, prompting Yahweh to inflict a three-year drought in a land where people are spurning him. Seizing the initiative, Jezebel imports 450 priests of Baal from her native Phoenicia and has many of Yahweh's prophets murdered ... Jezebel's reputation, however, elevates her notoriety beyond that of other women in the Scriptures. But how much is true? Old Testament stories originating in the mists of time may be rooted in reality, but they evolved into metaphor and parable with each retelling ... This biblical character assassination—if that's what it is —succeeded only too well ... among history's most famous female villains, fictional or real, the pagan queen of Kings 1 and 2 still rules as the most wicked and enduring of them all. (Satchell, 2008)

It is this portrait of Jezebel as a wicked slut that has been hung in the halls of popular imagination. She has become "a sort of shorthand, a quick and efficient allusion to sinfulness" (Gaines, 1999:147). More than that, she stands as a monument to *uniquely female* sinfulness and danger. She is every woman suspected of using her ability to arouse a man to get her own way. Jezebel is furthermore denounced for corrupting other women by example when they see how well her ploys work.

The queen also represents the kind of woman who wants to destroy a man's religious faith. Jezebel has been accused of expanding the worship of Phoenician gods by bringing priestess-prostitutes into her new home when she married Ahab, and "the lure of these legal, readily available, erotic encounters was more than the men of Israel could resist" (Dukhia, 2007:294). Thus, Jezebel not only inveigled her Jewish husband into worshiping false idols, she invented the religious honey-trap for Hebrew men. The queen was the ultimate shiksa nightmare.

Some modern evangelical Christians believe that even now Jezebelesque women are still luring men away from righteousness, breaking up churches and leading men off the Godly path and into the other burning bush. Likewise, the Islamic morality police, the Mutaween, devote themselves to making sure women remain covered lest the Jezebel-wannabes entice devote Muslim males into sin or sinful thoughts. Apparently men cannot be expected to persevere against temptation or be responsible for their own morality when faced with woman-flesh. Men must be *saved* from Jezebels.

Jezebel is reviled as the baddest of the bad, the lowest of the low, and the skankiest of the skanks, but she wasn't any of those things. Theological scholars, historians, and archeologists have found a plethora of information indicating that the stories of the queen are inconsistent, specious and imaginary. All the evidence points to the fact that Jezebel was guilty of nothing more than being the victim of one of the most virulent slut shaming campaigns the world has ever known.

What are the facts of the matter?

In the simplest terms, Jezebel was the daughter of Itho-Baal I, a Phoenician king. Her birth name was Itha-Baal, which meant "woman of the Lord" in Phoenician (Hazelton, 2009). Princess Itha-Baal was married to the Hebrew king Ahab roughly three thousand years ago. Their union sealed a trade agreement and peace treaty between Israel and Tyre. After Ahab's death, their son Joram (Jehoram is an alternate spelling) became the king of the Northern Kingdom. Their daughter Athaliah was married to the King of Judea as part of another peace treaty, and thus Ahab and Itha-Baal's grandson Ahaziah inherited the Southern Kingdom. Jehu, a trusted general, rebelled against both Judea and Israel, murdering both Joram and Ahaziah. Jehu and his comrades then rode to Jazreel to deal with the queen mother. Itha-baal's attendants dressed the queen in her best clothes and cosmetics to confront her would-be murderer. When she saw Jehu, Itha-Baal leaned out of a palace window and called him Zimri, the name of a famous Israelite traitor. Jehu's supporters then threw Itha-Baal to her death. From then on, her name was recorded in Hebrew as I-zevel (Jezebel), which sounded a lot like her given Phoenician name but meant "woman of dung" rather than "woman of the Lord" (Hazelton, 2009).

Marrying Jezebel was an astute political move by King Ahab. Ever since Israel had been split in the Northern Kingdom of Israel and the Southern Kingdom of Judea by civil war, what remained of Israel had been struggling to stabilize itself. It was only Ahab's father,

Omri, who had managed to pull the North out of political and military turmoil. Omri established a strong government and a renowned army, which his son Ahab inherited when he in turn became king of Israel. As king, Ahab expanded Israel's property by warfare, but he was no land-grabbing barbarian who saw the slaughter of neighboring peoples as the only way to increase the importance of his kingdom. He was a king who was also "anxious to share in the trade and the wealth of the nations around him" (Burnham, 1904:181). To that end, he sought an alliance with the Phoenicians, who dominated commercial activities in the region. The quickest way to seal the deal vis-à-vis political partnerships was through a wedding, so Ahab asked to make one of the Phoenician king Itho-Baal's daughters his bride.

Itho-Baal ruled the Phoenician city-state of Tyre, a rich metropolis built around sea trade. Tyre was not only wealthy; it was also a famous center for arts, culture, and learning. It was also the best place for Ahab to seek a Phoenician wife because Tyre had traditional ties to the Jewish people. The previous kings of Tyre had alliances with Hebrew kings David and Solomon and relations between the two nations had been friendly for decades. Tyre had been one of Israel's greatest trade partners under Solomon, and a flotilla of Israeli trading ships had been allowed to travel along with Tyre's merchant fleet. These trade ships had returned "every three years … carrying gold, silver and ivory, and apes and baboons" (1 Kings 10:22). The Bible also explicitly credits King Hiram of Tyre with praising the Lord (1 Kings 5:7), so the Phoenician nation was clearly respectful of the worship of Yaweh.

The strong connection between Israel and Tyre had even been made manifest in the Temple of Solomon itself. Most of the finer materials for the Temple had been imported from Tyre, along with skilled workers to help with the construction. In 2 Chronicles chapter 2 Solomon asks the king of Tyre for help, requesting the services of "a man skilled to work in gold and silver, bronze and iron, and in purple, crimson and blue yarn, and experienced in the art of engraving, to work in Judah and Jerusalem with my skilled workers, whom my father David provided. [8] "Send me also cedar, juniper and algum logs from Lebanon, for I know that your servants are skilled in cutting timber there. My servants will work with yours [9] to provide me with plenty of lumber, because the temple I build must be large and magnificent." In response the king of Tyre sent Solomon the craftsman Huram-Abi, a man of mixed Jewish/Phoenician heritage "whose mother was from [the tribe and/or city of] Dan and whose father was from Tyre."

Marriage to Jezebel also strengthened Ahab's status in his own country. For the king of Tyre to marry one of his daughters to Ahab was an acknowledgement that Ahab was the rightful ruler of Israel and worthy of a princess. Ahab was therefore obviously considered the Hebrew king by the same foreign powers that had acknowledged and befriended kings David and Solomon. Jezebel was an ideal political bride for the king of Israel and Ahab appears to have appreciated his luck.

Jezebel's value as a Phoenician princess meant that Ahab would have taken pains to make her (and thus also her powerful father) happy. One of the ways Ahab accomplished this was by building a temple for his new queen, dedicated to her religion, in order that she might continue to worship her deities in a familiar setting. This was not an unusual thing for a Hebrew king to do for his foreign-born wife, by any means (Miller, 1967:323). Common Jewish men who married

Phoenician brides let the women have their familiar altars, as well. It was considered basic marital courtesy. Nevertheless, the conservative Hebrew minority in Israel was *very* unhappy about the non-conversion of heathen brides and was especially miffed by Ahab's efforts to make his new queen feel at home.

Hebrew purists within Israel were against Ahab's marriage to Jezebel from the very beginning. In spite of the benefit the union would bring, having a former Phoenician princess as queen was seen as a threat to Yahweh's dominion. Conservatives were already concerned about the exogamous marriages to foreign, and thus idolatrous, women that many Hebrew men were making. The new brides brought their natal gods with them and conservatives believed that the women could easily tempt their husbands to worship these new deities with their seductive wifely ways. What if Jezebel used sex to bamboozle Ahab into following her religion? After all, there was precedent; King Solomon's non-native wives cajoled him into the worship of their gods (Nehemiah 23:23-27).

The fear of a negative influence that intermarriage could have on the purity of Yahwism was something that helped shape Jezebel's identity as a "harlot". In modern understanding the word harlot is a derogatory term for a woman accused of promiscuity, but the biblical use of the term simply denoted any woman born to gentile parents. The word harlot only became associated with sexual activity due to presumptions about the "low standard of morality prevalent among the non-Jewish peoples" (Klein, 1979). Jezebel was called a harlot because she was seen as a menace to Yahwism in the same way all alien brides were, not because she was slutty. There was never any suggestion, biblically or historically, that would indicate Jezebel had sex with anyone other than Ahab.

The only harlotry the queen is ever accused of is worshiping gods other than Yahweh and of seducing her husband with her exotic, non-Jewish wiles.

Despite the concerns of the fundamentalists, there is nothing to indicate that Ahab ever began to share Jezebel's faith. Ahab may have allowed Jezebel's devotions to her homeland deities to continue unabated but there is no evidence that he ever turned away from Yahweh to worship them with her. In fact, there is strong evidence that Ahab remained true to his Jewish beliefs. Ahab retained four hundred or prophets of Yahweh in his court to advise him and the names of his children are linguistically connected with Yahweh. His eldest son Ahaziah's name roughly means 'grasped or upheld by Yahweh', and his second son Jehoram's name means 'Yahweh is exalted'. Moreover, there is every indication that Ahab "tolerated Jezebel's religious ideas largely because his people has already accepted no few local Cannaanitish Baals who blessed the crops and vineyards, Yahweh being thought of as rather a desert God, although still peculiarly the God of Israel" (Clarke, 1924:226). Conservatives were therefore especially upset about Ahab's marriage to Jezebel because the worship of deities other than Yahweh, especially Baal, *was already occurring* in Jewish communities. The hardliners feared a non-Jewish queen would only exacerbate the situation.

For conservatives, Jezebel was a nightmare on several levels. Not only was she rich and powerful in her own right, she was a "strong-minded, determined queen, fearing neither God nor man", who was rumored to have "gained, from the first, a complete ascendancy" over her spouse (Burnham, 1904:181-182). In all likelihood this actually meant Ahab was smart enough to listen to his wife's expertise in Phoenician politics and trade. Nonetheless, suggesting that the king was being henpecked was yet another way for conservatives to illustrate to the average Israeli on the street that marrying outside Yahwism was a bad idea. Good women did not worry their pretty little heads about matters of state; they left that for the menfolk. The underlying conservative message was that those foreign bitches made horrible, bossy wives, unlike nice Jewish girls, so you should definitely marry the girl next door instead of some Phoenician hottie who didn't know Yahwism from a hole in the ground.

Another negative, from the point of view of the purists, was that Jezebel brought even more aspects of Phoenician culture to the new Israeli capital of Samaria. The practices of that sophisticated civilization were already much too widespread amongst Hebrews for the comfort of Jewish fundamentalists. Archeological remains of some ancient Israeli cities indicate that they were practically Phoenician cites (Dever, 2012). The Yahwistic intransigents felt, with good reason, that Phoenician culture was swamping Jewish identity. In many ways Israel was decidedly second best when compared to the neighboring nations. Phoenician ships were the best, their glass-making was undeniably superior, they excelled at bronze work, and their skills at dyeing cloth were legendary. Indigo was the clothing color of choice for Mesopotamian royalty and the people of Tyre had a lock on its manufacture and trade to such an extent it was known as "Tyranian purple". Phoenicians were the most powerful and influential people in the Mediterranean region and conservative Israelis didn't like it one bit.

If the queen further popularized Phoenician gentility, how could her gods not become more popular as well? Jezebel, after all, was more than the average follower of the Phoenician religion; she was well educated in her theology and very devout. The queen's father had been the high priest of Baal before he seized the throne and Jezebel had been raised in earnest veneration toward the gods of her people. How could she resist the urge to proselytize her religion?

Jezebel was the epitome of everything the conservative faction of Yahwism feared, and thus hated.

CHAPTER THREE

Much of the conservative discomfort with influences from Phoenician outlanders was predicated on the fact that at the time Yahweh and Baal were a little *too* similar, so that if "the nature and the work were substantially the same, the name mattered little" (Burnham, 1904:181). The names and images associated typically associated in non-Hebrew poems about the god Baal "was attributed to Yahweh at a relatively early point in Israel's religious history (Smith, 2002:56). Yahweh is called "the Bull of Jacob" in Genesis 49:24, which correlates to Baal's icon of a Golden Calf. In Psalm 68:4 Yahweh is called "Rider on the Clouds", which was a term also used for Baal. Some scholars have even "suggested that Psalm 29 was originally a hymn to Baal; its language is in any case strikingly familiar to a reader of the *Baal* cycle" (Coogan and Smith, 2012:15).

Theistic events were also similar in many places. For example, Yahweh defeated the Leviathan in a striking resemblance to the way Baal had achieved victory over a sea god called Yam (Routledge, 2012:99). Moreover, "like Baal, Yahweh revealed himself on a mountain in the midst of a storm; like Baal, Yahweh had a temple built of cedar. In the light of Canaanite religion, the character of the god of Israel looks like a composite" (Cogan and Smith, 2012:15).

To confuse matters further, some scholars argue "that *ba'al* was a title for Yahweh and that the cult of Baal coexisted with the cult of Yahweh" (Smith,

2002:65). The word *ba'al* is "used quite normally as a generic term meaning 'lord' or 'master' and applied to various male deities, but is also the personal name of a god and also ... the designation of autonomous and distinct superhuman personalities" (Moscati, 2001:123). Thus ba'al could have meant any male god, but could also have meant the masculine Phoenician deities Baal Saphon, Baal Malage, Baal Marqod, and the god of Jezebel's people, Baal of Tyre. Hebrew texts using the baalistic words *bb'l* (Lord is father), *b'l* (Baal/Lord), and *b'l'zkr* (Baal/Lord remembers) have had those words translated into modern tongues simply as Lord or God (Tigay, 1986). There is often no obvious distinction as to which specific deity, Yahweh or not, was being mentioned in some of the earliest Jewish records. Figuring out to what degree Baal and Yahweh were conflated is complicated by the profound linguistic entanglements.

Not only did the gods share verbal iconography and mythologies, Yahweh probably even have had a goddess consort named Asherah – just like Baal.

Asherah has long been dismissed from Judeo-Christina dogma, but archeological evidence shows her presence throughout Israel and the ancient Near East. Modern scholars postulate that the worship of Asherah may have occurred alongside Yahweh in the official Judahite religion, or even that Asherah could have been a "female hypostasis of Yahweh" (Ackerman, 1993:392). An archeological site in eastern Sinai, called Ajrud, found evidence of the cult of Asherah being linked to Yahweh from the time of Ahab's rule, in that there were inscriptions reading, "I bless you by Yahweh of Samaria and by his Asherah/asherah", "by Yahweh of the South and by his Asherah/asherah", and "I bless you by Yahweh of the South and by his Asherah/asherah" (Ackerman, 1993:393-394).

The goddess Asherah was associated with trees and groves, and was often "symbolized by a wooden pole or the image of a tree" (Dever, 2005:102). She was so strongly connected to trees and tree images (especially oak, palm, tamarisks, almond, terebinthes, and poplar) that the biblical mentions of planting trees near altars, shrines, or holy places, as well as the multiple mention of burials taking place near or under sacred trees, may be contextual remnants of her worship (Kien, 2000: 159-160). The menorah, the seven-branched candlestick used in some Jewish religious observances still in the modern era, appears to be modeled after the stylized "Tree of Life" that represented Asherah (Cohen, 2010:47).

The goddess was also represented by certain animals, such as the snake, lion, and ibex. In 2 Kings 18:1-4 Hezekiah was lauded for breaking "into pieces the bronze snake Moses had made, for up to that time the Israelites had been burning incense to it." Asherah moreover appears to have had greater prominence in the southern kingdom of Judah (Ackerman, 1993:398-401). Inasmuch as Asherah was linked to depictions of lions, could the goddess be the original reason for the lion symbol of the tribe of Judah?

There are also several passages in the Bible that suggest the worship of Asherah via her sacred trees. For example, when Jacob's father-in-law tried to trick him after promising him every spotted member of his flock, "Jacob ... took fresh-cut branches from poplar, almond and plane trees and made white stripes on them by peeling the bark and exposing the white inner wood of the branches. [38] Then he placed the peeled branches in all the watering troughs, so that they would be directly in front of the flocks when they came to drink. When the flocks were in heat and came to drink, [39] they mated in front of the branches. And they bore young that were streaked or speckled or spotted" (Genesis, 30:37-39). Why would Jacob use poles made from poplar and almond trees to work his sympathetic magic if it were not to call on Asherah, the feminine half of the God of Abraham, for aid? When Joshua reaffirmed the covenant between Yahweh and the Hebrews, he recorded it "in the Book of the Law of God. Then he took a large stone and set it up there under the oak near the holy place of the Lord. [27] "See!" he said to all the people. "This stone will be a witness against us. It has heard all the words the Lord has said to us. It will be a witness against you if you are untrue to your God" (Joshua, 24:26-27). The stone and oak are both thought to symbolize Asherah in ancient Yahwistic practice.

Acceptance for Asherah worship was also implied by what *wasn't* said in sacred text. When Jehu overthrew Ahab's son and became king of Israel, a religious structure built by Ahab to honor Asherah was left unscathed, which "suggests it was perceived as appropriate within official Yahwism" (Ackerman, 1993:394). In 1 Kings Chapter 18, four hundred and fifty prophets of Baal were slaughtered in Kishon Valley but there is no mention of an execution for the four hundred prophets of Asherah that had accompanied Baal's followers (Dever, 2005:211). Why would the prophets of Asherah, who were associated with Jezebel's court, be spared if they were not legitimate practitioners of Yahwism? It seems peculiar that devotion to Asherah was "not widely condemned in the prophetic literature, especially if her worship was so closely connected to that of Baal" (Hadley, 2000:23). The lack of prophetic criticism for the worship of Asherah is a strong indication that devotion to her was once a normal part of Yahwistic piety.

This opens up the possibility, even the likelihood, that Jezebel acted as a priestess of Asherah as part of her responsibilities as queen of Israel (Ackerman, 1998:184). As an official part of Yahwism, the goddess Asherah would have doubtlessly had state celebrations and rituals in her honor that would have been overseen or implemented by the highest ranking woman in the nation, which was obviously the wife of the king. Jezebel is mostly connected to Baal in popular culture, but it is practically a given that she was a follower of Asherah. Not only did four hundred prophets of Asherah "eat at Jezebel's table" (1 Kings 18:19), her father was recorded historically as being a priest of Astarte [Asherah] or a "priest of the Lady" (Moscati, 2001:153). That means that Jezebel would have been, at least in practice, a pluralistic Yahwist and a member of the state cult.

Nevertheless, Jezebel's worship of Asherah -- which would have been seen as a righteous act by the majority of the Israeli populace -- was terrifically problematic for the conservatives. With the queen bolstering the goddess, it would be even more difficult for Jewish extremists to convince the Hebrew people that Yahweh had no consort.

The fundamentalist arm of the Jewish religion was eventually victorious. The goddess Asherah, one of the oldest religious figure on record, "worshiped longer, and in a greater territory than any of the Greek goddesses ... has disappeared almost without a trace" (Kien, 2000:90). The veneration of Asherah, once an accepted component of early Yahwism, has ceased to exist in modern Judeo-Christian theology. How did that happen?

The same way Jezebel became a scheming whore – by rewriting history until it became the Truth.

The early biblical figures that condemned the presence of Asherah in the Yahwist religion were those conservatives who embraced deuteronomistic theology.

Unfortunately, for the followers of Asherah, it was the deuteronomistic theologians who would shape much of later Jewish doctrine. Complete monotheism "only became significant during the Babylonian exile [of the Jews] and was transplanted back to Judah on the return from exile. The Deuteronomistic History is in large part and attempt to backdate this monotheism to an early period when it was not truly present (Cohen, 2010:43). As a result of deuteronomistic editing, the idea that God has both a male and a female aspect was not just removed from the orthodox belief system, the very concept of it was lost to believers *because they decreed that it never existed in the first place*. The veneration of Asherah was repackaged as having *always* been counter to the will of Yahweh and having never been an acceptable part of Yahwism.

The anti-Asherah factions of the fundamentalist Hebrews quickly discovered that there was no "better way to give the cult symbol the stamp of Yahwistic illegitimacy than to associate it with Baal and his cult" (Olyan, 1988:13-14). The condemnation of Asherah worship is sometimes coded as "harlotry" associated with rituals that took place in shade of certain trees (Dever, 2005:214). Other biblical texts, such as some of those in Deuteronomy, were not so subtle in their disdain for Asherah (Dever, 2005:214). For example, Deuteronomy 16:21, 22 commanded that followers should "not set up any wooden Asherah pole beside the altar you build to the Lord your God, [22] and do not erect a sacred stone, for these the Lord your God hates." The sacred stone of the verse is a *massebah*, the same kind of pillar that was erected to honor Yahweh in earlier texts, such as Exodus 24:4 and Joshua 24:26-27. However, *massebah* could serve as a representation Asherah as well as Yahweh, and the deuteronomists wanted no such reminders of her. Over time, the worship of Asherah became sociologically linked with idolatry and paganism.

Signs of the deuteronomistic takeover are present in several places in biblical text. One such example is in the story of Judean king Asa and his grandmother Maakah. Asa was the grandson of king Rehoboam and his wife Maakah. During the reign of Rehoboam, "[22] Judah did evil in the eyes of the Lord. By the sins they committed they stirred up his jealous anger more than those who were before them had done. [23] They also set up for themselves high places, sacred stones and Asherah poles on every high hill and under every spreading tree" (1 Kings 14:22-23). When Asa came to power, he implemented the anti-Asherah policies of the deuteronomists, much to their delight. This included deposing "his grandmother Maakah from her position as queen mother, because she had made a repulsive image for the worship of Asherah. Asa cut it down and burned it in the Kidron Valley. [14] Although he did not remove the high places, Asa's heart was fully committed to the Lord all his life" (1 Kings 15:9-15).

Two things to notice about the story of Asa and Maakah are 1) the indication that the role of queen mother appears to have had a connection with the worship of Asherah, perhaps even as high priestess, since Maakah defied her grandson and continued to make iconography for the goddess and 2) Asa may have agreed with the Yahwistic monotheists but he did not destroy the "high places" devoted to Asherah. Why not? Was it because she was still too popular among the average Judean for the king to risk her total eradication?

Other kings did not follow in Asa deuteronomistic footsteps, and the influence of the conservatives can be seen waxing and waning among those in power. King Manasseh was a strong adherent to Asherah as a part of the Yahwistic religion and ruled Judah for more than fifty years. Manasseh replaced a carved Asherah pole in the temple of Solomon and rebuilt the "high places" his father, the former king Hezekiah, had destroyed. Manasseh's son Amon continued the pro-Asherah policies until he was assassinated by some of his officials. "Then the people of the land killed all who had plotted against King Amon, and they made Josiah his son king in his place" (2 Kings 21:24). Josiah grew up to be a staunch conservative and destroyed anything related to the devotion of gods who were not Yahweh, and anything to do with Asherah as well. When he died in battle, his sons Jehoahaz and Jehoiakim resumed the Asherah-friendly version of Yahwism, as did several kings after them until the conservatives finally wrested control over Yahwistic orthodoxy. The Temple of Solomon stood in Jerusalem for 370 years, and "for no less than 236 years (or almost two-thirds of the time) the statue of Asherah was present in the Temple, and her worship was part of the legitimate religion approved and led by the king, the court, and the priesthood and opposed by only a few prophetic voices crying out against it at relatively long intervals" (Patai, 1990:50).

    The kings were not the only members of the ruling family to adhere to Asherah as a part of their Yahwistic beliefs. Jehoiakim's wife, Nehushta, was also a follower of Yahweh's consort. Nehushta was the daughter of Elnathan and a native to Jerusalem; she was clearly not a foreign bride prone to serving foreign gods but she was nevertheless part of the cult of Asherah. A rough translation of Nehusta's name is "the serpent lady" and Asherah was known, among many other appellations, as Lady of the Serpent. Thus, the queen mother Nehushta can be probably "understood as a devotee of Asherah" (Ackerman, 1998:186). Goddess worship was clearly entrenched as a normative part of Semitic life.

Nor did Yahweh's consort go away quietly when the deuteronomists became the arbiters of the official state religion. Asherah remained in Jewish rituals long after she had ceased to be formally acknowledged as a part of Yahwism. There are biblical records of direct conflicts between those who still wanted to co-worship Asherah and those who wanted Yahweh to stand alone. The prophet Jeremiah told Jews living in Egypt that if they did not stop their reverence for Asherah then God would punish them. Defying the prophet, the people resisted this command:

[15] Then all the men who knew that their wives were burning incense to other gods, along with all the women who were present—a large assembly—and all the people living in Lower and Upper Egypt, said to Jeremiah, [16] "We will not listen to the message you have spoken to us in the name of the Lord! [17] We will certainly do everything we said we would: We will burn incense to the Queen of Heaven and will pour out drink offerings to her just as we and our ancestors, our kings and our officials did in the towns of Judah and in the streets of Jerusalem. At that time we had plenty of food and were well off and suffered no harm. [18] But ever since we stopped burning incense to the Queen of Heaven and pouring out drink offerings to her, we have had nothing and have been perishing by sword and famine." [19] The women added, "When we burned incense to the Queen of Heaven and poured out drink offerings to her, did not our husbands know that we were making cakes impressed with her image and pouring out drink offerings to her?" Jeremiah 44:15-19

Likewise, the prophet Hosea was in despair because the Israelites "consult a wooden idol, and a diviner's rod speaks to them. A spirit of prostitution leads them astray; they are unfaithful to their God. [13] They sacrifice on the mountaintops and burn offerings on the hills, under oak, poplar and terebinth, where the shade is pleasant. Therefore your daughters turn to prostitution and your daughters-in-law to adultery" (Hosea 4:12-13). It's fairly obvious that Asherah is being venerated in her sacred groves, and the prostitution/adultery/harlotry Hosea speaks of is her continued worship.

Clearly, the conservatives faced an uphill battle in eradicating Asherah from Judaism, even centuries after the death of Ahab and the establishment of deuteronomistic authority. The situation must have seemed especially dire for fundamentalists during Ahab's reign. As the queen of Israel, Jezebel's influence would have been seen as a formidable obstacle for the fundamentalist cause to overcome because she promoted and participated in the populist worship of Asherah. Doubtlessly, purists were convinced her relationship with Ahab played a part in his implied rejection of their theological demands.

Jezebel's veneration for Asherah was not the only concern for purists, inasmuch as she also remained faithful to Baal of Tyre. It must be said that the conservative factions may have had good reason to fear the spread of a state cult of Baal. The worship of Baal of Tyre, and other Phoenician deities, may have included the sacrifice of human infants. (This remains hotly disputed among scholars.) It's been theorized that babies or small children were placed into the hands of a bronze statue representing the god, and then rolled down into a pit of flames (Aubet, 2001). The children may not have been burned to death (if that helps); some historians recorded that the child's throat was slit before it was placed on the statue (Markoe, 2000).

Then again, the Hebrews themselves may have been already sacrificing children to fire in Yaweh's name. "Argument persists over the very use of the word *tophet*, which derives from a Hebrew Bible reference to a roasting area in the valley of Ben-Hinnom, where Israelite children were sacrificed by fire. This heinous practice was condemned by the prophet Jeremiah" (Markoe, 2000). Jeremiah, however, lived centuries after Jezebel. Although Jezebel might have seen nothing "wrong" with human sacrifice during her reign, she cannot be blamed for its continued practice so long after her death. A more likely explanation was that it was already entrenched in early Hebrew worship. Perhaps the conservatives were less concerned about child sacrifice than to which god the babies were sacrificed?

All the fears of the purists appeared to be coming true when Ahab began enacting policies that they considered to be flouting the will of Yahweh. It was expected that during war a conqueror would sacrifice captured enemy combatants in order to thank the deity who had provided his victory (Moore, 2003:106). Ahab, in conservative opinion, lacked the bloodlust of the truly devout and was appalling reluctant to slaughter thousands in Yahweh's name. 1 Kings Chapter 20 documents the king's sin against Yahweh:

[1]"Now Ben-Hadad king of Aram mustered his entire army. Accompanied by thirty-two kings with their horses and chariots, he went up and besieged Samaria and attacked it ... [13] Meanwhile a prophet came to Ahab king of Israel and announced, "This is what the Lord says: 'Do you see this vast army? I will give it into your hand today, and then you will know that I am the Lord.' ... [21] The king of Israel advanced and overpowered the horses and chariots and inflicted heavy losses on the Arameans. [22] Afterward, the

prophet came to the king of Israel and said, "Strengthen your position and see what must be done, because next spring the king of Aram will attack you again." ... ²⁶ The next spring Ben-Hadad mustered the Arameans and went up to Aphek to fight against Israel ... ²⁸ The man of God came up and told the king of Israel, "This is what the Lord says: 'Because the Arameans think the Lord is a god of the hills and not a god of the valleys, I will deliver this vast army into your hands, and you will know that I am the Lord.' ²⁹ For seven days they camped opposite each other, and on the seventh day the battle was joined. The Israelites inflicted a hundred thousand casualties on the Aramean foot soldiers in one day. ³⁰ The rest of them escaped to the city of Aphek, where the wall collapsed on twenty-seven thousand of them. And Ben-Hadad fled to the city and hid in an inner room. ³¹ His officials said to him, "Look, we have heard that the kings of Israel are merciful. Let us go to the king of Israel with sackcloth around our waists and ropes around our heads. Perhaps he will spare your life." ³² Wearing sackcloth around their waists and ropes around their heads, they went to the king of Israel and said, "Your servant Ben-Hadad says: 'Please let me live.' The king answered, "Is he still alive? He is my brother." ... ⁴² [an unknown prophet] said to the king, "This is what the Lord says: 'You have set free a man I had determined should die.[c] Therefore it is your life for his life, your people for his people.'" ⁴³ Sullen and angry, the king of Israel went to his palace in Samaria.

Fundamentalists were incensed at Ahab's "betrayal" of Yahweh. In their eyes Ahab had sinned when he forgave Ben-Hadad, because the king was denying Yahweh what conservatives insisted the deity wanted – heaps of slain humans. While Ahab's generosity appears, to the modern reader, to be an act of decency or even a foretaste of the loving God that Jesus would one day preach about, for conservatives the king's decision to spare his captives was nothing less than vile blasphemy against the Lord.

The fundamentalist faction was sent into a tizzy by Ahab's diplomacy. What did this act of mercy on Ahab's part portend? Was this the first step in the rejection of Yahweh in favor of another deity? Their worries soon centered on Jezebel. The queen was decidedly "zealous for her religion. It is understandable, then, why the more conservative Yahwists feared that this king (Ahab) who had so successfully disregarded the charismatic ideal also intended to replace Yahwism with Baalism as the official religion. Thus Jezebel, his Baalistic queen, became the symbol of their grievances" (Miller, 1967:323-324).

Conservatives were terrified Jezebel would lead all of Israel into the arms of Baal, displacing Yahweh as the God of Israel. As late as the twentieth century, theologians were still suggesting that Jezebel's devotion to her religion meant that there had been a real risk that the worship of Baal would be slowly substituted for the worship of Yahweh (Burnham, 1904:181). Deuteronomists saw the official tolerance for Baal's worshipers, the continued Jewish veneration of Asherah, and Ahab's impiety as the results of Jezebel's slutty manipulations. What would that Phoenician harlot convince Ahab to do next?

Queen Jezebel had become a lightning rod for fundamentalist anxieties.

The conservative Hebrew faction found their spearhead in Elijah the Tishbite. Samaria was in the middle of a long drought and subsequent famine when the prophet Elijah first approached Ahab. He challenged Ahab to bring the prophets of Baal and Asherah to Mt. Carmel to determine once and for all who was who was God, Yahweh or Baal. A sacrifice of a bull was set up for both deities, but only Yahweh rained fire from the heavens to consume the offering. Having established Yahweh's dominance, Elijah had the prophets of Baal (but not of Asherah) put to death.

The key point of the demonstration of Mt. Carmel was not that Yahweh was stronger than Baal; Elijah was asserting that *only* Yahweh actually existed and that all other gods were idols or figments of the imagination. Elijah had shown Yahweh's "rule over nature that eliminates the nature god Baal from consideration as a living deity" (House, 1998:261). Whereas other religions were welcoming of a polytheistic détente, believing that all gods and goddesses had validity to their adherents, Elijah and the conservatives demanded that people choose only the one true god Yahweh as the object of their veneration. Furthermore, they were willing to compel Yahwistic veneration at the point of a sword.

It is clear in the Biblical text that it was Ahab, the king, who did not capitulate to Elijah's demands to establish a theocratic reign. It was Ahab who would not strictly enforce the sole worship of Yahweh and forcibly prevent the worship of other deities within his kingdom. Nonetheless, only Jezebel is given credit for this refusal, as recorded in 1 Kings 19: 1-3. [1]"Now Ahab told Jezebel everything Elijah had done and how he had killed all the prophets with the sword. [2] So Jezebel sent a messenger to Elijah to say, "May the gods deal with me, be it ever so severely, if by this time tomorrow I do not make your life like that of one of them." [3] Elijah was afraid and ran for his life."

Jezebel was considered a force to be feared even by the mightiest of Yaweh's prophets.

CHAPTER FOUR

Apart from religious fears, there may have been legitimate grievances against Jezebel. The fundamentalist bias against her does not necessarily mean she has been totally slandered; just because she wasn't a harlot doesn't axiomatically mean she was a nice person. Based on the narrative in 1 & 2 Kings, Jezebel had an innocent man, Naboth, murdered so that she could seize his vineyard for her husband. Certainly, her behavior toward Naboth and her theft of his vineyard was reprehensible. Was Jezebel an evil queen?

Probably not.

For one thing, the veracity of story is suspect according to biblical scholars. There are two versions of the events regarding the theft of Naboth's vineyard (one found in I Kings 21 and the other in II Kings 4:25-26), and a studied "comparison of the two reveals important discrepancies regarding the type of property Naboth held, its location, the number of victims, the nature of the crime, the time of day of the crime, the presence or absence of a prophet, and Jezebel's involvement" (White, 1994:67). Moreover, the prophecy regarding Ahab's punishment for stealing Naboth's vineyard in I Kings 21:19 is fulfilled in 1 Kings 22:35-38, and yet the prophecy given in 1 Kings 21:21, 27-29, which indicated that Ahab's punishment would be put off until later and encompass the destruction of his descendants, is also reported to be fulfilled in 2 Kings 10:10,17 by Jehu's murder of Ahab's family (White, 1994:72). Each prophesy cannot be fulfilled simultaneously.

Even if the story had some basis in reality, it is not focused on Jezebel's iniquitousness. There is strong linguistic and historical evidence that the version given in 2 Kings is the older, and therefore more truthful, account of the theft of Naboth's vineyard (Rofe, 1988:96). This narrative does not condemn only Jezebel; it also presents the elders of the village as evildoers. It is the elders of the community, not the men that had given false statements against Naboth, who "lead Naboth from the city, stone him, and send the final report to the Queen. The circle of guilt spreads far beyond the queen herself" (Walsh, 199:1992).

Also adding to the implausibility of Jezebel's involvement with the theft of Naboth's property is the fact she is so ham-handed about it. When she writes to the elders of the unnamed town near Naboth's vineyard, in order to have Naboth framed for a crime and executed, she "reveals the whole plot in the letters to the notables instead of secretly hiring the false witnesses" (Rofe, 1988:91). Rather than the schemes of a cunning woman, this narrative has all the over-the-top nefariousness of a theatrical villain whose only purpose in the story is to be exposed and punished by the hero.

Ahab's unresisting compliance with Jezebel's schemes paints a very unattractive portrait of him, as well -- especially by the standards of the times. His dependence on Jezebel makes him look weak, henpecked, and as though he were a thief who is not even bold enough to steal but instead relies on a mere woman to steal for him (Rofe, 1988:93). Obviously, this is a deuteronomist dig at Ahab, but it is also more fuel on the fire burning Jezebel's memory at the stake. Jezebel had "usurped the power and prestige of the king" (Laffey, 1988). This is a very bad thing for a woman to have done to any husband of the era, let alone a royal one. A man who was dominated by his wife looked unmanly and foolish, but the wife who dominated him was perceived as unnatural and probably evil.

There isn't much plausibility in the idea that Jezebel was even peripherally the villain of the infamous land grab. Biblical scholars have provided strong evidence that it is "unlikely that Ahab, Jezebel, or Elijah were actually involved in the affair of Naboth's vineyard" (Miller, 1967:312). The whole incident appears to be manufactured in retrospect as "proof" of Ahab's weakness and Jezebel's wickedness in order to vindicate the fact the new king Jehu had murdered the queen, her son, and her grandson to get his crown. Ahab and Jezebel's presence in 1 Kings 21:21, 21-29 was most likely "authored by a supporter of King Jehu, probably a member of his scribal corps, shortly after the coup" (White, 1994:76) in order to create "a version of Ahab's crime that permitted a highly specific *ex eventu* prophecy of dynastic extermination designed to anticipate and legitimate Jehu's bloody usurpation" (White, 1994:75). Making Jezebel the main actor in the theft of Naboth's land was simply a justification for her murder that did not involve discussion of her loyalty to her religion or her devotion to her husband and sons. Furthermore, the story that Naboth's sons were also killed with him was probably "a conscious anticipatory justification for [Jehu's] slaughter of Ahab's entire family" (Miscall, 1989:79). Jehu attempts to soften his crimes with the idea that the children of Ahab and Jezebel deserve their fate as a direct result of their parents' mendacity and sinfulness.

Modification of sacred writings by later authors has never been uncommon. Biblical texts have been amended by scribes over the ages by with metaphors or descriptions that would add context for the perceived reader. During the narrative in Genesis when "Joseph was exalted by Pharaoh and made vizier of Egypt the scribe, writing a thousand years after the event, thought to underline Joseph's important by adding, 'And he made him ride in the second chariot which he had; and they cried before him, Bow the knee …' (Genesis 41:43). He was not to know that horses and chariots were unknown in Egypt in Joseph's day, before the Hyksos invasion" (Loewenthal, 1972:40). The purpose of adding horses and chariots was not to obscure or change the text, but rather to clarify it for the present audience. There are other places where biblical text has almost surely been altered by the scribes who were translating or copying the passages, although the "editors, as we may call them, used their imagination … with the best intentions" (Loewenthal, 1972:40).

Then there are cases where the text has been obviously been changed to correct a contradiction or to change the narrative. In 2 Samuel 24 the Lord commands king David to take a census of Israel and Judah, but then God punishes David for taking the census by sending a plague to wipe out seventy thousand Hebrews. A later scribe noticed that this didn't make any sense whatsoever, and thus rewrote the same event in 1 Chronicles 21 so that Satan was the one who had incited the king to commit census. Likewise, in John 8:1-11 there is the well-known story of the adulterous woman Jesus saved from the death penalty by saying "Let any one of you who is without sin be the first to throw a stone at her." However, this narrative is not found in any surviving Greek Gospels prior to the fourth century; there is a strong likelihood that someone added it in hundreds of years after the death of Jesus to illustrate Christ's compassion.

Taking the many examples of a biblical alterations or errantry into account, it is clear that the story of

Naboth's vineyard is very flimsy evidence for Jezebel's perfidy.

Jezebel's murderer patently needed to make up good excuses for his massacre of the royal family and theft of the crown, because Jehu was neither a popular nor respected king. There is archeological evidence that Jehu bowed down before Assyrian overlords and possibly even the Assyrian gods (Moore, 2003:99-100), something Ahab never did, and written history has not been any friendlier to Jehu than archeology has been. He was considered a repulsive figure by many theologians, even in antiquity. In his writings, St. Augustine castigated Jehu and speculated that he only overthrew the House of Omri because of "the lust of his own domination" (Moore, 2003:98). St Augustine was a man who disliked women intensely, because they had such delightfully tempting vaginas; he would have had no sympathy toward Jezebel to motivate his condemnation of Jehu. Clearly, Jehu's bad actions spoke for themselves.

There is ample evidence that Jehu's accomplices altered religious texts to justify and/or camouflage his terrorism (Moore, 2003:100). Biblically there are certain forms that are observed to demonstrate authenticity. When the dynasties of Jeroboam and Baasha were destroyed, it was clear that they were punished by Yahweh. The Lord had spoken first through Ahijah the Shionite in 1 Kings 15:29 and then through Jehu the prophet (who should not be confused with the Jehu who murdered Jezebel) in 1 Kings 16:11-12 (Miscall, 1989:73). In contrast, the narrative of Ahab's theoretical death in battle, after which the dogs were reported to have licked up his blood, "was described as a fulfillment of a word of the Lord, but there is no indication as to when the word was spoken or by whom" (Miscall, 1989:73).

Yahweh's appointment of Jehu as rightful king is also suspect. In the original text the man who anoints Jehu is described as "mesugga", which is translated as "madman" (Moore, 2003:110). There was no mention of Elijah or any other esteemed prophet of Yahweh until later. Even then, details are shady. Although the later texts about Jehu's rise claim to be quoting Elijah, the prophet's words and actions do not reflect Yahweh's commands in other writings. Elijah does not simply repeat the punishment that Yahweh told him was in store for Ahab, but instead "Elijah displaces the Lord's commission and delivers a sweeping and traditional condemnation of Ahab, his house (dynasty) and Jezebel which accords with all of Ahab's and Jezebel's actions" (Miscall, 1989:76). The way the text is written, Jezebel's death is not the will of the Lord, but the will of Elijah, and therefore also his spiritual heir, Elisha, who is considered the conduit of Jehu's Yahwistic kingship. Furthermore, the madman who anointed Jehu did he did not follow Elisha's supposed instructions and anoint Jehu "King over Israel"; instead he commanded Jehu to "destroy the house of Ahab" and included specific threats against Jezebel (Moore, 2003:103).

Moreover, when there are biblical records of his interactions with a named and important prophet of Yahweh, such as Hosea, things did not go well for Jehu. Hosea 1 it talked about explicit punishment for Jehu's sins: [4]"Then the Lord said to Hosea, "Call him Jezreel, because I will soon punish the house of Jehu for the massacre at Jezreel, and I will put an end to the kingdom of Israel. [5] In that day I will break Israel's bow in the Valley of Jezreel." Jezreel just happens to be the place where Jehu murdered what was left of Ahab's house, including Ahab's children, "as well as all his chief men, his close friends and his priests" (2 Kings 10:11).

Jezreel is also the place where Jezebel met her death at Jehu's instigation, and where the dogs ate her body.

There is an awful lot of biblical ink devoted to the death of Jezebel; much more than would normally be required to describe the death of a deposed king's mother. Why is this one particular woman such a focus for Jehu's animosity? When Joram asked Jehu if he had come in peace, Jehu responded "How can there be peace … as long as all the idolatry and witchcraft of your mother Jezebel abound?" (2 Kings 9:22). Why is she used to rationalize the destruction of Ahab's household more than the transgressions (falsified or not) of Ahab or his sons?

The biblical account of Jezebel's death, which was probably originally written by Jehu's lackeys, is full of symbolism designed to highlight her villainy and his righteousness:

[30] Then Jehu went to Jezreel. When Jezebel heard about it, she put on eye makeup, arranged her hair and looked out of a window. [31] As Jehu entered the gate, she asked, "Have you come in peace, you Zimri, you murderer of your master?" [32] He looked up at the window and called out, "Who is on my side? Who?" Two or three eunuchs looked down at him. [33] "Throw her down!" Jehu said. So they threw her down, and some of her blood spattered the wall and the horses as they trampled her underfoot.[34] Jehu went in and ate and drank. "Take care of that cursed woman," he said, "and bury her, for she was a king's daughter." [35] But when they went out to bury her, they found nothing except her skull, her feet and her hands. [36] They went back and told Jehu, who said, "This is the word of the Lord that he spoke through his servant Elijah the Tishbite: On the plot of ground at Jezreel dogs will devour Jezebel's

flesh."[37] Jezebel's body will be like dung on the ground in the plot at Jezreel, so that no one will be able to say, 'This is Jezebel.'"

First, there is the account of Jezebel's cosmetics. Jezebel has become so synonymous with her makeup that she has been nicknamed the "Painted Queen" (Loewenthal, 1972:21). Why did Jehu's scribes think the fact she dressed and styled herself as any highborn Phoenician woman would have was a matter important enough to be given a place in the religious record?

Some theologians have argued that Jezebel applied makeup in order to try to seduce Jehu, but this is blatantly improbable when taken in context (Olyan, 1985:205). Jehu had murdered Jezebel's son and grandson and was a Yahwist insurgent determined to suppress the religion of her homeland. These are not actions that typically make a woman's heart skip a beat; these are actions that will motivate a woman to stab you to death. Instead of wishing to appeal to Jehu, Jezebel's preparations were more likely to have been a display of her inherent majesty, a "defiant posture" and not a sign she was "trying to seduce Jehu" or was "even seeking mercy" from him (Olyan, 1985:206).

Regardless of Jezebel's motivations – real or imagined -- for wearing cosmetics, the fact she had donned makeup has been used for centuries to allegorize her sinfulness. Women have often been portrayed in Judeo-Christian theology as a colliery of the original Eve, who was the "author of sin" because she was foolish enough to defy God and eat from the forbidden tree of knowledge, (Polinska, 2000:48-49). Worse, Eve tempted Adam into joining her in her disobedience. Christian theologians of yore thought that since it was a woman who tempted a man into sin, and sin is the inability of the mind to control the body, it was women who introduced sin (and hence death) into the world. Judaism does not embrace this doctrine of "original sin", but conservative sections of the faith likewise see women as a threat to Jewish law because they compromise men's abilities to resist the baser human impulses. Even today, "women's sexuality continues to be viewed as disruptive and threatening" (Christ, 2002:90).

A woman's charms are considered perilous because they can be used to seduce and tempt men. Men have long been held as more logical and less emotional that women, but masculine stoicism apparently exists only outside of sexual congress. A "woman displaying her own beauty was considered immoral not because she failed to protect her own sexuality but because she failed to protect the sexuality of men ... man is a victim who succumbs to the insatiable carnal lust of woman" (Polinska, 200:49-50). For a woman to try to make herself appear attractive beyond what nature had provided her was considered more than a lack of modesty; it was also a sign of her spiritual deficiencies inasmuch as it revealed her *willingness* to harm men. Women are required to not only resist personal sexual temptation; they are also responsible for preventing men from experiencing that temptation as well. Therefore women, rather than men, are at fault for inappropriate masculine lusts (Polinska, 2000:49). This means that the woman is always the *real* perpetrator in any case of sexual impropriety unless she can prove otherwise.

Jezebel's eye makeup demonstrated her failure to be a moral gatekeeper and revealed her to be a "bad" woman. As such, she deserved her punishment. Just as modern rape victims are frequently slut shamed because they were "too provocative" – i.e. scantily dressed or flirty – and were somehow "asking" to be sexually assaulted, Jezebel was "asking" to be murdered by Jehu because she was dangerously sexual. When Jezebel put on her mascara she was enhancing and flaunting her beauty, which was a singularly feminine weapon that could only be used to drag men down to the base carnal level of women and force them to sin. This narrative means that Jehu didn't *really* murder a grandmother to gain power for himself; he slew a troublesome strumpet in order to save the men of the community.

Jehu's scribes indubitably went to great lengths to tie Jehu's coup with Yahweh's will. Even Jezebel's act of looking out of the window implied that her murder, and her family's murder, was justified. In Canaanite royal society, images of women in windows were often used to indicate they were the earthly representative of a goddess, including Asherah (Seeman, 2004:16). The "lady-in-the-window" motif was a common way to represent many goddesses throughout the Mediterranean and the Near East. Some scholars automatically assumed that the depictions were used to advertise temple prostitution, but it is much more likely that the images are "a manifestation of a widely diffused practice, the taking of commercial oaths before windows framing the images of a goddess" (Silver, 1995:15). Asherah has, as have other goddesses, been erroneously associated sacred prostitution to the present day, largely due to a long line of academics that were "unable to imagine any cultic role for women in antiquity that did not involve sexual intercourse" (Yee, 2003:88). However, for Jewish fundamentalists the act of looking out of the window would have been symbolically linked with the "harlotry" of goddess worship. That is one reason why when a woman looks out of window in a biblical text it almost always indicates a disaster or the "downfall of despised regimes or kin groups" (Seeman, 2004: 15).

If Jezebel, looking out of the window, was the representation of Asherah, then having the queen thrown down from the window served a twofold purpose. It wasn't just the queen who died. Jezebel's fall symbolically represented the destruction of Asherah worship in Yahwism (McKinlay, 204:91). Not only did the model of deviant womanhood meet her end, so did the deviant worship of the feminine consort of Yahweh.

Clearly the pro-Jehu revisionists were pulling out all the stops to portray Jezebel as the absolute nadir of womanhood, the sluttiest harlot to have ever plotted to deceive and destroy men. Why did her enemies feel the need to emphasis this to such an extent? Why wasn't it enough to simply reiterate that Jezebel was promoting a religious system that competed with the pure Yahwism that the prophet Elijah demanded the Israelites practice? Why didn't the storied theft of Naboth's vineyard provide enough justification for her downfall? Shouldn't have those two thing been plenty of reason to explicate her divine punishment? Banging the drum so hard over Jezebel's harlotries seems like overkill.

A clue as to why Jezebel's destruction needed to be so strongly linked with the anger of Yahweh may lay in the fact that she was in Jezreel when Jehu came for her. Why was she there? Samaria was the capital city and it held the temple of Baal. Shouldn't a Baalistic queen be in Samaria? Not if Jezebel was functioning as the "queen mother" and thus one of the primary priestess of Asherah. It is possible that Jezebel's, "cultic attentions in Jezreel … may have been focused on the state religion of the northern kingdom that paired the cult of Yahweh and the cult of Asherah" (Ackerman, 1998:185). This would mean that when Jehu murdered the queen she was acting as a priestess in the *legitimate* Yahwistic practice of Asherah veneration. If Yahweh didn't demand Jezebel's death, then Jehu would have been guilty of sacrilege (in the eyes of the non-deuteronomistic population) when he slaughtered the queen.

The deuteronomistic scribes who wrote Jehu's narrative portray the usurper as a Yahwistic purist, implying that *of course* he killed Jezebel because of her harlotries with Asherah. This portrait of Jehu is not in line with other biblical records, however. Not only did Jehu leave the shrine/statue/pole to Asherah standing in Samaria, it was still there when his son's reign ended (Patai, 1990:44). Either the worship of Asherah was a legitimate part of Yawehism, or Jehu let the worship of foreign deities continue unabated during his reign. Regardless of the choice, Jehu's murder of the rightful king appears to have been done for his own bloody ambition rather than for Yaweh's glory.

It is also possible that the further blackening of Jezebel's name was important because she publically compared Jehu to Zimri "you murderer of your master". Zimri was punished by Yahweh after he overthrew and murdered his king, and Jehu had committed the same crime. Comparing Jehu to Zimri was a serious insult and threat, considering that Zimri was rejected by the people and ruled for only seven days before being displaced by a better ruler (Olyan, 1985:204). Jehu had shot his lawful king *literally* in the back when Joram had trustingly agreed to meet him. Jezebel cannot have been the only one to notice that the new kid in crown was walking in Zimri's footsteps. She may have therefore been symbolically used to represent anyone who dared to remark on Jehu's semblance to Zimri. Her swift punishment and the fact her body was eaten by dogs, which was configured as a product of Yahweh's wrath, served as a warning of what would happen to anyone else who compared Jehu and Zimri. There was a twofold implication in her demise: 1) Yahweh would doom anyone who castigated Jehu for his regicide and slaughter and 2) anyone who noted the similarities of Jehu and Zimri *was like Jezebel*, and was therefore guilty by their association with a murderous, idolatrous slut.

The story of Jezebel's death also carefully avoids Jehu's direct murder of the queen. The image of a war-hardened general approaching the woman who had ruled Israel for more than thirty years, a grandmother whose son and grandson he had slain, and hacking her to pieces with a sword was not one Jehu's scribes wanted to put into the reader's mind. Instead, by having eunuchs throw her to her death, it is implied that her death was done by her own household and by the will of the people. See? Her own eunuchs didn't like her! Jehu just happened to call upon "the people" in a kingly way and command them to throw Jezebel out of the window, the same window that symbolized her connection to Asherah.

It wasn't enough for Jezebel to fall to her death, though. Jehu's scribes thoughtfully mentioned that her body was trampled by horses once it hit the ground. Why? Jezebel was clearly either dead or mortally wounded, because her blood had splashed on the wall. How did horses add to the narrative? In poems, songs and stories of the ancient Mediterranean and Near East the horse represented energy and action (Hannah, 2006:90-109). However, this energy was often represented as controlled by man only with the aid of the divine. For example, passages in the Iliad featured the words of a horse named Xanthus, who told Achilles that his death would come about "by force combin'd of God and man" (Hannah, 2006:100). There are many biblical examples of horses being sent by the Lord (Zechariah 1:7-11; 2 Kings 2:11) and passages where those who Yahweh wished to punish were trampled or threatened by horses as a final sign of God's disfavor (Judges 5:22; Jeremiah 6:23). The horses that trampled Jezebel are yet another effort to make it appear as though it was the Lord's will, rather than Jehu's, that killed her.

As a final indignity, when Jehu sent men to bury Jezebel's body they found that the dogs had eaten every part of her but her head, hands and feet. Jehu pointed out that this was exactly what the prophet Elijah had said would happen, and was thus God's will. Of course, Jehu's explanation of Yahweh's will applies to "the destruction of Jezebel's corpse" but does not encompass "her actual death, which was his work" (Miscall, 1989:80). Jehu and his scribes were perhaps not unfamiliar with "tweaking" confirmation of the Lord's will. There is a notable peculiarity, however. If Jehu was expecting dogs to eat Jezebel's body because Yahweh had commanded it via Elijah, then why he would send men to bury the body beyond the reach of dogs?

Dogs ate Jezebel's body in the biblical account for the same reason horses had trampled it; the dogs represented divine wrath. Additionally, dogs represented the vilest insult that Jehu's scribes could heap upon the queen's corpse. Dogs were both feared, in their guise as tools of war and as guards, yet loathed as contemptible dung eaters. That is why so many insults, even today, link the word "dog" with someone who is being conveyed as both a threateningly evil and/or disgusting object. Note that the word "bitch" is still thrown like a verbal rock at women who seem to be usurping masculine traits, such as competiveness or aggression (Hazelton, 2009:173).

Early Jewish interpretive tradition suggests the dogs did not eat certain parts of the queen's corpse because those "were the portions of her body that had been used for good" (Snyder, 2012:183) However, there is evidence that the account of Jezebel being devoured by dogs has been "doctored" to fit the cultural beliefs of the time, at the very least. The idea that dogs would not eat Jezebel's palms, skull, or feet is appears to be a cultural construction based on a widespread Middle Eastern belief that dogs are repelled by henna. Since applying cosmetics included using "henna as a colouring agent to [women's] palms, soles, nails, and hair", it was obvious to the person who recorded the story of Jezebel's murder that the dogs would have *necessarily* avoided eating the hennaed areas of her corpse (Loewenthal, 1972:21).

Jezebel, a Phoenician princess, Israeli queen and high priestess had met the most ignoble end her detractors could think of.

CHAPTER FIVE

Jezebel's life was over, but the queen did not go away quietly. Her name has become a byword for a woman's incitement of the "lusts of the flesh", or a temptation for the pleasures of the world rather than spiritual rewards. It also serves to represent women's unnatural, perhaps evil, "attempts to wield power" (Snyder, 2012:182). Ergo, the story of Jezebel encapsulates misogynistic beliefs about women and subconsciously excuses sexist behavior because all women are *potential* Jezebels.

In this vein, perhaps those who wrote about Jezebel's application of cosmetics before Jehu's arrival wanted to emphasize her femininity for reasons other than calling attention to her use of her physical charms. Was her femininity highlighted to make her "masculine" militaristic taunts for Jehu seem appallingly at odds with the "natural" behavior of her gender? Some theological scholars argue that Jezebel's primping conveys "the message that not only is this queen mother marked out to be the loser, but that such a powerful and assertive woman deserves what is coming to her [The reader is] meant to be shocked by the dissonance of a woman with all her femininity displayed being apparently engaged in a military encounter and uttering battle taunts. The writer wants his readers to understand that while this is indeed a woman in all the feminine senses, this is one who has not acted her part as a woman in Israel, and women who do not behave like women … must fall"

(McKinlay, 2004:81-82). Jezebel's death thus becomes the inevitable consequence of being an *unnatural* woman. A *bad* woman. A *slut*.

Jezebel's motive for dominating men is also portrayed as more than her personal ambition; the queen's evil encompasses gender ideology. She didn't just bully men to gain ascendancy over them; she was actively trying to damage all men and masculinity itself. Like their namesake, modern Jezebels are said to entice men in order to cause them harm. If a man overpowers (figuratively or physically) a Jezebel, then he is a victor over an evil power, not a villain who hurt a woman. In this way men who are "pickup artists" are reconfigured as semi-heroes who are cleverly tricking Jezebels into giving up their power, in contrast to the mendacious misogynists they really are. The pickup artist's adversarial relationship with women can be considered reasonable, provided that all women are present or potential Jezebels.

Likewise, fear of Jezebel explicates why men who are sexually promiscuous cannot be sluts. The twisted cultural logic goes like this: Only women who are Jezebels have premarital sex. Therefore any woman granting a man sexual access is a Jezebel. Since a Jezebel has ability to lure men into coitus, the sex act *was not his fault* because he was seduced by her overwhelming harlotry.

Sometimes the "seduction" used by a Jezebel is her unprotected, unconscious body being available for predation. Men who rape can rely on the jury to wonder if the woman was a Jezebel-type who "asked for it" in some way and/or got what she "had coming to her". Often a rape victim must prove that her sexual assault wasn't the punishment she received for tempting a rapist. Rape culture maintains that if she was metaphorically standing at the window putting on makeup, then what did she expect?

There is even a racial aspect to the term Jezebel. The three most common stereotypes attached to black women in America media are the Mammy, the Sapphire, and the Jezebel (Mance, 2006). Although Mammy's happy servitude and Sapphire's acerbic hatefulness are problematic enough, it is in Jezebel that we find the slut shaming *specifically* of black women for the crime of being desirable. Jezebel lies at the intersection of race and gender, doubling the power of the label to harm. The concept that black women were more sexually indiscriminate and available than their white counterparts allowed society to pretend they were willing participants of their own victimization. This idea provided the reasoning behind a culture that has "tolerated and even encouraged the white, male sexual exploitation of black women servants ... the seductress Jezebel undermines men's control (especially white men's control) over their own sense of sexual propriety through her primal and irrepressible erotic advances " (Mance, 2006:474-475). In sum, it was totally the black woman's fault if white men were moved to sexually assault her because she had tempted them like the Jezebel she was.

Jezebel's reputation isn't becoming a more benign as time passes, either. If anything, she is being upgraded from witch-whore to flat out demon.

Some modern evangelical Christian pastors caution their fellow believers about the "Jezebel spirit", which is a "demonic spiritual force ... one of the most powerful demons" (Benson, 2012: vii) that infested/motivated the evil ancient queen. The demonic spirit of Jezebel is compared to "witchcraft" (McGowan, 2007:14) and fundamentalist Christians are warned that, "Jezabelic activity in the church is Satan's use of man's carnal nature to bring the church to the place of being dysfunctional … It is important we recognize that the attack of the Jezebel spirit is uniquely wrapped in the carnal nature of man … the Jezebel spirit loves to use the seduction of harlotry, adultery, and fornication as a way to accomplish its purpose with harlotry" (Richter, 2005:31, 64, 88).

Some of the beliefs about the Jezebel spirit link directly to sexist sociocultural paradigms. For example, one of the signs that the Jezebel spirit is present in a woman is that she lacks proper submission to the authority of her father and/or husband. Not only does the Jezebel Spirit goad a woman into refusing to obey a man, it motivates her to try to rule over *him*. This spirit of Jezebel is "the spirit in women today that says, "I will not have a man rule over me – not in my home, not in the church, not on the job, and not in government" … It's called the Feminist Movement today, but at the beginning of this century, they were called suffragettes" (Henson, 2009:9-10).

(Feminism is part of a demonic spirit encouraging women to overthrow and terminate the "right" of men to rule over women in the home, church, job, and government? I've never personally, as a feminist, knowingly been the agent of a demonic spirit, yet I must admit that I am actively colluding with other feminist in trying to topple the belief that men should axiomatically rule over women. As an Episcopalian, I have a way to test the hypothesis that I am infested with a jezebel demon: I can have my priest anoint me with holy water. Holy water is well known to have a negative reaction when in contact with a demons. Therefore, if it burns upon application then I'll know I am riddled with demonic spirits. However, if it doesn't burn then I am going to assume God is totally okay with women's equality.)

Evangelical women are also cautioned to learn from Jezebel's bad example. The queen was *dreadful* at acting with wifely submission to her husband. Jezebel was emasculating, and her "cosmetics couldn't make up for her ugly attitude toward her husband. Some of our [evangelical Christian women] men may be viewed as competent and capable in every setting but their own home. It may be our strong –willed nature – and not their weak-willed one – that makes them appear "less than". Let's pray for a gentler, more supportive spirit … If we want warrior-poets for husbands, let's treat out men as if they're already toting mighty shields and sharpened quills" (Higgs, 2004:187). In order to avoid being a slatternly jezebel a woman needs to remain compliant to her husband's authority. Only a wicked tart would fail to prop up the king in his castle and allow her hardened heart make her husband's personal resolve appear limp.

Jezebel's demonic spirit is furthermore present in women's uncontrolled sexuality. If a woman confides to someone that she is having sex out of wedlock, a "Jezebelite will assure the woman that it is okay if she is in love, easing the guilt and glossing over any godly conviction the woman might feel" (LeClaire, 2013:18). I wonder: is slut shaming therefore holy, if only the ungodly fail to do it? There is no word on whether or not a Jezebelite would offer a fornicating man the excuse of "boys will be boys" to ease his guilt and gloss over his godly convictions.

Then again, why is premarital sex connected with Jezebel (either historical or demonic) at all? For all of Jezebel's many biblically recorded sins, none of those trespasses were sexual in nature. Jezebel was not involved in physical promiscuity or non-spiritual prostitution. So why is she so conflated with illicit sex? Why isn't her name synonymous with haughty rather than harlot? Larceny rather than lust? Why, in short, has she been slut shamed?

As I explained earlier, most often a woman is slut shamed for the sin of contradicting gender ideology. It's only *after* she is called a slut that her sexual ethics get called into question. That's what we have going on with Jezebel. The fallacious line of reasoning is that since the queen was a bad girl she was QED a slut and since she was a slut she was obviously sexually promiscuous. It should be noted that the more a woman perturbs the powers that be, the trampier she is considered. That's how Jezebel wound up with the reputation as the sluttiest slut to have ever slutted up the world.

Jezebel was a cultural offender on two levels. Firstly, she was a threat to the religious domination of *the solely masculine version* of Yahwism. The idea of hypostatic male/female duality of God was anathema to Elijah and the other prophets. Feminine forms of the divine, like Asherah, naturally indicated that women had a role in religious life, including the role of priestess. Women who were priestesses had power and authority of their own that was independent of men's social control. Asherah had to be destroyed, even though as a hypostasis of Yahweh she was of the same essence and was simply the female "face" of the Lord, because she gave women power. Asherah not only *symbolized* a woman with power over men, she opened the door for women to gain *actual* power over men in her religious function. Furthermore, a god/goddess equal duality made the subjugation of women seem less like the will of heaven. Jezebel upheld devotions to Asherah; since the goddess was a threat to the masculine domination of Yahwism then so was the queen by proxy.

The queen's continued veneration of Asherah also meant that Jezebel had refused to lose her natal identity. Jezebel walked, talked, dressed, and worshiped like a Phoenician. This was interpreted as favoritism of her birth family over her marital family. When women in the Bible display loyalty to their husband and his kin it is synonymous with their loyalty to Yahweh, and when they remain attached to their ethnic and familial roots they are "associated with religious backsliding or the success of foreign deities" (Seeman, 2004:26). The queen's adherence to the religion of her childhood made the conservatives afraid that Jezebel would have no qualms about displacing Yahweh with the gods of her fathers.

Secondly, Jezebel flouted and subverted the gender ideology that women were naturally passive and modest and only interested in domestic concerns. Rather than being a meek wife, Jezebel was a force to be reckoned with. Instead of being afraid to accentuate her beauty lest she cause the men around her to succumb to lust, the queen adorned herself in ways that would make her attractiveness even more noticeable. If good women are naturally timid, then Jezebel was bad because timid was the last word anyone would use to describe her. The queen was too *manly* for a woman and it upset the cultural applecart.

Jezebel's destruction served as a warning to women on both fronts. It told a woman that if she did not adhere to a particular *form* of Yahwism, then she would suffer a horrible death. Additionally, it implied that if she was not subservient and demur like a good girl, then she would be despised as a harlot and no one would mourn her death. So women had better toe the line, hadn't they?

Now we have established that Jezebel was slut shamed for breaking the rules about cultural, not sexual, norms and analyzed what her slut shaming was meant to accomplish. But what, you may ask, has the slut shaming and death of an ancient queen got to do with modern slut shaming?

Jezebel's slut shaming is relevant because her story normalizes the messages that women receive regarding the punishment for female transgressions. The queen's name is a familiar one, even if the details of her fall from grace aren't. She is called, and thought of as, a wicked queen and a harlot. She is presumed to have been as sexually voracious as her reputation suggests. The subtext of her story is that since Jezebel was a tramp she was a bad person *who deserved death*. By thinking of her as a filthy whore, gone is any chance to view her murder as anything other than a righteous execution. Ergo, the slut shaming of Jezebel serves as a narrative and metaphor for a particularly destructive cultural belief about what happens to troublesome strumpets. Jezebel's story reminds us that all sluts will get what's coming to them.

Alyssa Funke was a 19 year old straight-A student at the University of Wisconsin-River Falls. She had recently appeared in a porn film for the website CastingCouch-X, was recognized by a former high school classmate, and had become the center of a concentrated slut shaming campaign (Kingkade, 2014). Alyssa, like too many other young women, committed suicide as a result of vicious slut shaming. Nonetheless, her death was not enough for her attackers. Dr. Jill McDevitt, a noted sexologist, pointed out that, "Even though she's dead, men continue to tweet at her remarks that simultaneously shame her for saying yes to sex, relish her death, and delight in masturbating to her video. The tone I read over and over again was "She filmed herself having sex, so she deserved to die. I enjoyed watching her have sex, but she still deserved to die."

The comments about Alyssa are as vile as they are heartbreaking. A commenter calling himself James Andrew Mayes tweeted that she "killed herself because she can't handle the fact she's a fucking whore. Nobody even gives a fuck. P.s fapped [masturbated] to your vid" (McDevitt, 2014). A man identified as Nicholas@NuckyAintSHIT tweeted that he was rofl [rolling on floor laughing] about the "comments to that porn star that off'd herself"(McDevitt, 2014). Someone posting as EAGLES_4_LIFE, a supporter of the Philadelphia Eagles sports team, sneered that "In a week, no one will give a damn about the porn slut whose dead!!" (McDevitt, 2014).

In the opinions of these people, and many others, Alyssa Funke was justly given the death penalty for the crime of having had herself videotaped consensually having sex. They were metaphorically ready to throw her out of the window and let the dogs eat her body because she was a so-called slut.

Audrie Potts was also slut shamed to death. She was just 15 years old when she hanged herself on Sept. 10, 2012. A little more than a week before she had gone to a party at a friend's and had (like many teens before her), decided to get drunk. Thinking she was safe among friends, she drank herself into a stupor. However, her safety was an illusion, as she discovered later when she woke up mostly nude and with obscenities written all over her skin.

Not only had Audrie suffered sexual assault by three boys she thought of as being her friends, one of the boys had filmed the gang rape on his phone and shared the images with several people. She confronted him on Facebook, violently upset that "whole school knows. . . . Do you know how people view me now? I fucked up and I can't do anything to fix it. . . . One of my best friends hates me. And I now have a reputation I can never get rid of" (Burleigh, 2013). Humiliated and hurt, Audrie thought ending her life was the only way she would ever escape the pain of being slut shamed.

Amanda Todd was also 15 years old when she committed suicide to escape the relentless slut shaming she endured because of a photo of her breasts. Her ordeal started when she was flattered into "flashing" her breasts during a live streaming web chat. A screen-capture picture of her breasts was then circulated at her school, and the slut shaming rained down upon her. Miserable and depressed, she switched schools in an attempt to start fresh.

Unhappily, Amanda was soon contacted on line by a man who revealed he had the semi-nude picture of her and tried to blackmail her. He threatened that he would share the image with everyone she knew if she did not put on an erotic performance for him via webcam. He taunted Amanda,

"U already forgot who I am? The guy who last year made you change school. Got your door kicked in by the cops. Give me 3 shows and I will disappear forever. you know I won't stop until you give me those 3 shows." (UPI, 2012) When she refused, the extortionist made good on his threat. The kids at Todd's new school not only got the pictures, they also helpfully shared with each other in order to maximize her humiliation.

The photo was taken when Amanda was a 13 year old child, only in the 7th grade. This made the photographer a pedophile and the image of child pornography. Did Canadian law enforcement officials trace this pedophile -- who was actively attempting to sexually extort a minor -- and have him punished to the extent allowable? Did they go after people who had received the pictures, warning them they would be charged with possession of child pornography if they didn't delete the image?

Nope.

Amanda Todd's mother contacted the Royal Canadian Mounted Police of British Columbia multiple times, but she got a lackadaisical response at best. It wasn't until after the teen's suicide that the RCMP made the investigation a top priority. Until then, she was just another slut getting socially punished for showing her breasts.

The messages from Amanda's stalker continued, and he moved on to the fertile ground of Facebook. He even created a Facebook profile using the picture of her nude breasts as his icon. Amanda's mother reported that,

"The Internet stalker she flashed kept stalking her … Every time she moved schools he would go undercover and become a Facebook friend … He went online to the kids who went to (the new school) and said that he was going to be a new student - that he was starting school the following week and that he wanted some friends and could they friend him on Facebook … He eventually gathered people's names and sent Amanda's video to her new school." (Bleaney, 2012)

Facebook, which has been amazingly vigilant when removing inappropriate pictures of breastfeeding mothers from its site, has conversely been notoriously lax about removing pages named "Bikini Jailbait" that feature sexualized pictures of underage girls (Sharps, 2012). It is perhaps unsurprising that Amanda's stalker found Facebook to be one of the most efficacious ways of harming the teen.

Amanda was, by this time, suffering severe psychological effects from her torment. She began cutting herself as a form of self-harm, as well as using alcohol and drugs. Human beings in their teens are not renowned for their rational decision making, even at the best of times, so it is hardly shocking that Amanda made some poor choices in this state of mind.

    A boy she had known at a former school kept in contact with her, and Amanda considered him to be one of her few friends. Amanda was unaware that this boy had a girlfriend, and their relationship escalated until she had consensual sex with him. When the fact that they had had sex was discovered, the boy's girlfriend brought him and more than a dozen other teens to surround Amanda while she physically assaulted her. Some of the witnesses even filmed Amanda being beaten (Villalva, 2012).

    Amanda assault is a graphic display of slut shaming. Why didn't the girlfriend attack the boy who had 'hooked up' with Amanda? After all, he is the one who had broken a promise and was unfaithful. Amanda was attacked because of the still-pressing *need* to have a boyfriend. Whether the girl who assaulted Amanda realized it or not, it wasn't all about how much she "loved" her boyfriend, either. If you are a woman without a male partner your power has been weakened. Having a boyfriend means you are pretty enough to attract a male, and girls have been trained since birth to think that being pretty should be their major life goal. The boy who slept with Amanda was a valuable sociocultural commodity for the attacker, while Amanda was a threat to that resource. Slut shaming Amanda was a win-win for the assailant; she protected her territory while simultaneously displaying her willingness to defend the cultural definition of "good girl". Beating the crap out of Amanda certainly gave the attacker more social leverage than dumping a cheating boyfriend.

    The attack, understandably, gave Amanda emotional damage far worse than the physical bruising.

She was so upset she tried to commit suicide then, by drinking bleach. Her peers acted with all the sensitivity of malicious rocks. Upon learning of Amanda's suicide attempt, they sent her Facebook messages taunting her and saying she deserved the beating. One budding psychopath even went so far as to comment, "I hope she dies" (Villalva, 2012). Even when Amanda changed schools, these former classmates began tagging her in photos on Facebook with messages that included, "She should try a different bleach. I hope she dies this time and isn't so stupid" (Villalva, 2012).

Hounded by slut shaming and at the end of her emotional endurance, Amanda Todd hung herself on October 10, 2012.

Less than two weeks later yet another 15 year old girl took her own life because she could not bear the agony of slut shaming for even one second more. On October 22, 2012 an orphan in the foster system named Felicia Garcia committed suicide by throwing herself in front of a commuter train. She was being unceasingly tormented by slut shaming over the rumor that she had had group sex with four football players from Tottenville High School, Repulsively, a group of her fellow students, "described by witnesses as members of the football team", stood around her taunting her right up to the moment of her death. (Rosario, 2012).

Tottenville High School initially responded to Garcia's death with platitudes and by moving a planned Friday night football game to Monday. They also banned supporters from attending Monday's game, because they wanted it to be "more subdued" (Chapman, et al., 2012). Personally, I suspect this is code for the fact Tottenville didn't want the football players' tender ears to hear the mean words people might say to them regarding bullying.

A few weeks later, doubtless the result of public outcry, the Tottenville High School decided to do something other than twiddle its thumbs and banned several of the top football players from participating in the Public Schools Athletic League playoffs. "The school's principal John Tuminaro denied the players bullied Garcia before her death — but admitted their suspensions may be linked to the ongoing [investigation into Felicia's death]" (Abramson, 2012). So far it is the only punishment anyone has received for emotionally torturing Felicia Garcia to death. Missing the playoff games hardly seems a fitting consequence for ending a life.

Certainly not everyone on the team felt remorseful about Garcia's death. Joshua Rainey, the sophomore quarterback for the Tottenville Pirates, sent out a rage-filled tweet:

"EVERBODY WHO IS BLAMING THE FOOTBALL PLAYERS S-- & MIND YOUR BUISNESS !!" (Chapman et al., 2012).

Notice the lack of defense for his team members' actions? He merely wants people to shut up and *mind their own business*. Perhaps he thinks his teammates did nothing wrong? Clearly he does not consider slut shaming a girl to death to be a community concern, especially when it involves censure for the football team. People are being *mean* to the football team simply because they were instrumental in a young girl's death and as far as Joshua Rainey is concerned, this isn't *fair*. Rainey's tweet is a fine example of the outraged pity-party a certain kind of male can throw when his privileges are threatened. The Good Old Boy network is not amused by threats to its shadow crown.

Sometimes slut shaming brings a more explicit manner of death than suicide. Aya Baradiya, a 20 year old university student from Palestine, was murdered by her uncle because he believed her to be dishonoring her family with her slutty behavior (Sherwood, 2011). In her uncle's opinion, Aya had an inappropriately close relationship with her fiancée. Mashael Albasman was murdered by her Kuwaiti father, Faleh Ghazi Albasman, because he believed "Mashael had been very disrespectful, she had been talking on her phone and he maintained that was inappropriate in his culture" (Pleasance, 2014). Rania Alayed, a 25 year old mother of three, was murdered by her husband and his brothers because her spouse became "unhappy when his wife started college and began wearing make-up" like a slut (BBC News, 2014).

These kinds of murders among South Asians and Middle Easterners are known as "honor killings", but when similar crimes are committed against European or North American women it is called "domestic violence". The motivations for domestic violence murders are the same as honor killings – a woman (95% of the time it is a woman) has done something a relative or her husband does not like. Usually that something is seeking autonomy; the most common reason for this type of murder is that the woman dared to leave her abuser. Jealousy and rage that a woman's sexuality is her own is the primary reason men kill their intimate partners (Adams, 2007). Nor do Western nations necessarily punish the crime as it would the murder of a stranger. In 2012 England's most senior judge ruled that "juries should be allowed to consider whether a victim's infidelity was a possible provocation for murder" (Doughty, 2012). One can only infer that in the judge's opinion killing a slut is not quite the same as killing a good girl.

Like Jehu's scribes, some people still believe that a woman's failure to meet gendered expectations is a justification for her death, either by her own hand or at the hand of her society. They believe that the dead woman got what she deserved. She had it coming to her, the slut. The eerie parallels between Jezebel's murder and modern honor killings/domestic homicides shine a light on the ugly fact that not enough has changed in the last three thousand years.

CHAPTER SIX

Famed for her beauty and her bewitching sensual allure, Cleopatra has been the subject of art, literature, and drama for millennia. She has been made immortal by Roman historians and Shakespeare alike. She is the woman who is accused of seducing Julius Caesar and Mark Antony, manipulating them for her advantage in international policy. She was rich and successful and cunning and sexually dominating and exotic--all the qualities of a very Bad Girl indeed.

However, she is also remembered for being driven to suicide by the defeat and death of the man she loved. Only 39 years old, Cleopatra clasped a venomous snake to her breast and died rather than live without Mark Antony. (Granted, it is more likely that she killed herself in order to avoiding being paraded through Rome during Octavian's Triumph, but that isn't as emotionally stirring, so let's skip it for now. It has no place in the legendary lovers' status of Cleopatra and Mark Antony.) In her willing sacrifice the Bad Girl showed that she had been tamed by her love for one man. Her sexual passion had been channeled through an approved filter of True Love and Romance, and she thus became a "tragic" figure as well as a naughty woman.

Cleopatra's putative Death for Love nonetheless serves the cultural narrative about what happens to women who aren't Good Girls. Like with Jezebel, if Cleopatra had not been strong and influenced politics, if she had remained in her proper sphere of docile domesticity, then she wouldn't have *had* to die. She, the narrative implies, *asked for it* by vamping her way into Roman power structures. Yet in contrast to Jezebel, Cleopatra's death is considered lamentable because it implied that she had become a real girl, having learned to value her lover more than her throne.

Cleopatra, the redeemed slut who was still punished with death, the Cleopatra portrayed in films by Hollywood sex-goddesses Theda Bara and Elizabeth Taylor, is the Cleopatra most people know. She is one half of Antony & Cleopatra, lovers who are a monument to the erotic and exotic.

She is, of course, mostly poppycock.

Who was Cleopatra *really*? If she wasn't the gorgeous, glamorous seducer of Roman rulers or the femme fatale of the Middle East, who was she? If she didn't dissolve pearls in vinegar, flog her minions, and twist hapless men enslaved by lust around her little finger, what did she actually do during her reign?

Historians and biographers would love to know more about that, as well. There is very little factual information about Cleopatra that survived the sacking of Alexandria. What is known about her is often the distorted view of Roman historians eager to justify her demise, the defeat of Mark Antony, and the Imperial takeover of Egypt. Moreover, the historians were often writing sensationalized versions of her life centuries after her death so that whatever bits of fact that had remained on record were sacrificed for dramatic storytelling. Playwrights and poets, of course, took great license in their depictions of her. The "real" Cleopatra is too often buried under a pile of persiflage or a mountain of mumbo jumbo for anyone to be very sure of very much. Nevertheless, the facts that *are* known depict a very different woman than the one you've seen on the silver screen.

Cleopatra was actually the seventh Egyptian queen by that name. Not that she was Egyptian. In point of fact, she was a tenth generation member of the Ptolemaic dynasty and was therefore ethnically Macedonian Greek. Nor was she a queen. From her point of view she was a female pharaoh, a living descendant of the sun god Ra, and she didn't let either her own subjects or the Romans forget it. Queens, it would seem, are paltry beings when measured against a female pharaoh; pale moons compared to the strong desert sun.

She ruled Egypt for more than two decades and she did it well. Cleopatra "knew how to build a fleet, suppress an insurrection, control a currency, alleviate a famine" (Schiff, 2010) and how to gain some independence for her country in spite of the grip the Roman Empire had on the entire Mediterranean region. She did everything she could to keep Egypt from becoming just another conquest of Rome, including allying herself personally and politically with two of the strongest power players in the ancient world. Although neither man was able to maintain his position long enough to secure Egypt's future, no one can deny Cleopatra did the best she could with the allies fate gave her.

How did this savvy politician and resourceful leader become reduced to merely scheming eye-candy and a sensuous man-trap in the popular imagination?

It all started with the Romans.

Ptolemy XII, Cleopatra's father, had retained his throne by expediently bribing and kowtowing to the Roman general Pompey the Great, who was at the height of his power in the last century before the birth of Christ. The mighty general had crushed the slave rebellion of Spartacus and was one of the founding members of the first Triumvirate to rule the Roman

Empire. Pompey's influence had kept Egypt from being officially conquered and annexed by the Empire, but the cold fact was that Ptolemy XII was a subordinate of the famous general, to whom he owed his continued survival. When Ptolemy XII passed away in 51 BC the Roman Empire was on the brink of being torn in two by the civil war between Julius Caesar and Pompey. Pompey, however, looked like the better bet in that he had been named sole Consul by the Roman Senate and Caesar was busy fighting in Gaul.

It was into this international mess and the death of the Roman Republic that 18 year old Cleopatra was thrust as co-ruler of Egypt, along with her 10 year old brother and husband, Ptolemy XIII. Strong, determined, and smart, Cleopatra was the de facto leader of Egypt. However, it wasn't long before her brother's power-hungry "advisors" -- the eunuch Pothinus, his rhetoric master Theodotus, and the commander of the royal guard, Achillas -- overthrew Cleopatra and sent her fleeing into Syria with her allies. There, while Pothinus ruled Egypt in all but name as regent for Ptolemy XIII, Cleopatra spent the next couple of years raising an army and planning to take her diadem back by force. Things didn't look hopeful for her, though. Pothinus wasn't going to go quietly.

Julius Caesar unknowingly rolled the dice in Cleopatra's favor when he defeated Pompey the Great in the Battle of Pharsalus in 48 BC. Pompey fled to Egypt, understandably expecting some help from Ptolemy XIII, who had an army of 20,000 men ready and waiting. Unfortunately for Pompey, the young pharaoh was not the true master of his domain and three shadow-kings were determined to please the oncoming Caesar. Pothinus and Theodotus, along with Ptolemy XIII, watched Achillas murder Pompey as the former general was rowed toward the Egyptian shore in a small boat.

On that day Pompey learned that there was nothing more dangerous than someone who owed you a tremendous debt.

In an attempt to curry Caesar's favor, the regents presented him with Pompey's severed head upon his arrival in Alexandria two days later. This backfired spectacularly. Caesar had been pardoning his enemies as a gesture of goodwill, and as Pompey had once been his ally and son-in-law, Caesar was not disposed to like his murderers, and he speedily had the non-royal conspirators put to death.

Alexandria, meanwhile, was not disposed to like Caesar. The populace was deeply concerned that he would become their new master and Egypt would be just another puppet kingdom under Roman rule. Alexandrians had not liked Ptolemy XII's subservience to Pompey, and they didn't like Ptolemy XIII's subservience to Caesar. They also, thanks to a dedicated propaganda campaign on Ptolemy XIII's side, wanted nothing to do with Cleopatra. There were riots in the streets and clashes with Caesar's soldiers.

Believe it or not, Caesar's first thought wasn't to get Alexandria and Egypt under his thumb. What he wanted most was to get the whole place calmed down and exporting stuff to Rome again. With that in mind he summoned Cleopatra and Ptolemy XIII to him, in the hopes that he could get the siblings back into the co-ruling marriage they were *supposed* to have.

Ptolemy XIII was close to Caesar in proximity, but his absolutely worthless advisors cautioned the young pharaoh to refuse to go out of pique. Caesar was the lower ranked person and thus should be going to Ptolemy XIII instead of summoning him. This witless bit of snobbery meant that Ptolemy XIII missed out on his chance to win Caesar over and turn him against Cleopatra.

Cleopatra was much too smart to let protocol strip her of an advantage. She was happy to go to Caesar; but how? Her brother's troops were trying to kill her. She couldn't just waltz into the palace.

Although legend has it that Cleopatra was smuggled into the palace to see Caesar in a rolled up carpet, it was much more likely that her faithful Sicilian retainer, Apollodorus, tied her up in a sack and hauled her into the royal residence on his shoulder. Nor did she strike Caesar with her beauty when she was decanted. Women are not typically at their most decorous when they have been hauled in a sack. Moreover, Caesar was a world-weary and promiscuous 52 year old Roman who had seen it all and slept with most of it. Cleopatra was a 21 year old exiled ruler who was probably still a virgin. She wouldn't have known how to seduce a man like Caesar even if she had been willing to try.

(This is slightly off topic, but I want to take a moment to point out the snide remark supposedly made by Curio the Elder suggesting that Caesar was "every woman's man and every man's woman" was balderdash. Romans thought there was nothing "homosexual" about being the man who penetrated another male's body, either orally or anally, so there is a distinct possibility that Caesar would have "used" other men (or teenaged boys) this way. However, the Romans were savage in their condemnation of an adult male who would allow himself to be penetrated; such a man would be called a *pathicus*, a *cinaedus*, or the very crude *scultimidonus* among other derogatory things. By calling Caesar "every man's woman", Curio was insulting him and suggesting that Caesar was penetrated during intercourse. That was something that lesser beings – such as women, slaves, boys, actors, and gladiators -- did during sex. It is highly unlikely that Caesar would have put his reputation for virility at risk by permitting another man to "use him as a woman".)

What Cleopatra was, however, was charming. She had charisma to burn. What she lacked in sexual experience she made up for in conversational skill. She was so engaging that everyone knew it was "impossible to converse with her without being instantly captivated by her" (Plutarch In Clough, 1875). Her only hope of survival was to turn Caesar's distaste for Ptolemy XIII into support for her reign. She didn't seduce him -- she *persuaded* him.

Caesar decided to back the personable female pharaoh, and at first it looked like he made a mistake. The populace was not happy. Moreover, it meant a guerrilla war in Alexandria while simultaneously still trying to become undisputed dictator of Rome in the face of Senate objections. To make matters more complex, Ptolemy XIII's younger sister, Arsinoe IV, joined forces with Achillas, the murderer of Pompey, and turned the war into a three-way battle for the throne. It was a tug of war that Caesar and Cleopatra nearly lost. At one point Caesar was forced to set his own ships on fire to escape rival Egyptians, and the conflagration spread into the city until it burned down the famous Library of Alexandria.

Nevertheless, Caesar continued to fight for Cleopatra. One reason may be that he had cemented his alliance with Cleopatra in the bedroom, as evidenced by her pregnancy in November.

This was normal operating procedure for the times. Alliances were sealed with marriages and/or physical intimacy. If Cleopatra had been a man, Caesar would have 'married' a sister or daughter but Cleopatra's gender meant that she would become the physical as well as symbolic vessel for their political union.

It wasn't until the Battle of the Nile in February of 47 BC that Caesar and Cleopatra finally wrested control from her sibling and half-sibling. Arsinoe's forces had already betrayed her and given her to Caesar by the time Caesar's allies, Mithridates of Pergamum and Antipate of Judea, arrived with military back-up and helped Caesar defeat Ptolemy XIII's troops. Ptolemy XIII himself was said to have drowned while attempting to flee across the Nile, leaving Caesar the uncontested victor.

Caesar promptly set up Cleopatra as co-ruler with her remaining half-brother – who was of course named Ptolemy. As tradition demanded, Cleopatra was married to her co-ruler Ptolemy XIV. Nevertheless, she ruled alone and continued her physical relationship with Caesar. Likewise, Caesar did not seek to divorce his wife in Rome and marry Cleopatra. They were allies more than "lovers". A few months after the Battle of the Nile, Caesar left Egypt, leaving behind a heavily pregnant Cleopatra but maintaining their cordial relationship with no hard feelings.

Cleopatra gave birth to Caesar's only son on June 23, 47 BC. She named her son Ptolemy XV Caesar, in a blatant advertisement of his paternal lineage. The people of Alexandria nicknamed the child Caesarion, or "little Caesar". Historians of antiquity recorded that "according to certain Greek writers, this child was very like Caesar in looks and carriage" (Suetonius, 2004). Cleopatra, in an astute PR move, took advantage of the fact that Caesarion was born at the beginning of the Nile's summer flooding to link her name indelibly with Isis in the eyes of her subjects. It was the tears of Isis that were said to flood the life-giving Nile, and people were already celebrating her annual feast. Cleopatra, with Caesarion on her lap like the iconography of the gods Isis and Horus, wore the traditional crown consisting of solar disk and cow's horns to remind all who saw her that she *was* the embodiment of the goddess. She furthermore had coins minted that depicted Caesarion as Horus to reinforce his connection with the son of Isis and to not-so-subtly point out that if Caesarion was Horus then Cleopatra was Mother Isis.

Isis also served as Cleopatra's doppelganger in another way. Isis was the Lady of Abundance, and Cleopatra stood between her subjects and famine by opening the royal granaries during times of scanty harvests. Frankly, Cleopatra's responsibilities were so heavy that she might as well have *been* Isis. "She not only dispensed justice, commanded the army and navy, regulated the economy, negotiated with foreign powers, and presided over temples, but determine the prices of raw materials and supervised the sowing schedules, the distribution of seed, the condition of Egypt's canals, [as well as] the food supply" (Schiff, 2010).

Caesar returned to Rome at the end of July 46 BC, eagerly looking forward to a four day Triumph in his honor in the autumn. Determined to show his continued support for Cleopatra, and perhaps because he missed her company, Caesar invited her to Rome to see the show. She, of course, brought their son Caesarion. Oddly enough, she also brought her young husband (Vagi, 2000). Possibly she didn't want him give him an opportunity to try to usurp her rule by leaving him home without her.

Rome was delightfully aghast when Caesar installed her, their son, and her retinue in Caesar's own villa on the banks of the Tiber. The populace quickly decided that they didn't like the foreign queen. She was too… not-Roman. She also seemed to have undue influence over their dictator. Not only was she staying in his home, he had commissioned a gold (or gilded) statue of Cleopatra to stand alongside the statue of Venus within the inner sanctum of the Temple of Venus Genetrix he had just dedicated. Romans began to speculate that Caesar planned to divorce his wife, marry Cleopatra, move the capital of the Empire to Alexandria, and to declare himself a god-monarch in the Hellenistic style (Gruen, 2003).

How could the citizens of Rome explain the very popular Caesar's very unpopular ambition? Easy. They decided that Cleopatra was a flagrant hussy who had bewitched Caesar with her womanly wiles. How else could she be influencing him? With her brains? By using his own lust for power? Pshaw! It had to be harlotry.

Certainly historians from antiquity embraced the idea that Cleopatra enslaved the elderly general with exotic sex techniques and possibly even sorcery. Plutarch wrote that when Caesar first saw Cleopatra he was "captivated" by the "bold coquette" and then "succumbed to the charm of further intercourse with her" (Marr 2012). Plutarch also blamed the Alexandrian war on the Egyptian queen, claiming Caesar only entered that "unnecessary" war "for love of Cleopatra" and thus exposed himself to all kinds of "shame and dangers" (Canfora, 2007). Moreover, Cleopatra was part and parcel with the cult of Isis, which was spreading like wildfire throughout Rome. The cult of Isis was deeply suspect, since conservative Romans thought it encourage sexual deviance (especially in women). Surely an Egyptian woman who was an avatar of Isis would be raunchy sex personified?

Some of the Roman antipathy for Cleopatra leaked through during Caesar's Triumph. The Triumph began on September 21st and the celebrations carried on until early October. During one part of the event Caesar paraded Cleopatra's captive sister Arsinoe through the streets as a captive enemy, after which she should have been strangled. However, the crowd's sympathy for the young woman – a known rival for Cleopatra's throne – was such that Caesar thought it best to give her sanctuary at the Temple of Artemis in Ephesus rather than death. From her island semi-prison Arsinoe continued to have a disruptive influence in Egyptian politics, declaring herself queen of Egypt and finding Roman backers, much to Cleopatra's disgust.

Then, as now, there was a general "understanding" about proper or ladylike behavior. For the Romans, a Good Girl was modest, a hard worker, wanted children rather than adornments, didn't call attention to herself, and was deferential to men. Cleopatra could not have violated these norms more if she had set out to deliberately defy them. She was grandiose, arrogant in her assurance of herself as a female Pharaoh, liked luxury, liked to have fun, wore make-up, bedecked herself with enough jewelry to fund an army, and wasn't very deferential to anyone. Cleopatra, was the general Roman consensus, *must* be a Bad Girl because she certainly wasn't a Good one.

Cleopatra did not stay in Rome continuously from 46 until 44 BC. Rather, she made at least two trips (Gruen, 2003). The Romans must have been relieved when the Egyptian Hussy set sail for Alexandria in the spring of 45. Caesar was less so. Suetonius, a Roman historian, claimed that Caesar wasn't content to let Cleopatra, "with whom he often feasted until daybreak", leave Rome "until he had ladened her with high honours and rich gifts, and he allowed her to give his name to the child which she bore" (Suetonius, 2004). The Romans must have been equally dismayed to see her return again in the autumn, to be with Caesar after his return from Spain.

The famous Roman statesman Cicero certainly wasn't happy to have her back in Rome. He was later to write that "The arrogance of the queen herself when she was living on the estate across the Tiber [Caesar's villa] makes my blood boil to recall ... I hate the queen" (Ashton, 2009). Once can only surmise that the Egyptian queen acted like a queen and didn't give the crotchety but brilliant old man enough deference. Cleopatra's "insolence" was the crux of her problem with more Romans than Cicero. She had no idea how to be the meek but witty Roman paragon of womanhood. She saw no reason to pretend she was anything other than a demi-goddess amongst provincial barbarians.

Cleopatra's life was about to take another dramatic turn in March of 44 BC. More specifically, her fortunes would change on the Ides of March.

Julius Caesar was stabbed to death by conspirators on March 15, on the feast day of the goddess Anna Perenna. The spring festival occurred in the hope that Anna Perenna would, when appeased with a few prayers and some sacrificial animals, grant people a happy year until her next feast day. It was also, like May Day in the Celtic world, a chance to eat and drink and, if one was lucky, perhaps even fornicate outside in the fresh air. It was a day for celebrating, relaxation, and good cheer. No one would have expected an assassination and massive political upheaval to mark the festivities.

After Caesar's death, Cleopatra and her entourage left for Egypt in a hurry. This was wise. For one thing, she didn't know if she and Caesarion would be next on the conspirators' hit list. Not only was she Caesar's lover and ally of whom the Romans disapproved, it was an open secret her son was fathered by Caesar. It's no wonder Cicero described Cleopatra's leave-taking as a "flight" from Rome (Jones, 2006). Additionally, the city had become a madhouse anyone would be wise to escape. The conspirators made no plans for filling

Caesar's slippers after they stabbed him, and thus all of Rome was in turmoil with no one to steady the helm. After her coming of age in Alexandria, Cleopatra would not have viewed an unstable city as anything other than a personal threat.

To further complicate matters, Cleopatra was pregnant again. A pregnant queen was one who could "complicate Rome's future. Unlike Caesarion, this second child had been conceived on Roman soil. All of Rome knew it to be Caesar's. What if Cleopatra bore a boy, and chose to press her case … she could derail the succession. She was "perfectly poised to do so" (Schiff, 2010). Sadly, Cleopatra did not bear the child (whether the loss was a miscarriage or stillbirth or neonatal death is unknown) so we can never know what she would have done if the baby had been male.

Even if she hadn't been eager to set sail for Alexandria, she would have had to vacate Caesar's estate anyway. On the March 17th reading of his will, Caesar left the villa and the land around it as a public park to the citizens of Rome, making Cleopatra an instant squatter. Nor was his will kinder to her in other ways. He left her nothing, and failed to acknowledge Caesarion or bequeath anything to his biological son or child-to-be. This should not be made much of, however; it was illegal for a Roman citizen like Caesar to bestow anything to non-Romans (Schiff, 2010). Even if he had been wildly enamored of Cleopatra, he knew his will would have been contested and invalidated if he tried to provide for her or their child. Moreover, the fabulously wealthy queen didn't need his money. What she and their children needed was his protection, and that was gone.

CHAPTER SEVEN

By late May the queen was back in Egypt. She was 26 years old, and without her most potent friend to assist her. Her sister, Arsinoe, was rallying Roman backers and trying once more to usurp her throne. Cleopatra was well aware her sister was more popular in Rome than she was. What if Rome invaded Alexandria and put Arsinoe in as the new puppet queen? For that matter, what would happen if her husband/brother made a power play while she was politically vulnerable? With Caesar dead, she was alone and eager to dispatch any potential threats within reach; she did not hesitate to act with ruthlessness to add to the security of her crown. Thus, she "promptly had her younger brother, Ptolemy XIV, murdered, so she could replace him as co-reagent with her own 4-year-old son Caesarion, who she married in the Ptolemaic fashion" (Vagi, 2000). Egyptian politics was a game without mercy; Cleopatra gave none and expected none for herself.

In the wake of Caesar's assassination, Rome devolved into a civil war. Caesar's heirs and proponents were pitted against Caesar's murderers. The Senate passed a law called the *Lex Titia*, which created a Triumvirate of Caesar's great-grandnephew Octavian (later Caesar Augustus), Caesar's devoted supporter Marcus Aemilius Lepidus, and Caesar's distant cousin and friend Mark Antony. Cleopatra formally sided with the Triumvirate but mainly stayed home and took care of Egyptian business. There was plenty on her plate in

Alexandria without having to worry about Rome's shenanigans.

Nevertheless, Roman shenanigans were inescapable. After the Triumvirate's troops, marshaled by Mark Antony, soundly defeated the armies of Caesar's murderers at Philippi in Greece in 42 BC, Rome was able to once again turn its greedy eye toward Egypt. In 41 BC a third of the Triumvirate, in the form of Mark Antony himself, summoned her to the city of Tarsus in Cilicia.

Mark Antony had, beyond doubt, met Cleopatra when she stayed in Caesar's villa in Rome. There is, however, absolutely no indication that the two were romantically involved. If they had so much as given each other a lingering glance, the gossipmongers in Rome would have spread the word. Cleopatra's critics would have pounced on any hint of impropriety, especially while she was pregnant. If they could have cast doubt on the paternity of her fetus, they would have done so forthwith. The fact that Mark Antony and Cleopatra were never linked in the public mind during her sojourn in Italy is nearly a guarantee they had not been intimate when Caesar wasn't looking.

That was then; Tarsus was now. Mark Antony was one of the most powerful men in the world. He had almost certainly met Arsinoe's allies in Rome and abroad, and perhaps even Arsinoe herself. He had declared Arsinoe the regent of Cyprus in 44 BC, not long after Caesar's untimely end. Arsinoe was "to hand", so to speak, and would theoretically be easier to control. Cleopatra would have needed to win Mark Antony over and win him over quickly. She would have used every weapon in her arsenal to convince him she was the queen he wanted to see in Egypt, and that would have included sex if needs be.

According to Plutarch, Cleopatra arrived in Tarsus armed for bear, vis-à-vis seduction and awe. The Egyptian queen came into the city by:

> "sailing up the River Cydnus in a barge with gilded stern and outspread sails of purple, while oars of silver beat time to the music of flutes and fifes and harps. She herself lay all along, under a canopy of cloth of gold, dressed as Venus in a picture, and beautiful young boys, like painted Cupids, stood on each side to fan her. Her maids were dressed like Sea Nymphs and Graces, some steering at the rudder, some working at the ropes. The perfumes diffused themselves from the vessel to the shore, which was covered with multitudes, part following the galley up the river on either bank, part running out of the city to see the sight. The market place was quite emptied, and Antony at last was left alone sitting upon the tribunal; while the word went through all the multitude, that Venus was come to feast with Bacchus for the common good of Asia." (Plutarch in Clough, 1875)

Plutarch also spared nothing in telling the tale of how Cleopatra made emotional mincemeat out of Mark Antony, and had him eating out of the palm of her hand:

> "The next day, Antony invited her to supper, and was very desirous to outdo her as well in magnificence as contrivance; but he found he was altogether beaten in both, and was so well convinced of it that he was himself the first to jest and mock at his poverty of wit and his rustic awkwardness. She, perceiving that his raillery

was broad and gross, and savoured more of the soldier than the courtier, rejoined in the same taste, and fell into it at once, without any sort of reluctance or reserve. For her actual beauty, it is said, was not in itself so remarkable that none could be compared with her, or that no one could see her without being struck by it, but the contact of her presence, if you lived with her, was irresistible; the attraction of her person, joining with the charm of her conversation, and the character that attended all she said or did, was something bewitching. It was a pleasure merely to hear the sound of her voice, with which, like an instrument of many strings, she could pass from one language to another; so that there were few of the barbarian nations that she answered by an interpreter; to most of them she spoke herself, as to the Ethiopians, Troglodytes, Hebrews, Arabians, Syrians, Medes, Parthians, and many others, whose language she had learnt; which was all the more surprising because most of the kings, her predecessors, scarcely gave themselves the trouble to acquire the Egyptian tongue, and several of them quite abandoned the Macedonian. Antony was so captivated by her that, while Fulvia his wife maintained his quarrels in Rome against Caesar by actual force of arms, and the Parthian troops, commanded by Labienus (the king's generals having made him commander-in-chief), were assembled in Mesopotamia, and ready to enter Syria, he could yet suffer himself to be carried away by her to Alexandria, there to keep holiday, like a boy, in play and diversion, squandering and fooling away in enjoyments

> that most costly, as Antiphon says, of all valuable, time." (Plutarch in Clough, 1875)

Plutarch's descriptions are certainly captivating, and may even have an element of truth, but they should perhaps be taken with a grain or two of salt. The author was himself a toddler when Cleopatra sailed up the Cydnus, so we know it isn't a firsthand description of the events. Even if Plutarch had been there it was in his best interest to play to the crowd, as it were. His words were written as much to please the Roman Emperors and the Roman public as they were for the historical record. Octavian had become the Emperor Caesar Augustus and even after his death the power in Rome remained Imperial. It was crucial that Octavian's enemies be remembered as 'the bad guys'. Mark Antony had done a little too much for his country to be entirely discounted, so a safe way to hedge criticism against him was to depict him as a great man who had tragically gone to the dogs. A man whose love of frivolity set him up to be seduced and manipulated by Cleopatra, a "ruinous monster" and man-eater that enticed him to his doom (Thompson, 2011).

If Cleopatra was going to be the downfall of a powerful Roman, she needed to be a foe worthy of Rome. A hero is only as good as the villain he defeats. It was important, therefore, that Cleopatra's destructive capabilities on men be presented as the most devious womanly wiles possible for a female beast.

Historical facts suggest that Cleopatra's initial effects on Mark Antony were not as strong as Plutarch assured his readers they were. In spite of hyperbolic assertions that Cleopatra "captured his heart" (Blackaby, 2009) and "won him over in just one night" (Thompson, 2011), Antony showed no real signs of love. He had no qualms about leaving the queen when his winter's pleasures were over, even though she was pregnant with his child. (It would turn out to be "children" since she gave birth to twins, but there is no record of either of them knowing she was carrying more than one fetus at the time.) He also showed no compunction about staying away from her, and his twins, for the following four years.

That's not how a man who is obsessed with his paramour acts.

There are no signs Antony was pining for Cleopatra while he was away from her either. In the autumn of 40 BC he met with the two other members of the Triumvirate in Brundisium, a moderate-sized but important coastal city with a busy port that served as the de facto jumping off point when Romans went to either to Greece or the Near East. There Mark Antony, Octavian, and Lepidus renewed the Triumvirate and divided the known world amongst them. Lepidus was essentially granted Africa (excluding Egypt) by the two more powerful members of the trio. Octavian took the West, and Mark Antony called dibs on everything to the East of Scodra in Illyria, which is now modern Albania (Goldsworthy, 2010). Egypt and the rich city of Alexandria where Cleopatra lived were now in Antony's territory.

To seal the deal Antony married Octavian's freshly widowed older sister, Octavia. Unlike Cleopatra, Octavia was an ideal Roman wife. She was loyal to Mark Antony and worked to keep peace between himself and her brother far longer than she should have, considering his philandering. Initially their marriage seemed to be working. He had coins struck with her profile on them (she is believed to be the first woman so honored in Roman history) and she bore him the first of two daughters in 39 BC. Inasmuch as Octavian was "deeply attached to his sister" (Everitt, 2007) and

Octavia herself was incredibly well-respected and popular in Rome, it would have behooved Antony to have maintained the marital cordiality. Until 37 BC, when he resumed his relationship with Cleopatra, there was no reason to think he wouldn't.

Early evidence of Antony's undying love for Cleopatra may have been lacking in 40 BC, but he was nonetheless influenced by his persuasive and charming Egyptian lover. He may not have loved her enough to stay with her, but he did Cleopatra the favor of having her sister Arsinoe murdered. He furthermore gave her several nice perks in the Treaty of Brundisium. Antony not only returned Cyrenaica to Egyptian control, he additionally gave Egypt the Roman province of Cilicia and big chunks of newly conquered Syrian territory (Thompson, 2011). Thanks to Antony's generosity, Cleopatra now ruled over an Empire as large as that of her greatest Ptolemaic forbearers.

Cleopatra kept close tabs on Antony while they were apart. The queen received reports from "an Egyptian astrologer she had infiltrated into Antony's household" (Preston, 2009), and it would be very surprising if she didn't have other spies as well. However, her long-distance stalking of Antony was no different than that of other powerful figures during the time period and it shouldn't be construed as a symptom of her love for Antony. She needed the information for political reasons, and it didn't necessarily reflect her personal feelings about him.

Cleopatra and Antony wouldn't see each other again until the winter of 36-37, when she accepted his invitation to visit him in Antioch. Not that it is indicative of planning on Antony's part to arrange a meeting with his lady love. Rather, it was circumstantial.

Antony and Octavian has just finished making the Treaty of Tarentum, and Antony had set sail for the East with his wife. Octavia, who was pregnant with their second daughter, became ill on the Greek island of Corfu (Streissguth, 1999). Antony dispatched Octavia back to Rome, since traveling with a military campaign wasn't the best situation for an ailing and gravid wife. It was therefore simply by chance that Antony wound up in Antioch sans spouse. There, many heads of state were invited to call upon him, including Egypt's queen. Unburdened by his wife, Antony was ideally situated to resume an affair with Cleopatra.

By the time she left Antioch, once more pregnant, in the spring of 36 BC she had convinced Mark Antony to be a very loyal ally indeed. He acknowledged that her two youngest children had been were his as well, and had given the queen plum pieces of real estate, including important coastal trade cities such as Kyrene, even more land in Cilicia, Phoenicia, and Syria, the entire kingdom of Iturea in northern Palestine, and the island of Crete (Burstein, 2007). They may even have gotten married.

It is unknown if Cleopatra physically brought her twins by Mark Antony, Alexander and Cleopatra the Younger, with her to Antioch. What is known is that not long after she arrived in the city Antony claimed both children as his own. The twins were renamed Alexander Helios (Alexander the Sun) and Cleopatra Selene (Cleopatra the Moon), a symbolic statement of their newly cemented paternity.

Equally unknown is the veracity of a marriage between Antony and Cleopatra. They may have been married in the Egyptian style, or they may have merely participated in an ornate ceremony to reinforce their alliance (Southern, 2012). It can't be said for sure. All that can be accurately said of it is that Octavian capitalized on it.

Polygamy was forbidden in Rome, and a marriage with a non-Roman citizen was legally invalid and no marriage at all. News of Antony and Cleopatra's marriage scandalized Rome. He was already married to Octavia, a good Roman matron whom he impregnated on a semi-annual basis and the idea that he would betray her (and by extension, Rome) in order to 'marry' some Egyptian tart enraged the public. They could handle the fact that Octavia and Cleopatra would both give birth to one of Antony's children in 36 BC, but even an illegal sham of a marriage to that trashy Oriental tramp was beyond enduring. To all outward appearances, Antony had gone native, abandoning his Roman roots for Eastern gold.

But was his apparent favoritism to Cleopatra really all for her benefit? Cleopatra was incontestably not the only Eastern potentate to get bounteous gifts of land from Antony, and many of these rulers were retained by Octavian after Antony's death (Southern, 2012). He really didn't give her more than was reasonable in the circumstances. He refused to give her Judea (which he had promised to Herod), no matter how nicely she asked him.

Why was he so generous with her, if not for love? The more likely truth is that although Antony's grants to Cleopatra may have restored Egypt to its former glories, it wasn't Cleopatra's needs that Antony was thinking of. He was thinking of himself. Egypt was to "form the heart of a great eastern empire which he hoped to rule" (Holbl, 2001) and to strengthen Egypt was to bolster Antony's plans.

Nor are the coins he ordered struck with Cleopatra's portrait on one side and his on the other symptomatic of his great love for the queen. He had done something similar for Octavia just a few years before and he was manifestly not head over heels for his wife. Rather, the coins denoted to what extent "the orient was now viewed as one domain under one ruling couple" (Holbl, 2001). Antony was co-opting Cleopatra's legitimacy as a hereditary ruler of Egypt, while simultaneously giving her the backing of Rome, in order to tighten his grip of the region.

It must be admitted, though, that they were unquestionably lovers. Nothing confirms physical intimacy like a pregnancy, and in the autumn of 36 BC the queen of Egypt once more bore Antony a son, whom she named Ptolemy Philadelphia. She gave birth alone in Alexandria, because the baby's father was busy in a disastrous war with Parthia. Not long after the birth of her fourth child she and a fleet of ships had to sail for Libya to pick up Antony and the beggared remains of his army. Together, Antony and Cleopatra returned to her capital so he could lick his wounds and plot afresh.

Whatever Antony's feelings were for the intelligent and personable queen, he still found it easy to live without her by his side. In the spring of 35 he headed off once more to Syria, planning to launch an attack into Armenia from there.

Mark Antony may or may not have lost his heart to Cleopatra, but he certainly seemed to have lost his grasp of Roman real politick. His still-legally-wed wife, Octavia, attempted to save his skin by joining him in Syria in 35 BC and allowing him a chance at reconciliation with her and through her reconciliation with her powerful brother and the Roman people. She made sure he knew that she brought with her gifts of gold and soldiers to refresh his troops, which was either a bribe for his affection or a signal that she still considered herself bound to him. In a huge PR blunder, Antony sent a messenger to intercept her, "accepting the gifts but instructing Octavia to return to Rome" (Burns, 2006).

This, naturally, went over a treat with the Romans. Antony had spurned his very popular and very matronly wife for an exotic chippie from the East! It was an insult to all Roman womanhood. The Romans just *knew* that his cruelty toward Octavia was done at the behest of Cleopatra, the aforementioned exotic chippie:

> "Cleopatra perceived that Octavia was advancing on her and feared that if Octavia added to her decorum and [Octavian's] power the pleasure of her company and her support of Antony, she would be untouchable and would have total command of her husband. So Cleopatra feigned passionate love for Antony and made her body waste away wither a strict diet. She fixed her gaze on him every time he came near and, when he left, she appeared to swoon and sink down. She contrived that he should often see her weeping, the quickly wiped away the tear and hid it, as if she wished to escape his notice." (Plutarch in Jones, 2006)

It shouldn't surprise you to know this probably wasn't true. In fact, the odds are extremely good that Cleopatra wasn't even in Syria at the time, and it was Antony's decision alone to tell his wife to stay away. As is often the case, reality held less interest for the Romans than the titillating story of the Egyptian queen's perfidious manipulation of man flesh.

Regardless of who was to 'blame' for Antony's decision, it was a bad one. After that boneheaded action, the public was well primed for the propaganda regarding Antony and Cleopatra that was about to be pumped into Rome via Octavian and his allies.

And pump propaganda they did.

Unlike their countrymen who would be born after the reign of Caesar Augustus, the Romans of Antony's time still held simplicity as equivalent to Roman manhood. They were deeply invested in the concepts of *mos maiorum* – their traditions – and *pietas* – fulfilling one's obligations (Spielvogel, 2014). Neither traditions nor responsibilities included such sissified behaviors as showing off and being silly and getting emotional about stuff. Real Romans, it was felt, were serious about things. That's why Octavian's poisonous slanders about Antony and Cleopatra focused so heavily on extravagance and frivolity. It was both un-Roman and unmanly for Antony to be led into frippery and whimsy by an Oriental trollop.

What made the slanders so effective was that in some of them there was a tiny grain of truth. Cleopatra had been raised to understand showmanship and spectacle were essential for rulers, and the dramatic personality of Mark Antony took to pageants and displays like a duck to water. Nonetheless, many of the things about Antony and Cleopatra's time together that have been recorded as fact by ancient historians is most likely pure piffle.

For example, there is the tale of how Antony:

> "went out one day to angle with Cleopatra, and, being so unfortunate as to catch nothing in the presence of his mistress, he gave secret orders to the fishermen to dive under water, and put fishes that had been already taken upon his hooks; and these he drew so fast that the Egyptian perceived it. But, feigning great admiration, she told everybody how dexterous Antony was, and invited them next day to come and see him again. So, when a number of them

had come on board the fishing-boats, as soon as he had let down his hook, one of her servants was beforehand with his divers and fixed upon his hook a salted fish from Pontus. Antony, feeling his line give, drew up the prey, and when, as may be imagined, great laughter ensued, "Leave," said Cleopatra, "the fishing-rod, general, to us poor sovereigns of Pharos and Canopus; your game is cities, provinces, and kingdoms." (Plutarch, in Clough, 1875)

This fish story had a nice one/two punch for its Roman audience. First, it made Antony seem like a self-aggrandizing fribble who thought he was bright when he was actually a bit dim. Good thing he lost to Octavius then, huh? Secondly, it showed how that she-devil Cleopatra could outsmart him at every turn, even as she flattered him. To be bamboozled and surpassed by a mere woman! Antony was a poor excuse of a man to let it happen, and Cleopatra's ability to do it made her a threat to Roman manhood everywhere, ensuring the belief that whatever happened to her, she deserved her fate without question.

Plutarch was not the only classical author to present this view of Antony and Cleopatra's relationship. Cassius Dio noted that Cleopatra had:

> "enslaved [Antony] so completely that she had persuaded him to act as gymnasiarch for the Alexandrians; she was saluted by him as 'queen' and as 'mistress', and she had Roman soldiers in her bodyguard, all of whom had her name inscribed upon their shields, She visited the market-place with Antony, presided with him over festivals and at the hearing of lawsuits, rode with him on horseback even in the cities, or

else was carried in a litter, while Antony followed on foot together with her eunuchs. He also referred to his headquarters as 'the palace', sometimes carried an Oriental dagger in his belt, wore clothes which were completely alien to Roman custom, and appeared in public seated upon a gilded couch or chair. Painters and sculptors depicted him with Cleopatra he being represented as Osiris or Dionysus and she as Selene or Isis, and it was this practice more than anything else which gave the impression that she had laid him under some spell and deprived him of his wits." (in Scott-Kilvert, 1987)

Notice that Antony had to follow her on foot with her eunuchs? Cassius Dio wasn't being subtle with his insinuations of Antony's emasculation by that royal floozy, was he?

Then there was the infamous account of the pearl-in-vinegar by Pliny the Elder (in Bostock):

"There were formerly two pearls, the largest that had been ever seen in the whole world: Cleopatra, the last of the queens of Egypt, was in possession of them both, they having come to her by descent from the kings of the East. When Antony had been sated by her, day after day, with the most exquisite banquets, this queenly courtesan, inflated with vanity and disdainful arrogance, affected to treat all this sumptuousness and all these vast preparations with the greatest contempt; upon which Antony enquired what there was that could possibly be added to such extraordinary magnificence. To this she made answer, that on a single entertainment she would expend ten millions of sesterces. Antony was extremely desirous to learn how that could be done, but looked upon it as a thing quite impossible; and a wager was the result. On the following day, upon which the matter was to be decided, in order that she might not lose the wager, she had an entertainment set before Antony, magnificent in every respect, though no better than his usual repast. Upon this, Antony joked her, and enquired what was the amount expended upon it; to which she made answer that the banquet which he then beheld was only a trifling appendage to the real banquet, and that she alone would consume at the meal to the ascertained value of that amount, she herself would swallow the ten millions of sesterces; and so ordered the second course to be served. In obedience to her instructions, the servants placed before her a single vessel, which was filled with vinegar, a liquid, the sharpness and strength of which is able to dis- solve pearls. At this moment she was wearing in her ears those choicest and most rare and unique productions of Nature; and while Antony was waiting to see what she was going to do, taking one of them from out of her ear, she threw it into the vinegar, and directly it was melted, swallowed it. Lucius Plancus, who had been named umpire in the wager, placed his hand upon the other at the very instant that she was making preparations to dissolve it in a similar manner, and declared that Antony had lost—an omen which, in the result, was fully confirmed."

It's hard for the modern audience to understand just how destructive that story was to the reputations of Antony and Cleopatra. Pearls were the most extravagant jewels imaginable in Rome and extravagance went hand in hand with decadence. Pliny accused Cleopatra of having pearl earrings worth 420 talents a piece, the fiscal "equivalent of a Mediterranean villa [hanging] from each ear" (Schiff, 2010). The idea that Cleopatra would dissolve and drink a pearl worth that much money was breathtakingly outrageous to the staid Romans of the time. It was the essence of her Oriental feminine cunning, because no other woman would "be so frivolous, so wanton, so ready to enchant a man that she would pluck a pearl from her lobes, dissolve it in vinegar, and swallow it, to beguile a man with magic and excess" (Schiff, 2010).

In the spring of 34 BC Mark Antony set out to conquer Armenia and in the fall of that same year he returned triumphant to Alexandria with Artavasdes, the king of Armenia, bound in silver chains. This, of course, required a rousing celebration and suitable pageantries from the rulers who were proclaiming themselves the apotheosis of Osiris/Dionysus and Isis/Aphrodite:

> "Antony himself, in saffron robes, garlanded with ivy beneath a golden crown, wearing long high-heeled boots and brandishing the *thyrsos* – the ivy-wreathed wand tipped with a pine cone that was a symbol of Dionysus – had chosen to present himself to the Egyptians as that deity made flesh rather than as a conquering soldier of Rome. The imagery was of the great god of the east about to meet his goddess. Long lines of marching legionaries followed Antony's chariot along the city's wide, colonnaded streets. Together with swaying, wooden-wheeled

wagons loaded with booty, including, it is said, at least one solid-gold statue" (Preston, 2009).

Regardless of the exaggerations, the couple's actions in Alexandria surely weren't helping them win any hearts in Rome. Cleopatra would have seen nothing wrong with such a display; it would have been practically conventional. Antony, however, should have known better than to indulge in this kind of over-the-top dramaturgy if he wanted to keep the Romans on his side.

Worse, from Rome's point of view, was Antony's public display of dynastic intentions. For the Romans, these intentions:

> "seemed a theatrical piece of insolence and contempt of his country. For, assembling the people in the exercise ground, and causing two golden thrones to be placed on a platform of silver, the one for him and the other for Cleopatra, and at their feet lower thrones for their children, he proclaimed Cleopatra queen of Egypt, Cyprus, Libya, and Coele-Syria, and with her conjointly Caesarion, the reputed son of the former Caesar, who left Cleopatra with child. His own sons by Cleopatra were to have the style of kings of kings; to Alexander he gave Armenia and Media, with Parthia, so soon as it should be overcome; to Ptolemy, Phoenicia, Syria, and Cilicia. Alexander was brought out before the people in the Median costume, the tiara and upright peak, and Ptolemy, in boots and mantle and Macedonian cap done about with the diadem; for this was the habit of the successors of Alexander, as the other was of the Medes and Armenians. And, as soon as they had

saluted their parents, the one was received by a guard of Macedonians, the other by one of Armenians. Cleopatra was then, as at other times when she appeared in public, dressed in the habit of the goddess Isis, and gave audience to the people under the name of the New Isis." (Plutarch in Clough, 1875)

On December 31, 33 BC the Triumvirate was officially over, and it was clear that there would be no new treaty. Cleopatra met Antony, who had gone off to consolidate his ground forces in Anatolia, at Ephesus in early 32 BC. Of the 800 ships ready for war, 200 were supply ships brought by Cleopatra. She also brought 20,000 talents with her, enough money to fund 19 legions (Holbl, 2001).

Rome was ripping itself apart. Both of the consuls who were elected in January of 32 BC and several hundred senators fled to Antony's side after Octavian threatened to use force against Antony's supporters. Octavian, even with his propaganda machine in full force against his rival, was having trouble mustering enough troops to attack Antony, and was thus hesitant to declare war; not even Antony's formal divorce from Octavia was enough to incite a battle (Chauveau, 2004). Octavian was also raising taxes and slashing public services as he amassed a war chest, which didn't make him beloved by the Romans. Antony was winning the popularity contest. Octavian needed an ace in the hole and he needed on badly.

What was a wannabe-dictator to do?

Fortunately for Octavian, he had the perfect scapegoat: Cleopatra. As an exotic Grecian woman from Egypt she was tailor-made for Roman-centric propaganda.

Cleopatra was nearly everything the average Roman man on the street distrusted; she was Greek, she was Egyptian/Oriental, and most egregious of all… she was a woman. Roman historians and writers were already biased against her even before it became expedient to cast her as Octavian's justly defeated nemesis. Cleopatra was the exact opposite of the Roman male ideal; she was the epitome of the outrageous.

Romans both mimicked and maligned the Greeks. Romans conquered Greece, enslaved its people, sneered at its customs, and then paradoxically copied its culture. As the Roman Empire became Hellenized, Greek became the most commonly spoken language and Grecian teachings became the bedrock of Roman intellectualism. Nevertheless, the Romans did not trust the Greeks, maintaining that Greeks were naturally sneaky (Schiff, 2010). I suspect that they disliked the way their Greek slaves could frequently outsmart them, a trait which has been cross-culturally considered by slave owners as evidence of a duplicitous character in the humans they own.

As they did with Greek culture, Romans curled their collective lips at the Egyptian way of life and then copied it assiduously. To the Romans, "Egypt was a symbol of the exotic, just as the Orient was for nineteenth-century Europeans" (Ellis, 1992). Furthermore, Egypt didn't leap to adopt Roman culture. Egypt retained so much of its own sociocultural identity that mighty Rome found itself forced to be more "tolerant" of a foreign culture it sought to conquer. Egypt was also rich. Romans imported wheat, olive oil, glass, gold, silver, and turquoise from Egypt by the ton (Thompson, 2011). Taxes on these material goods meant that wealth, like the Nile, flowed upward. Cleopatra was one of the most prosperous monarchs to ever reign anywhere, at any time. She was far richer than even the richest Roman. The Romans really didn't like the idea that that Egyptian civilization was older and wealthier than Rome. That seemed quite uppity in a country full of non-Romans.

There was almost nothing else on Gaia's good earth that Romans despised more than Eastern strumpets – except for Roman men who allowed themselves to be bossed around by Eastern strumpets. All Octavian had to do was firmly link her name with Antony's in the public mind and make it seem like Antony was dancing to her tune then … BOOM, Antony's reputation would sink like a rock.

Octavian took a bold risk and seized Antony's will. Suetonius recorded that, "the better to show that his rival had fallen away from conduct becoming a citizen, he had the will which Antony had left in Rome, naming his children by Cleopatra among his heirs, opened and read before the people." Stealing and reading a will was both illegal under Roman law and expressly forbidden in Rome's state religion. Octavian was counting on the will being so inflammatory to Roman feelings that they ignored the wicked lawlessness of its being read in the first place.

In a marvelous piece of serendipity, Antony's will was indeed inflammatory. It not only acknowledged his children with Cleopatra, but also asseverated that her son Caesarion was fathered by Julius Caesar and instructed that Antony's body should be interred in Alexandria rather than Rome. If Octavian had written the will himself, he could not have hoped for a more damning document in the eyes of the Roman public. It was almost as if though the whole thing were a forgery created for Octavian's own purposes!

Rumors regarding Antony's intentions ran through Rome like wildfire:

"Calvisius, a dependent of [Octavian], urged other charges in connection with Cleopatra against Antony; that he had given her the library of Pergamus, containing two hundred thousand distinct volumes; that at a great banquet, in the presence of many guests, he had risen up and rubbed her feet, to fulfill some wager or promise; that he had suffered the Ephesians to salute her as their queen; that he had frequently at the public audience of kings and princes received amorous messages written in tablets made of onyx and crystal, and read them openly on the tribunal; that when Furnius, a man of great authority and eloquence among the Romans, was pleading, Cleopatra happening to pass by in her chair, Antony started up and left them in the middle of their cause, to follow at her side and attend her home." (Plutarch in Clough, 1875)

Romans initially suspected that Calvisius was making stuff up, because the stories he was spreading were too far-fetched. Antony, war-hero and friend to Caesar, an Egypt-whipped cat's paw for Cleopatra? Surely not!

Octavian's PR machine ground on however, and made fine meal for Roman consumption. Antony, it was said, was becoming "more than ever a slave to the passion and the witchery of Cleopatra" (Cassius Dio In Scott-Kilvert, 1987). Cleopatra was driving away more and more of Antony's Roman allies, old friends whom he now allowed to suffer "insolent usage" in her court to please the queen (Plutach in Clough, 1875). The will that was supposedly Antony's was continually used to flog the public into outrage. Octavian's biographers would later insist that the winds of popularity started to blow against Antony in Rome. Cassius Dio assured his readers that "Romans in their indignation [began] to believe that the other reports in circulation were also true, to the effect that if Antony should prevail, he would bestow their city upon Cleopatra and transfer the seat of power to Egypt ... For she so charmed and enthralled not only him but also the rest who had any influence with him that she conceived the hope of ruling even the Romans" (in Scott-Kilvert, 1987).

Did the majority of Romans really believe that Antony, a loyal son of the city, would move the capital of the Empire from Rome to that hot-house of sin, Alexandria? Only the records of the anti-Antony faction are left, so it is impossible to be sure. However, even Mark Antony's supporters knew who *really* to blame if such a treacherous thought had actually entered his head. It was Cleopatra's fault, of course!

Thanks to Octavian's propaganda and the natural mistrust of the Romans for Oriental potentates, Cleopatra became the one thing everyone agreed to hate. The female pharaoh of Egypt was no longer merely a "ruinous monster" who had destroyed Antony; she was a "calamitous danger" to Rome itself (Holbl, 2001). She had to be stopped at any cost before she brought down the Empire! But who was the stalwart man who could save the citizens of Rome from the predations of the voracious Whore of the Nile?

Octavian was clearly the only answer to that question.

CHAPTER EIGHT

In the autumn of 32 BC, Octavian very publically went to the temple of the goddess of war, Bellona, where he had priests sacrifice pigs to this important Roman deity. He then dipped a javelin into the blood of the sacrifice and led his audience to the Field of Mars. There, he cast the javelin to signify he was starting a war with a *foreign* enemy. It was Cleopatra, the femme fatale who had destroyed Mark Antony with her insidious charms, whom Octavia claimed to be fighting. His message was that Rome was attacking Egypt; Octavian was certainly not attacking Antony in a palpable bid to become Emperor! No need to worry about that, citizens of Rome!

Above and beyond Antony's diminished but persistent popularity, it was a smart move on Octavian's part to keep Antony out of the declaration of war. He was giving Antony enough rope to hang himself. Octavian and his allies knew "full well that [Antony] would become an enemy in any event, since he certainly was not going to prove false to her and espouse [Octavian's] cause; and they wished to have this additional reproach to put upon him, that he had voluntarily taken up war on the side of the Egyptian woman against his native country, though no ill-treatment had been accorded him personally by the people at home" (Cassius Dio in Scott-Kilvert, 1987).

Octavian, with the Senate's backing, also "had a decree made, declaring war on Cleopatra, and depriving Antony of the authority which he had let a woman exercise in his place [Octavian] added that [Antony] had drunk potions that had bereaved him of his senses, and that the generals they would have to fight with would be Mardion the eunuch, Pothinus, Iras, Cleopatra's hairdressing girl, and Charmion, who were Antony's chief state-councilors" (Plutarch in Clough, 1875).

In regards to manipulation, it was a brilliant decree. By claiming that Antony had been drugged with "potions" by Cleopatra, Antony's ensnarement by the queen became a sign of the treacherous evil of foreign magic rather than any weakness in Roman masculinity. Even Antony's friends could therefore desert him with clean consciences; he was no longer the Antony they had known. He was now the hollow shell filled with Cleopatra's poisons and must be defeated by Octavian for the good of all. To symbolize how far Antony had slipped off true, he was said to be taking advice from not only a queen, but also eunuchs and hairdressing girls. Antony, according to Octavian, had become everything that a real Roman man was *not* because he had been ensorcelled by a devious and exotic slattern.

The war between Mark Antony and Octavian finally moved from rhetoric to battle in the spring of 31 BC. Cleopatra, who was heavily invested in the outcome of the war in more ways than one, joined Antony's military counsels. This would turn out to be a bad idea, in hindsight.

Cleopatra favored defense, a strategy that "clearly indicated that [she] was primarily concerned with Egypt and obviously was not interested in marching on Rome as Octavian's propaganda had alleged" (Holbl, 2001). She also believed that the war should be fought primarily at sea, inasmuch as Antony and Egypt had conspicuous naval superiority over Octavian's warships. To defend with one's greatest source of strength is not a foolish choice per se, but it was against the aggressive nature of the Roman military. What Cleopatra failed to understand is that they couldn't just fight Octavian off. To win the war she and Antony would have to win Rome itself. This would have seemed like madness to Cleopatra, since she was aware that the city would break out into terminal riots if the Romans though she was ruling them in any way.

Most historians believe that, with the best of intent, Cleopatra talked Antony out of using his greater military forces to invade Italy and attack Octavian. Instead, nearly 100,000 of Antony's troops whiled away the summer on the other side of the Ionian Sea in the region of Epiros. His fleet was snug and safe from attack in the Gulf of Ambracia, which could only be accessed by sea via a small straight. The promontory called Actium overlooked the straight, and it would give the upcoming clash between Octavian's and Antony's forces its name.

Within the Gulf of Ambracia, Antony's troops and warships were safe from surprise attacks, but they were also appallingly easy to blockade. Supplies were not getting through, which meant hungry soldiers. Antony's men were also suffering from the heat and the malarial outbreak which the mosquitoes that infested the area were kind enough to share with nearly everyone. There was also tension between the troops. The Romans under Antony's command were unhappy about fighting with the Thracians, Greeks, Polemics, Medians, and Cretans alongside them. Antony's troops grew increasingly anxious and unhappy.

Worst of all, from their point of view, was Cleopatra's presence.

"That she occupied a vital position in camp and did little to apologize for that position is clear; as Egypt's commander and chief, she believed war preparations and operations to be her duty ... She was unwilling to be silenced ...It is impossible to say what came first, the Roman humiliation at Cleopatra's presence, or Cleopatra's superciliousness with the Romans. Antony's officers were said to be ashamed of her and of her status as equal partner. His closest companions objected to her authority ...Even the trusted Candidius, who had earlier argued on her behalf, wanted her gone ... [but] Antony would not send her away as "his ears, it seems, were stopped by his infatuation" ...Slaves and client kings alike abandoned the cause" (Schiff, 2010).

As summer ended, Antony was left with two choices. He could either abandon his ships and fall back further into Greece or he could abandon his troops and use his fleet to break out of the gulf and return to Alexandria. Cleopatra was decidedly in favor of a naval battle, and in the end that is what Antony chose to do.

Outflanked and outnumbered during the battle, Antony saw that his fleet had very little chance of winning the encounter. From the outset he had probably been preparing to get as many of his ships as possible back to Alexandria, to recoup and retrench (Anglim, 2003). Antony put Cleopatra and the supply ships in a rear squadron, and then used his remaining fleet to hold off Octavian's navy so that the queen and sixty ships could escape with a good head start. Antony and the surviving ships followed suit.

It was a bad defeat for Antony, but it wasn't all that Octavian had hoped for either. Rather than a decisive victory that ended the war, Octavian had egg on his face and Antony had lived to fight another day. However, Octavian was one of the best spin-doctors in history. He spread the word that:

> "the fortune of the day was still undecided, and the battle equal, when on a sudden

Cleopatra's sixty ships were seen hoisting sail and making out to sea in full flight, right through the ships that were engaged. For they were placed behind the great ships, which, in breaking through, they put into disorder. The enemy was astonished to see them sailing off with a fair wind towards Peloponnesus. Here it was that Antony showed to all the world that he was no longer actuated by the thoughts and motives of a commander or a man, or indeed by his own judgment at all, and what was once said as a jest, that the soul of a lover lives in someone else's body, he proved to be a serious truth. For, as if he had been born part of her, and must move with her wheresoever she went, **as soon as he saw her ship sailing away, he abandoned all that were fighting and spending their lives for him,** and put himself aboard a galley of five ranks of oars, taking with him only Alexander of Syria and Scellias, **to follow her that had so well begun his ruin and would hereafter accomplish it**. She, perceiving him to follow, gave the signal to come aboard. So, as soon as he came up with them, he was taken into the ship. But without seeing her or letting himself be seen by her, he went forward by himself, and sat alone, without a word, in the ship's prow, covering his face with his two hands" (Plutarch in Clough, 1875).

That story stuck to the historical record like white on rice. To this day, most people think that Cleopatra sailed away from battle after her soothsayers declared that omens revealed Antony's demise and that Mark Antony then abandon his fleet to chase after Cleopatra.

Cassius Dio further embellished the tale of Antony's unmanly enslavement to Cleopatra. According to him, prior to the naval engagement Octavian had given his men a stirring speech, telling them:

> "For that we who are Romans and lords of the greatest and best portion of the world should be despised and trodden under foot by an Egyptian woman is unworthy of our fathers, who overthrew Pyrrhus, Philip, Perseus, and Antiochus, who drove the Numantians and the Carthaginians from their homes, who cut down the Cimbri and the Ambrones; it is unworthy also of ourselves, who have subjugated the Gauls, subdued the Pannonians, advanced as far as the Ister, crossed the Rhine, and passed over the sea into Britain. Would not all those who have performed the exploits I have named grieve mightily if they should learn that we had succumbed to an accursed woman? Should we not be acting most disgracefully if, after surpassing all men everywhere in valour, we should then meekly bear the insults of this throng, who, oh heavens! are Alexandrians and Egyptians (what worse or what truer name could one apply to them?), who worship reptiles and beasts as gods, who embalm their own bodies to give them the semblance of immortality, who are most reckless in effrontery but most feeble in courage, and who, worst of all, are slaves to a woman and not to a man, and yet have dared to lay claim to our possessions and to use us to help them acquire them, expecting that we will voluntarily give up to them the prosperity which we possess? Who would not lament at seeing

Roman soldiers acting as bodyguards of their queen? Who would not groan at hearing that Roman knights and senators fawn upon her like eunuchs? Who would not weep when he hears and sees Antony himself, the man twice consul, often imperator, to whom was committed in common with me the management of the public business, who was entrusted with so many cities, so many legions — when he sees that this man has now abandoned all his ancestors' habits of life, has emulated all alien and barbaric customs, that he pays no honour to us or to the laws or to his fathers' gods, but pays homage to that wench as if she were some Isis or Selene, calling her children Helios and Selene, and finally taking for himself the title of Osiris or Dionysus, and, after all this, making presents of whole islands and parts of the continents, as though he were master of the whole earth and the whole sea? All these things seem marvellous and incredible to you soldiers, as I am well aware, but you ought therefore to be the more indignant. For if that is actually true which you do not believe even when you hear it, and if that man in his luxurious indulgence does commit acts at which anyone would grieve who learns of them, would it not be reasonable that you should go past all bounds in your rage?"

In Rome, Octavian's victory at Actium was portrayed as a symbol "of the great struggle of the West against the East, of liberty against despotism, honesty against corruption, frugality against opulence, simplicity against sophistication, and virtue against depravity … It also represented, to Romans, the defense of Roman laws against the arbitrary despotism of the

East ... [Whereas Cleopatra] flaunted her riches and used her empire to gratify herself, the Roman ethic prescribed parsimony and insisted that the purpose of empire was not to indulge the whims of the powerful" (Gress, 1998). In a nutshell, Rome was told it had won because it wasn't prone to Eastern dissipation. Any modern reader even remotely familiar with the excesses that Octavian's reign as Caesar Augustus would usher in to the Roman culture will doubtlessly find this ironic in the extreme.

In spite of assumptions to the contrary, Antony did not follow Cleopatra back to Alexandria like a hopeful puppy. Instead, he sailed to Cyrenaica, where he planned to coordinate a counter-attack on Octavian. He had every reason to expect a warm welcome there. Lucius Pindarius Scarpus, the governor of Cyrenaica, had been given his position by Antony. Sadly, like Pompey, Antony was to discover that gratitude was in short supply among those he had helped. Scarpus, upon hearing of Antony's defeat at Actium, had turned his coat and gone over to Octavian. Rather than assisting Antony, Scarpus killed his messengers and refused to allow him to dock. Only when faced with this betrayal, and with his options curtailed, did Antony return to Alexandria and Cleopatra.

Once the word got out that Octavian had won Actium, Antony's client kings and friends almost trampled each other in their rush to Octavian's side. Now Egypt was surrounded by suddenly hostile armies and was left wide open from both sides for Octavian's eventual assault.

Cleopatra, being above all things pragmatic in the face of adversity, decided the best course of action would be to put as many miles between herself and Octavian as possible. She convinced Antony that by using the technological skills of the Egyptians they could move ships and treasure 40 miles overland to be launched into the Red Sea. From there, they could go sail through the Gulf of Aden and into the Arabian Sea, possibly going as far away as India to plan their future. Unfortunately for Cleopatra, her ships would have to be drawn to shore in the territory of the Nabateans. Her mortal enemy, King Herod of Judea, had recently conquered the Nabateans thanks to Cleopatra's sabotage (Schiff, 2010). The Nabateans were miffed about that. They were so miffed about it that they set fire to each one of Cleopatra's ships as it was beached.

Escape via the Red Sea was no longer one of her options. Nor could she count on Antony. With his defeat at Actium and his friend's abandonment, the mighty general had lost heart. While Cleopatra schemed and plotted with her allies in the region, Antony retreated into a small hut near the bottom of the Alexandrian lighthouse. On top of everything else she was doing, the queen also had to coax her lover out of his despair.

It is this juncture that Cleopatra revealed herself to be a parent unlike her Ptolemy forebears; she actually loved her offspring. The proud queen of Egypt stooped to beg Octavian for the lives of her children. She sent Octavian a throne, a crown, and a scepter of gold and offered to abdicate – to even kill herself -- if he would spare her children and allow her son Caesarion to be recognized as pharaoh after her banishment or death. Octavian's private response was chilling: "he would be perfectly reasonable with her [provided she would] arrange for Antony's execution or at the very least his exile" (Schiff, 2010).

So why didn't Cleopatra hand over Antony's head in a basket? The short answer is that she had no guarantee that Octavian would (for a change) actually keep up his end of the agreement even if she was willing to kill her closest ally. That's not even taking into account the PR fallout if she murdered her husband to appease a Roman oppressor. The longer answer is that whatever she and Antony might have felt for each other in the beginning of their association they appear to have fallen genuinely in love with one another by its end. Cleopatra was caught between the devil and the deep blue sea.

In the fall of 30 BC Antony had recovered enough to join Cleopatra in negotiations with Octavian. Using envoys, "Antony reminded [Octavian] of their friendship and kinship, made a defense also of his connection with the Egyptian woman, and recounted all the amorous adventures and youthful pranks they had shared together … [Antony] **offered to take his own life, if in that way Cleopatra might be saved** … Antony dispatched … his son Antyllus with much gold. Caesar accepted the money, but sent the boy back empty-handed, giving him no answer." When none of these offers got a response from Octavian, Antony finally challenged his rival to single combat. Octavian, being an intelligent man, chose not to meet such hardened soldier in a combat.

Romans had no love for losers while they were alive, although they often mourned them later. Antony was clearly the loser and Octavian was manifestly the winner. Thus, during the final battle with Octavian's forces, Antony's troops defected in masse. In his despair, Antony "retired into the city, crying out that Cleopatra had betrayed him to the enemies he had made for her sake". This was irrational in the extreme, but Antony was a man at the very end of his mental reserves.

In response, Cleopatra locked herself and two trusted women into her mausoleum and supposedly sent Antony word that she was dead. Perhaps she wanted him to remember he loved her before he harmed her in his madness, but later historian Cassius Dio would accuse Cleopatra of faking her own death as a way of slyly planting the idea of suicide into Antony's head. Whatever Cleopatra's intentions, when Antony believed that she was dead he stabbed himself in the stomach with his own sword. Unfortunately, it was only *after* he had inflicted this mortal wound that he found out Cleopatra was alive. Mortally wounded, Antony asked to be brought to her:

> "Cleopatra would not open the door, but, looking from a sort of window, she let down ropes and cords, to which Antony was fastened; and she and her two women, the only persons she had allowed to enter the monument, drew him up. Those that were present say that nothing was ever more sad than this spectacle, to see Antony, covered all over with blood and just expiring, thus drawn up, still holding up his hands to her, and lifting up his body with the little force he had left. As, indeed, it was no easy task for the women; and Cleopatra, with all her force, clinging to the rope, and straining with her head to the ground, with difficulty pulled him up, while those below encouraged her with their cries, and joined in all her effort and anxiety. When she had got him up, she laid him on the bed, tearing all her clothes, which she spread upon him; and, beating her breasts with her hands, lacerating herself, and disfiguring her own face with the blood from his wounds, she called him her lord, her husband, her emperor, and seemed to have pretty nearly forgotten all her own evils, she was so intent upon his misfortunes" (Plutarch, in Clough, 1875).

CHAPTER NINE

As much as she was overcome by Antony's death, Cleopatra was still not down for the count. Instead, she was wisely staying inside the heavily fortified mausoleum on a pile of treasure with which to manipulate Octavian. From her stronghold she demanded, "that her kingdom might be given to her children." She threatened to burn in the mausoleum to the ground – destroying along with it all the loot she had collected -- if Octavian tried to take her by force. Octavian was not a fool and knew Cleopatra wasn't bluffing. Even in utter defeat she was still a formidable adversary.

Since brute strength wouldn't work, Octavian tried sweet talk. He promised to let her bury Antony with full honors (something incredibly important to both the Romans and the Egyptians) and let her know he was treating her children by Mark Antony well. (Her oldest son, Caesarion, had already been sent toward India with a lot of money and a theoretically trusted tutor to help him and was presumably out of Octavian's reach.) All Octavian claimed he wanted from her was that she come back to live in the palace and be reasonable about negotiations.

What happened next may actually be one of the more factual accounts of Cleopatra. Her personal physician, Olympos, wrote a first person account of the next few days that became the basis of Plutarch's account (Holbl, 2001):

Antony "was buried with royal splendor and magnificence, it being granted to [Cleopatra] to employ what she pleased on his funeral. In this extremity of grief and sorrow, and having inflamed and ulcerated her breasts with beating them, she fell into a high fever, and was very glad of the occasion, hoping, under this pretext, to abstain from food, and so to die in quiet without interference. She had her own physician, Olympus, to whom she told the truth, and asked his advice and help to put an end to herself, as Olympus himself has told us, in a narrative which he wrote of these events. But Caesar, suspecting her purpose, **took to menacing language about her children, and excited her fears for them, before which engines her purpose shook and gave way,** so that she suffered those about her to give her what meat or medicine they pleased."

It is fairly plain that when Cleopatra had given up on else, even her own life, she was still trying to keep her children safe. Is she remembered as a devoted mother, one who was willing to sacrifice anything for her children? Nope. She is remembered as the sexy chippie who seduced Caesar and Antony. In a slut shaming culture no other deed, no matter how laudable, can outweigh the 'dishonor' of woman who had had sex and maintained her own power.

At this point all Cleopatra appeared to have wanted for herself was to die rather than be dragged through Rome in chains for Octavian's Triumph. Octavian, just as fiercely, wanted her alive to drag through Rome in chains for his Triumph. In order to achieve her goal Cleopatra needed to trick Octavian into guarding her loosely enough that she could get her hands on a suitable means of suicide. She did this by convincing him she really, really wanted to live:

"Some few days after, [Octavian] himself came to make her a visit and comfort her. She lay then upon her pallet-bed in undress, and, on his entering in, sprang up from off her bed, having nothing on but the one garment next her body, and flung herself at his feet, her hair and face looking wild and disfigured, her voice quivering, and her eyes sunk in her head. The marks of the blows she had given herself were visible about her bosom, and altogether her whole person seemed no less afflicted than her soul. But, for all this, her old charm, and the boldness of her youthful beauty had not wholly left her, and, in spite of her present condition, still sparkled from within, and let itself appear in all the movements of her countenance. Caesar, desiring her to repose herself, sat down by her; and, on this opportunity, she said something to justify her actions, attributing what she had done to the necessity she was under, and to her fear of Antony; and when Caesar, on each point, made his objections, and she found herself confuted, she broke off at once into language of entreaty and deprecation, as if she desired nothing more than to prolong her life. And at last, having by her a list of her treasure, she gave it into his hands; and when Seleucus, one of her stewards, who was by, pointed out that various articles were omitted, and charged her with secreting them, she flew up and caught him by the hair, and struck him several blows on the face. Caesar smiling and withholding her, "Is it not very hard, Caesar," said she, "when you do me the honor to visit me in this condition I am in, that I should be accused by one of my own servants of laying by some women's toys, not meant to adorn, be sure, my unhappy self, but that I might have some little present by me to make your Octavia and your Livia, that by their intercession I might hope to find you in some measure disposed to mercy?" Caesar was pleased to hear her talk thus, being now assured that she was desirous to live. And, therefore, letting her know that the things she had laid by she might dispose of as she pleased, and his usage of her should be honorable above her expectation, he went away, well satisfied that he had overreached her, but, in fact, was himself deceived." (Plutach in Clough, 1875)

After all they had been through Octavian still made the mistake of underestimating her. He would have expected any Roman man to have been eager for death in a similar circumstance, but he could not see the same honor-driven wish in a woman who was Oriental and Greek. Every Roman knew that Eastern people, especially the woman, had little honor and needed great Romans to lead them into nobility. Cleopatra was well aware of this Roman weakness and played Octavian like a cheap fiddle.

Would the Imperial historians admit that a Roman man was outwitted yet again by a Greco-Egyptian woman? Pish-tosh! Cassius Dio, indignant that such a thing could even be conceived, garnished the tale of Octavian's last visit with the queen to demonstrate Roman mastery over tricky Oriental women. According to Dio, Octavian was employing a clever ruse to make Cleopatra think he had fallen in love with her. No matter how Cleopatra wheedled and flattered and tried to evoke sympathy, she just could not bluff Octavian. Cassius Dio assures the reader that Cleopatra "was greatly distressed because [Octavian] would neither look at her nor say anything about the kingdom nor even utter a word of love, and falling at his knees, she said with an outburst of sobbing: "I neither wish to live nor can I live, [Octavian]. But this favour I beg of you in memory of your father, that, since Heaven gave me to Antony after him, I may also die with Antony. Would that I had perished then, straightway after [Octavian]! But since it was decreed by fate that I should suffer this affliction also, send me to Antony; grudge me not burial with him, in order that, as it is because of him I die, so I may dwell with him even in Hades."

It seems peculiar that Cleopatra would so openly beg for death and yet Octavian wouldn't be suspicious of her attempted suicide. Dio solves this problem by shifting blame onto "others", as in other "to whose charge she had been committed, had come to believe that she really felt as she pretended to, and *neglected to keep a careful watch*, she made her preparations to die as painlessly as possible." See? Not Octavian's slip-up at all. Of course, in this same account Dio also called Julius Caesar Octavian's "father" so its accuracy is perhaps less than exact.

Regardless of whose eyes she pulled the wool over, Cleopatra made good on her determination to die. On her last day of life, she:

> "sent to Caesar a letter which she had written and sealed; and, putting everybody out of the monument but her two women, she shut the doors. Caesar, opening her letter, and finding pathetic prayers and entreaties that she might be buried in the same tomb with Antony, soon guessed what was doing. At first he was going himself in all haste, but, changing his mind, he sent others to see. The thing had been

quickly done. The messengers came at full speed, and found the guards apprehensive of nothing; but on opening the doors, they saw her stone-dead, lying upon a bed of gold, set out in all her royal ornaments. Iras, one of her women, lay dying at her feet, and Charmion, just ready to fall, scarce able to hold up her head, was adjusting her mistress's diadem. And when one that came in said angrily, "Was this well done of your lady, Charmion?" "Extremely well," she answered, "and as became the descendant of so many kings"; and as she said this, she fell down dead by the bedside." (Plutarch in Clough, 1875).

Although Octavian thought she had had an asp smuggled into her room in a basket of figs and died from its bite, no one was really sure how she arranged her death. Even Cassius Dio admits that, "No one knows clearly in what way she perished, for the only marks on her body were slight pricks on the arm. Some say she applied to herself an asp which had been brought in to her in a water-jar, or perhaps hidden in some flowers. Others declare that she had smeared a pin, with which she was wont to fasten her hair, with some poison possessed of such a property that in ordinary circumstances it would not injure the body at all, but if it came into contact with even a drop of blood would destroy the body very quietly and painlessly; and that previous to this time she had worn it in her hair as usual, but now had made a slight scratch on her arm and had dipped the pin in the blood." (Cassius Dio in Scott-Kilver, 1987).

Regardless of how it was accomplished, Cleopatra -- the last woman to rule Egypt -- was dead.

Cleopatra had slipped out of Octavian's grasp, and "though much disappointed by her death, yet could not but admire the greatness of her spirit, and gave order that her body should he buried by Antony with royal splendor and magnificence. Her women, also, received honorable burial by his directions. Cleopatra had lived nine and thirty years, during twenty-two of which she had reigned as queen, and for fourteen had been Antony's partner in his empire. Antony, according to some authorities, was fifty-three, according to others, fifty-six years old. His statues were all thrown down, but those of Cleopatra were left untouched; for Archibius, one of her friends, gave Caesar two thousand talents to save them from the fate of Antony's." Plutarch in Clough, 1875)

After Cleopatra's death, Antony's ex-wife, Octavia, displayed true compassion and poise by taking on responsibility for the upkeep and safety of her dead husband's children by Cleopatra (Burns, 2006). Octavian had much less class and empathy, however. Rome's new Caesar had Cleopatra's three youngest children paraded beside their dead mother's statue in his Triumph in 29 BC. The twins were ten and their little brother was only four years old. By the time of his Triumph, Octavian had already had both Antony's son Antyllus and Cleopatra's son Caesarion brutally murdered after they were betrayed by their unscrupulous tutors. Cleopatra's remaining sons, ominously, "vanished from the historical record soon after entering Octavia's care" (Tyldesley, 2011). Two little boys would have been easy prey for the most powerful man in the Western world and it could have easily looked like one of the myriad childhood illnesses had killed them. Frankly, I would be more surprised by proof Octavian *didn't* murder his sister's wards than by proof to the contrary.

In spite of all Cleopatra could do only her daughter would survive long enough to marry and have children of her own. Cleopatra Selene was married to Numidian prince Juba II, a client king of Octavian's who ruled the country of Mauretania in northwestern Africa. As a child Juba had also been paraded through Rome in chains during the Triumph of Julius Caesar and had also been subsequently raised in Octavia's household. Juba became a "rex literatissimus", a scholar-king, respected by such notaries as Pliny the Elder and Plutarch (Roller, 2004). From all evidence he and Cleopatra Selene had a strong marriage. Their court was culturally rich and was honored for its sophistication throughout the region. Before her death (the date is unknown but it appears to be around 5 BC), Cleopatra Selene bore at least two children: Ptolemaios, who ruled Mauretania until he was murdered by Caligula, and a daughter named Drusilla whose fate after her marriage is largely unknown. After Ptolemaios's death, there is no further historical record of Cleopatra's descendants. It seems all that is left of Cleopatra is the memory of her deeds.

How is this mighty pharaoh remembered?

Is she remembered for the intellectual renaissance she encouraged in Alexandria? It was under Cleopatra's auspices that the "only indigenous school of philosophy" appeared in Alexandria (Schiff, 2010). Among the great thinkers Cleopatra encouraged and supported were the renowed orator Philostratus, the preeminent skeptic Aenesidemus of Knossos, and the lionized author Didymus. She was the patron of the Temple of Hathor, which housed the first known medical center devoted to obstetrics and gynecology.

Is she remembered for the astute way she handled an outbreak of famine and bubonic plague in the spring of 43 BC? She opened her granaries and distributed wheat free to the starving populace of Alexandria, and gave a general amnesty to those who had protested tax collection. Some scholars suggest that it was Cleopatra herself who sent one of her court physicians, Dioscordides, to accompany Poseidonius and examine the strange new disease causing glandular swelling and death throughout Egypt and Libya (Little, 2007). Dioscordises, who is often mistakenly described as a physician in the Roman army living 100 years later, wrote at least some of the De Materia Medica with Cleopatra's funding. The De Materia Medica would be used by healers for nearly 2000 years.

Is Cleopatra remembered for her building projects? She is carved on the walls of the Temple of Dendera, she completed the works of her father in Edfu, and she commissioned a shrine in the form of a ship at Koptos. She also authorized building the Caesareum above the harbor, which "would ultimately constitute a precinct unto itself, of porticoes, libraries, chambers, groves, gateways, boardwalks, and courts, fitted with exquisite art" (Schiff, 2010). She also started a gargantuan Temple of Isis, "which would have dwarfed everything else in Alexandria but which was unfinished at her death and was probably never completed" (Trow, 2013).

Is she remembered for her clemency toward the Jewish community in Alexandria? In spite of the claims of Josephus, a Jewish historian who was determined to please the Romans, Cleopatra did not discriminate against Hebrews in her kingdom. Instead, "Jews were involved in all levels of government, even the surprisingly efficient police force, and it was a Jewish army that had backed her and Caesar in 48" (Trow, 2013). Octavian, unlike Cleopatra, would not be able to keep anti-Semitism in Alexandria on a leash when he took over after her death (Smallwood, 2001).

Is Cleopatra remembered for any or all of these accomplishments?

Of course not. She was a Bad Girl. Thus, she is at best remembered as a tootsie who eventually fell in love with a loser and offed herself. When historical biographer Vicky Alvear Shecter spoke at a high school she played a word association game and the name "Cleopatra" evoked the responses "Queen" "Egypt" "Slut" "Whore", causing Shecter to reflect that, "The spirit of Augustus Caesar must have danced a little jig of victory because 2,000 years after his propaganda war against the queen, we are still maligning her with insults related to her ultimately unknowable (and irrelevant) sex life" (Shecter, 2010). Cleopatra has inspired hard-core porn films with names like *Cleopatra's Bondage Revenge* and *Venus of the Nile* (Solomon, 2001). Thanks to historical slut shaming Cleopatra, "will always be known as the seductress from the East who lured two of Rome's greatest men away from their duties … [rather than] a heroic and brilliant patriot, and the last major threat to the Roman Empire" (Mahon, 2011).

Despite all that she accomplished using her brain, all most people remember her for what she might have done with her vagina.

CHAPTER TEN

What, exactly, did Cleopatra *do* to inspire history to remember her as more of a sex kitten than pharaoh? Why is she so viciously slut shamed? Sexually, she had two long term monogamous partners, one of whom she married formally in accordance to her religious traditions. Although both her lovers had numerous other women in their lives and were not monogamous themselves, there is no evidence whatsoever that Cleopatra ever looked for physical intimacy outside of these two men. She was, on the contrary, loyal to both her partners until their death. What sexual promiscuity did she indulge in that gives her such a slutty reputation? If she was sexually conservative, what is it that she did to make her a harlot?

She did what all sluts do: she broke a gender based cultural taboo and did things no woman is *supposed* to be able to do.

Women are supposed to be weak. Cleopatra was strong. Cleopatra made decisions with a ruthless pragmatism that makes a mockery of the idea of tender-hearted womanhood. She was daring where women are said to be cautious, bold where women are said to be timid, and fierce where women are said to be demure. Cleopatra usurped masculine prerogatives with ease when a Good Girl should have fainted from affronted sensibilities. Moreover, women are supposed to be sexual objects, the targets of male desire. Cleopatra used her sexuality as a tool for cementing political bonds. Women are supposed to be docile, yet Cleopatra was active. Women are supposed to depend on men, nevertheless men depended on Cleopatra. Women are supposed to be retiring, but Cleopatra remained undaunted. Women are supposed to be feminine with feminine attributes, while instead Cleopatra was feminine with *masculine* attributes.

Perhaps the Romans could have forgiven Cleopatra for being an affluent Greco-Egyptian. They could have possibly even forgiven her for being influential in Roman politics, provided she bought a Roman citizenship and strived to emulate Roman manners. Yes, forgiveness may have been possible, if only Cleopatra had been born with a penis. As a Greco-Egyptian *woman*, however, she was a menace.

Women, according to Classical thought, were just all kinds of wrong. Men were considered to be rational, humane, philosophical and able to rise above the demands of the flesh. In contrast, women were emotional, animalistic, unreasonable, and a slave to their biology.

All the "proof" that women were inherently inferior came from the belief in a decisive split between the mind and the body. Humans, it was argued, had a body and a soul/mind. The body was a bestial thing driven by appetites; the soul/mind was for art, learning, and communing with the gods. The body was the seat of all things lowly and vulgar, while the mind was the home of all that was good and civilized (Bordo, 1999). Plato, whose influence as a philosopher cannot be overstated, considered the human body a mere prison that caged and limited the rational soul, an obstacle man strove to overcome. Plato declared that the soul was always striving to become "pure", and that souls were reincarnated over many lifetimes. One could, according to Plato, see what kind of soul one had by the way one lived one's life. Women, he explained, always harbored an impure or adulterated soul in their filthy bodies. He warned that if a man wasn't good, his soul might come back in a woman's body. Women, the disgusting creatures, just could NOT overcome the body to concentrate on the higher ideas of the mind (Spelman, 1999).

Thus, the idea that women and the body are inextricably linked in a way men were not rooted itself in the very heart of the Western philosophic heritage. The theory that men were synonymous with the soul/mind and women were synonymous with the animalistic body became unquestionable fact. With Plato, the philosophical and sociocultural link between men/mind and women/body became the "Truth". Aristotle, a firm believer in the wisdom of Plato, carried this Truth further, eventually arguing that women lacked a *rational* soul because of their close association with the body (Allen, 2005). Their souls were something less cerebral and noble than men's souls.

Not only did the female body house inadequate, irrational souls, ancient physicians and philosophers thought that there was something unquestionably weird about the not-male body itself. Galen, a Greek physician who was considered the utmost authority on biomedicine, considered the uterus to be an inverted scrotum which had not descended in the female due to the lack of proper male 'heat' (Thompson, 1999). Until the later Renaissance the female reproductive organs would continue to be conceptualized an inside-out model of male reproductive organs. This meant that women were, from birth, 'men gone wrong'. Like Galen, Aristotle also imagined that women were "mutilated males". This understanding of women as mutilated/deformed men meant that women were conceptualized on some level as "monsters", their feminine bodies a horrible admixture of human and animal.

This monster/woman image has the deeper implication in that women's bodies are anomalies which must be *feared and restrained.* Nevertheless, most men coveted access to female bodies and all men needed women in order to beget heirs. Women were thus a distressingly necessary evil. The deviant but desirable non-male body of a woman therefore "shares with the monster the privilege of bringing out a unique blend of fascination and horror" (Braidotti, 2013). This simultaneous attraction and repulsion felt toward the female body has been postulated to be the key to misogynists' secret dread and fear of women right up to the present day (Gilmore, 2011).

But these are now modern times! We've moved far beyond Galen and humoral theory of medicine. Surely the female mind isn't still thought of as less rational than a male one. Surely the female body isn't still thought of as some kind of deviant not-man thing, right?

Not so much.

An analysis of philosophical texts revealed that "the terms associated with the feminine are persistently marginalized by comparison with those associated with masculinity, as when the rational powers of human beings are habitually regarded as more valuable that their emotional skills (James, 2000). Women not only continue to be anecdotally perceived as less rational and more emotional in comparison to "masculine" minds, it is often treated as a scientific reality despite the fact there is no *real* evidence, peer-reviewed or otherwise, to prove this (Griffiths, 1988). Researchers David Geary and Giljsbert Stoet "found that numerous studies claiming that the stereotype, "men are better at math" had major methodological flaws, utilized improper statistical techniques, and many studies had no scientific evidence of this stereotype" (Science Daily, 2012). In contrast, hard evidence of mathematically equality has proliferated. An international study examining school math performance conclusively refuted "once and for all that girls and women have less ability to succeed in math and science because of their biology. Janet Mertz, senior author of the study … and an oncology professor at the University of Wisconsin-Madison, reduced her findings to the simplest terms … It's nurture, not nature, that holds women back in math" (Brenoff, 2011).

    The erroneous but persistent belief in greater masculine rationalization has serious sociocultural consequences. Girls have been less encouraged to pursue STEM (science, technology, engineering, and math) subjects from kindergarten to graduate school (Maynard, 2012). The dearth of women in STEM occupations in turn reinforces the concept that men are gifted with superior abilities in math and science. Not too long ago the president of Harvard University publically excused the lack of STEM professors by declaring that biological differences explained why there were fewer women teaching science (Goldenberg, 2005). The ovaries, not gender bias in hiring, were the real culprit preventing women from getting jobs at Harvard.

    Women are still often described in scientific narratives as acting at the behest of fixed biological imperatives (Birke, 1999). By strange coincidence these biological imperatives just happen to exactly match the current gender ideology. Frequently feminist scientists must bestir themselves to rip apart yet another flawed, specious bit of "research" claiming to have proved that women and men are pre-programmed by nature to act exactly like Western sexism tells them they *should* act

(Tang-Martinez, 1997). As more women enter the scientific fields, more of the accepted paradigms about human/animal behavior are called into question by a new plethora of hard evidence. For instance, longitudinal studies by noted primatologist and anthropologist Dr. Sarah Blaffer Hrdy rebuffed the accepted convention that men "inherently" dominated women by demonstrating that most primates form social cores around females which, "have far more long-term influence than does the ephemeral power politics of males" (Hrdy,1999).

Additionally, repeated scientific studies have demonstrated that the so-called alpha males are not the ones that are most successful in passing along their genes. In biology, reproduction is the only real measure of success. Females and 'non-alpha' males are the clear winners of the reproductive arms race. The attentions of the gentler beta males inspires the females to voluntary copulate with them much more frequently, especially during times of greatest fertility. Even though the alpha males can command sex the female preference for beta males means that is the nice guys who pass on their genes to the next generation. Although alpha males can superficially appear to subjugate other members of the group, the most aggressive and dominating males turn out to be the natural losers in the long run because fewer of them survive and those that do have less offspring. Male domination cannot be 'inherent' for the simple reason that fewer males inherit it.

Most gendered beliefs are buried so deeply in the human psyche by enculturation that people don't realize how much it affects their perception of reality. Scientists, regardless of their theoretically disinterested and objective stance, can be influenced by their culture just like anyone else. For example, biology continues to be described and thought of in a way that echoes the 'natural' roles of women, much like Plato did millennia ago. Dr. Emily Martin was one of the first medicos to point out that biology textbooks described a female's egg as passively awaiting the male's active sperm – just like women were supposed to be passive and men active – in direct contrast to what *actually* occurs. Knight-like sperm do not swim and penetrate the awaiting damsel of the egg. Sperm thrash their tails in an attempt to prevent getting stuck to cells in the female reproductive tract. When a sperm bumps into an egg, the zona (outer coating) of the egg grabs the sperm and holds it while its tail continues to wiggle helplessly. The egg and the sperm then both release enzymes that softens the zona so the flailing of the sperm and the chemical bonds of the egg can work *together* to get the sperm inside. Without the egg's aid, penetration does not happen; if "an egg is killed by being pricked with a needle, live sperm cannot get through the zona" (Martin, 1999). Doctors and biologists 'saw' the egg/sperm interaction through a gendered lens without even being aware that their view was distorted.

    The subconscious influence of gender ideology is why the woman's body remains conceptualized as more animalistic and more natural than a man's, just as it was in Cleopatra's era. It is implied, or even stated outright, that that women are more controlled by their bodies than men. Women are often portrayed as slaves to their hormones and cannot overcome that wretched uterus. It may not wander anymore, but it still controls the ladies. When Doctor Louann Brizendine asked how research finding varied for female test subjects, she was told point blank by a male professor that females were never used because "their menstrual cycle would just mess up the data" (Brizendine, 2007). Men are apparently uninfluenced by their hormones. People never seem to think that men's performances are jeopardized because their testosterone makes them 'naturally' too aggressive.

The influences of gendered beliefs *matters* because if people never break away from the idea there is an inherent and "right" behavior for men and women determined by their bodies then, "women who enter professions that are typical of men are therefore seen as unnatural and going against their biology; so too are men who take up professions using abilities considered to be typical of women. These "unnatural" women and men are considered to threaten the fabric of society, as seen and maintained by those (scientists, politicians, business leaders, and the gender public) who see genes as paramount in causing sex difference in behavior. The notion that genes cause sex differences has more to do with social attitudes than scientific proof" (Roger's 2001). Thus, gender inequality becomes an unalterable thing so there's no point in trying to change it. In turn, the cultural narrative insisting that women make less money and are excluded from positions of power because their girly bits make them better suited to the domestic and emotional sphere is further entrenched as a biological absolute that only freaks dispute.

If these sorts of beliefs about women continue to the present day, imagine how strong those ideologies were in Cleopatra's lifetime. For men in the ancient world, women were scary enough when they were poor and helpless; a rich, powerful ruler like Cleopatra was terrifying. Her lingering reputation as a siren is due to the fact that "Cleopatra stood at one of the most dangerous intersections in history: that of women and power" (Schiff, 2010). It is her gender, not her skills in the bedroom, that has inspired so much of the slut shaming thrown her way.

It must be admitted, however, that Cleopatra's limited sex life did help make her a target for condemnation. It is not because of the mere fact she engaged in intercourse, though. She was and is reviled because she treated sex in a very "unfeminine" way. Her sexual liaisons with Julius Caesar and Mark Antony might have been more forgivable if she let them rule *her*, as opposed to being the one influencing their policies. Cleopatra not only resisted being controlled by men; she appears to have actually reversed the 'natural order' and controlled men. When women appear to control men, they become a danger to the definition of manhood.

    Power and control are areas of intense vulnerability for men in patriarchal societies. All men may benefit from aspects of a male-dominated society, but a few men at the top have power over the many men who are lower down the socioeconomic ladder. That means that most individual men *are already struggling with a feeling of powerlessness* (Kimmell, 2010). Culturally, men are taught to "seek security, status, and other rewards through control, [and] to fear other [people's] ability to control and harm them (Johnson, 2005). A loss of control equals vulnerability and vulnerability tends to make people feel afraid. Fear is an incredibly strong motivator for behavior, and is often expressed in forms of anger or aggression. The patriarchal and systemic forces that are the true source of male anxiety are not necessarily obvious. What is obvious are the nonconforming women who may be undermining a man's sense of masculinity. For insecure men, insubordinate women who do not follow the cultural norms of gender have taken away even more of the power they already felt was insufficient. Therefore, women who cannot be controlled, "risk the wrath of men, who may feel undermined, abandoned and even betrayed" by their perceived disobedience and disregard of male authority (Johnson, 2005). Cleopatra is the symbolic manifestation of this feminine hazard to men and masculinity. If good girls make men feel safe and bad girls make men feel scared, then Cleopatra is very bad girl indeed -- a total slut.

    Slut shaming is, at heart, driven by the fear of emasculation. By calling dissident women sluts, culture is able to punish them for being a threat to manhood and a menace to the larger patriarchal structure. Slut shaming drives these dangerous women to the social margins, where they can do the least damage to the status quo. Women who are culturally noncompliant are repulsive enough; a woman who actively 'overpowers' men (especially with her sexuality) is bloodcurdlingly horrific. Cleopatra continues to be slut shamed because her 'masculine' behaviors in the past remain terrifying in the twenty-first century.

CHAPTER ELEVEN

Anne Boleyn's relationship with Henry VIII has become a romantic saga for the ages. In any good saga, both hero and antihero have to be larger than life and epic in virtue and villainy. Anne Boleyn has had the rare privilege of serving as both the innocent and the evildoer in her own story, overshadowing Henry to the point where he has become a mere background for her tale.

Anne has, on occasion, been treated as a sympathetic figure in popular culture. James Maxwell Anderson's 1948 play, *Anne of a Thousand Days*, and the 1969 movie based on it show Anne as a brave woman who was Henry's obsession and eventual victim. More often, Anne is depicted as a power-hungry woman determined to do well for herself, like in Hillary Mantel's books *Wolf Hall* and *Bringing Up the Bodies*. Sometimes Anne is characterized as a hardhearted hussy willing to indulge in any sexual depravity in order to get a crown, as she was in Philippa Gregory's novel *The Other Boleyn Sister* and the movie of the same name.

For the last 500 or so years, the most popular version of Anne's life has her playing the role of sultry harlot, a woman willing to use her sexuality as the bait to trap a king. At the very least, it has been taken for granted that she wanted to be queen and manipulated Henry in order to achieve her goal. She looms in the public mind as "the most popular femme fatale, far outranking Cleopatra or Catherine the Great of Russia"

(Smith, 2013). Inasmuch as Anne has been cast as a sly temptress making a gambit for the throne, her execution seldom engenders pity. It is either shrugged off as happenstance when you gamble in the big leagues or seen as just deserts for a wily home-wrecker.

One of the drawbacks in this Anne-as-siren narrative, (other than the lack of accurate information) is that Henry has been reduced to a chump who took more than a decade to figure out he was being played for a love-struck fool. Michael Kimmell, a sociologist who studies gender, points out that men display masculinity in part by showing their dominance over women, and women who won't be dominated threaten masculinity (Kimmell, 2010). Men who appear to be dominated by women are subject to ridicule even today, and it was a thousand times worse in the 16th century. Henry was mocked throughout Europe because he couldn't "command" Anne. How much of Anne's reputation as an artful trollop has been an exaggeration to explain her supposed emasculation of Henry VIII? She unmanned a manly king, so she was clearly a bad woman. Bad women are sluts; QED Anne must have been a slut.

Historical facts suggest that in reality Anne Boleyn was a woman constrained by circumstance, one whose greatest crime was that she had the audacity to resent her lack of options. Why then is she such a lightning rod for salacious allegations? Is it a by-product of the human enjoyment of scandal? Is the fallacious idea that Anne and her brother had incestuous sex simply more entertaining because of the shock value? Who was Anne Boleyn, really? Was she a vamp or victim or something in between? No one can say with absolute surety, but there are bits of the historical record on which to base speculative conclusions about her personality and character – with *speculative* being the key word. Historians cannot even agree 100% on the year in which she was born, let alone who she was as a person.

Eric Ives, who wrote *The Life and Death of Anne Boleyn* – which is the definitive historical biography of Henry's second wife – is of the opinion that Anne's birthdate was circa 1501. Since he was the preeminent scholar on this topic, I'm willing to believe him. She was most likely to have been born in Blickling, the Boleyn estate in Norfolk, the daughter of a courtier to Henry VII and the maternal granddaughter of the Earl of Surrey. Her grandfather was reinstated as the 2nd Duke of Norfolk when Anne was still in her teens, and by the time she came to Henry VIII's court in either late 1521 or early 1522 her grandfather was still a presence at court and the king's treasurer. Her maternal uncle, the newest earl of Surrey, was also at hand and a member of the king's council.

There has been a certain amount of historical snark about the fact that Anne's paternal lineage were founded on the marital successes of a rich merchant, but her blood was sufficiently blue for her to have a place as one of the queen's ladies in waiting. Like everyone else in England during this time period, Anne made much of her highborn antecedents. Her coat of arms proudly displayed her upper crust connections. David Starkey sniffs that, "as a remote descendant in the female line", Anne's right to display such arms was "debatable", and postulates that her heraldry was a sign she "tried too hard and asserted too much". Notwithstanding Starkey's implicit condemnation of her ambition, Anne would have been a foolish anomaly for her time if she didn't emphasize her noble heritage. Ostentation and bloodlines were the way you announced your worth, and more importantly they determined how you were valued in that era. Moreover,

Henry VIII owed his throne to his 'remote descent in the female line' to John of Gaunt. Descent in the female line was certainly advantageous when applicable to Henry, so why not to Anne?

It wasn't as though her father, Thomas Boleyn, was hawking wares in the streets either. Her dad had served as a squire of the body to Henry VII and as an ambassador to Henry VIII. He was in line for the fortunes of both the Boleyn and Hoo families, as well as half of the Ormonde estate (Ives, 2004). There was even a shot at becoming Earl of Ormonde someday, if he kept in Henry VIII's favor. Even better, Thomas Boleyn was very much in Henry's favor … perhaps too much.

Cardinal Wolsey, the man actually running Henry's kingdom for him, didn't seem to like the way Henry's favorite courtiers were getting plum offices without having to beg and bribe Wolsey first. Thomas was one of the courtiers to get smacked down by Wolsey in 1519, when the cardinal sent Boleyn a letter letting him know that instead of getting controllership of the royal household he would be getting nothing without Wolsey's say-so. The miffed Cardinal made it clear that in the course of "implementing" the king's wishes, he had quite a lot of leeway to yank a courtier's chain. Thomas had to write Wolsey a letter pleading for his support, and only after his "abject submission thus on file and a clear recognition that while the king might promise it was Wolsey who performed" (Ives, 2004) that Boleyn got the post.

Although Anne would later get the "credit" for destroying Wolsey, the Cardinal had also managed to alienate her father and her powerful uncle, the duke of Norfolk. Wolsey made plenty of enemies on his own who would have happily pushed him off fortune's cliff once it was clear he was on the edge of it. Why is it

Anne, rather than another adversary -- or Wolsey's own culpability -- that gets the blame for his downfall? Again, she is the best villain for the piece because portraying her as a hard-hearted vengeful harlot reinforces the idea she wasn't a 'proper' woman. In this way Anne is rendered as a harpy who destroyed men, rather than a woman who successfully fought back on male terms. Maintaining the narrative of Anne's unnatural lack of feminine virtues is so important that it trumps any contradictory historical information. The slut-shaming of Anne Boleyn pulls the lives of other historical figures into her orbit, warping them just enough to fit the party line.

Very little is known about Anne's earliest years, except that the family was (or at least the Boleyn offspring were) moved to Hever Castle in Kent around 1505 and it is there that she is considered to have spent her childhood. The first time she really pops up on the historical radar is when she was sent to live at the court of Archduchess Margaret of Austria, the regent for the would-be Holy Roman Emperor, Charles V. This was a definite coup for the Boleyn family. Margaret of Austria was one of the most important women in the world, and "the elite of three or four countries vied to put their sons and daughters" (Starkey, 2009) in her care in order to polish up their courtly educations.

Thomas Boleyn, like all ambassadors, was able to be charming and agreeable. I suspect Anne got her famous charisma from her dad. The man was able to become a close confidant of kings and royal dignitaries, which indicates he had his fair share of social appeal. Margaret of Austria is one of the many who were won over by Boleyn when he visited her court as an ambassador to the Netherlands in 1512-1513. She was so impressed with him that she allowed him to inveigle a spot for one of his children in her household. As soon as possible after returning home he sent Anne off with an entourage to the Archduchess Margaret, and had his daughter securely in place by the summer of 1513.

Of his three children, why did he choose Anne? George, Anne's little brother, was perhaps too young to go. Maybe Thomas already had plans for George in the English court? If so, it worked because George was one of the king's pages by 1515, when he was about 10 years old. However, Thomas did have another daughter, a daughter a year older than Anne to boot. Even if Mary had already become ensconced in England as a lady in waiting for the queen, of which there is no evidence, she could have been sent to Austria and her spot at court could have been passed on to Anne. Why wasn't Mary first pick for Margaret's court? It is almost certain that, like all ladies of quality, she was spending time with a noble relative or patron to get some "finishing" of her own, but that wouldn't have been a real impediment for sending her to the Netherlands.

Perhaps Thomas Boleyn saw glamour in Anne that reminded him of his own abilities to delight others, and was betting that she would one day be a cynosure in court circles? He would have never thought she would be queen; that would have been ludicrous. But did he hope that her birth, talents, brains, and pizzazz would mean a stellar marriage? Gain her influence with the queen, as he had influence with Henry? Lead others in fashion, and win hearts over to causes her family supported? What was it about his younger daughter that made him willing to bet on her?

Whatever it was, Thomas Boleyn's faith was justified. Anne appears to have been a hit with the archduchess Margaret, who wrote to Thomas Boleyn to let him know what a good impression his daughter was making. In her letter she assured him that, "I find her so well behaved and agreeable for her young age, that I am more obliged to you for sending her than you are to me [for receiving her]" (Starkey, 2009). Yes, some of that was the normal flattery of the era. Nevertheless, it is effusive enough to indicate that Anne had truly delighted Margaret. There is no hint of the famed temper and peevish behavior Anne would be credited with as Henry's inamorata.

Anne had been staying with the archduchess for only a year when her father wrote Margaret to tell her Anne had to return home. Henry's sister, Mary Tudor, was leaving to marry the king of France, Louis XII, soon and had specifically asked for the Boleyn sisters to be part of her retinue. Mary was born in 1496 and was only few years older than the Boleyn girls. They would all be teenagers together and, since she was marrying a man three decades older than she was, Mary would need friends her own age to converse with. Moreover, the new queen had trouble speaking French even though she had been tutored in it for years but both the Boleyn sisters were fluent in that language and could serve as interpreters who were loyal to Mary's interests. Thomas Boleyn would have seen this as a heaven sent opportunity for his girls to advance.

Anne's sister sailed to France with the new queen, arriving in early October, but Anne had to travel overland to meet them there. Mary Tudor's ladies had hardly unpacked her bags before drama commenced. Louis XII got into an almighty row with Lady Guilford, an older woman in charge of the queen's attendants from England and Mary's beloved former governess. In a snit, the bridegroom had most of the English ladies shipped back to London. The Boleyn sisters, however, "survived the purge" (Starkey, 2009). Whatever else may be said of Anne and her siblings, they certainly knew how to make themselves agreeable to those in power.

It was a short reign for the new queen. Louis XII died on New Year's Day of 1515. Rumor had it he had exhausted himself to death by dancing with his beautiful redheaded queen, either vertically or horizontally. Regardless of how it came about, Mary was now a widow and a great source of tension in France. If she was pregnant and the infant was a boy, the king who had recently taken the crown, Francis I, would have to step down. If she wasn't pregnant, then Francis was in no doubt of his throne and Mary would be thrown back on the marriage-go-round for diplomatic advantage.

The young dowager queen turned out not to be pregnant. Both Henry and Francis wanted to marry her off to their advantage. In an attempt to keep her in France, the new king flirted a little too hard with Mary and caused consternation for the widow and her attendants. Francis was only 21 and a well-known skirt-chaser, so it is easy to sympathize with Mary about her worries. Henry, meanwhile, sent Charles Brandon, the Duke of Suffolk and one of Henry's dearest friends, to go get Mary and bring her back. What neither Henry nor Francis realized was that Mary herself was in love with Brandon and that she was determined her next marriage would be to the handsome nobleman. By sending Brandon to rescue her from the French king, Henry sent the fox into the henhouse. Or perhaps Mary was the fox in this case, and Brandon the hen she was determined to catch?

The kerfuffle that resulted in Mary and Brandon's clandestine marriage was international and extreme. Brandon came close to losing his head, widowing Mary again and putting her hand in marriage back into Henry's arsenal of diplomatic weapons. Henry loved his best friend and his sister too much to do something that extreme, but he was sufficiently irked to make them pay a crippling fine. The duke and the former queen duchess returned to England, and Mary Boleyn appears to have gone with them.

Anne Boleyn did not leave for England when her sister did. Instead, Anne was invited to remain in France as the lady in waiting of the newest queen, Claude. Like Anne, Claude was in her mid-teens. Unlike her husband Francis, Claude was both pious and chaste. Anyone who has been "tempted to picture Anne in regular contact with the blatant sexuality of Francis I's household" (Ives, 2004) has been incorrect. Claude, and most of her ladies, were models of sincere virtue.

There was another influential woman at Francis I's court whom Anne probably met and openly admired: Marguerite of Angoulême, the elder sister of Francis I and the future queen of Navarre. Known as the "Mother of the Renaissance", Marguerite was "highly visible in virtually all aspects" (Cholakian and Cholakian, 2013) of royal life. She was profoundly intelligent, highly educated, lavish in bestowing her opinions, bold as any man, and an ardent supporter of the Reformation. I cannot say for sure that Anne Boleyn viewed Marguerite as a role model, but let's not pretend there aren't some clear echoes of Marguerite's behavior in Anne's decisions. Anne would later write to Marguerite that her "greatest wish, next to having a son, was to see you again" (Lindsey, 1996).

During the years Anne resided in France, Henry VIII finally had a legitimate heir who survived birth and infancy; Princess Mary was born on February 18, 1516. From Henry's point of view it wasn't wholly good news, though. The legitimate heir to his kingdom was a girl yet a woman had never been able to rule England before. There was a real and reasonable risk that if she took the crown upon Henry's death it would lead to another civil war. Henry was not wrong to fear for the future of his country if he had only a daughter to reign after him. In hindsight, we know he worried for naught. Mary not only became queen, she did it through military usurpation and ordered the execution of the legal heir she had overthrown as boldly as any prince could have done. Mary was ruthless and determined-- a Tudor through and through.

Anne Boleyn didn't return to England until the winter of 1521/1522. She was so well liked by the French court that the king himself wrote Henry to express his displeasure about the loss of "the daughter of Mr. Boullan … who was in service to the French queen" (Starkey, 2009). Cardinal Wolsey placated Francis I by explaining that Anne was needed for an important marriage negotiation, which was the truth. In 1521 Wolsey was brokering a deal that Anne should marry James Butler, the heir to the Earl of Ormonde, in order to end the dispute between the Butlers and Thomas Boleyn over the inheritance of the Ormond fortune. The proposed alliance failed, however, for reasons historians are still trying to puzzle out.

It surely could not have been over some objection to the bride herself. Anne was a luminary from the minute she was introduced to the English court. She was, according to witnesses, "beautiful, [with] an elegant figure and eyes were even more attractive … Such was their power, that many men were hers to command … You would have never taken her for an Englishwoman in her manner and behavior … but a native-born French lady" (Starkey, 2009). She became a lady in waiting for the queen, Katherina of Aragon. (Henry's first wife often signed her name "Katherina" and I use that spelling in deference to her probable preference.) Anne rose in popularity so quickly that she was given a role in the Shrovetide pageant in March, alongside the king's sister. The theme centered on courtly love, and

Anne was one of the eight ladies representing the ideal qualities of noblewoman. She was, appropriately enough, the allegory of Perseverance.

As for Anne, with the Butler marriage kaput she was free to shop the marriage market at court (within reason). Inasmuch as her "excellent gesture and behavior did excel all other" women in the court (Lindsey, 1995:53), this wouldn't have been a strain on her resources.

Anne Boleyn had what we would now call 'star power'; that certain extra something that made her stand out. She wasn't an idealized beauty, but she more than made up for that with her double helping of sex appeal (Ives, 2004:43-45). Although she has been accused of cruelly ensnaring men with her glamorous flirtations, it is a wholly unfair way to characterize her forays into courtly love. For women of Anne's time her "job" was to flirt and win hearts. The only way highborn women could help their families, secure their economic stability, and influence policy was by using their attractiveness to make men, who had all the power, fall in love/lust with them. Should she be hated simply because she was very, very good at her job?

She is also victim to the "slut if you do, bitch if you don't" school of misogyny. On one hand, Anne Boleyn was a nasty vamp if she had sex with the men who wanted her. On the other hand, Anne Boleyn was a cold-hearted prick tease and manipulator if she *didn't* have sex with the men she charmed. Simply by being desired, Anne is placed in a no-win situation. Men desired Anne Boleyn but could not have her and she has been punished for it ever since.

There is no evidence at all that Anne had premarital lovers. Nevertheless, her chastity did not mean she was a frigid courtesan who tormented men with sexual frustration in order to keep them hooked on her.

Instead, she was a woman who was aware that her only power over her own fate was the power of her attractiveness in influencing men's desires yet with the understanding that sex before marriage would ruin any chance she had of marrying a man of her socioeconomic class. She *had* to flirt, and *had* to remain a virgin. She had no choice, in any meaningful sense of the word, in the matter. This is not even taking into account that Anne was of a very religious nature and would have been extremely unwilling to have sex without a church-blessed marriage. Queen Katherina's piety is always mentioned in her reluctance to release Henry, but Anne's piety is almost never mentioned in her reluctance to embrace Henry.

Anne's personal magnetism would eventually be her undoing, but it also came close to giving her a marriage with the eldest son of one of the most powerful men in England, the Earl of Northumberland's heir, Henry Percy. It appears to have been a love match, with sincere affection on both sides. Sadly, it was not to be.

According to George Cavendish, who loyally served Cardinal Wolsey as a gentleman-usher and was a firsthand witness to the events, it was Henry VIII who ruined that future for her. Henry ordered Wolsey to put Percy through the wringer until he gave up Anne. There is also a chance that Wolsey didn't like anyone making marriage plans without being called upon to broker them himself and used the king as an excuse, as he had done before. Cavendish was devoted to Wolsey and wrote the Cardinal's biography in the 1550s. It is not beyond possibility that he may have fudged the details to make Wolsey look more sympathetic. Did Wolsey crush the couple's happiness out of sheer pique and power-envy, much the way he denied Thomas Boleyn a controllership several years prior? Or was Cavendish correct in laying the blame at Henry's feet? Whoever was responsible, the result was the same; Wolsey forced Percy to renounce his engagement to Anne.

It is a common mistake to think that Percy gave up Anne easily. That is simply untrue. The young man held out so long against Wolsey's threats and bullying that the Cardinal had to ask Percy's father to help badger Percy into renouncing his love. Percy's father was the ultimate tool to pressure the young lover: "Percy would have been under tremendous pressure to obey his father's commands. It is almost impossible to overstate the cultural pressure which existed to respect one's elders, particularly one's parents, and to submit to authority figures. Absolute obedience to one's parents and social superiors was drummed into people from their earliest youth. For Percy to have defied his father and married Anne anyway would not have been seen as 'romantic'; it would have been seen as an ignominious betrayal of common decency, marking the young man as a scoundrel, and the young couple would have suffered grievously for it" (Kramer, 2012). Percy didn't have a "choice" the way the modern reader often thinks he did. It was a foregone conclusion that Percy would bow to his father's rage and marry the woman his father had chosen for him.

Percy therefore married Mary Talbot, at his father's behest, sometime between the spring of 1525 and the summer of 1526 (Starkey, 2009). The resulting marriage was miserable, which is not really too surprising.

Percy may have *had* to marry Mary Talbot, but there would have been some cultural censure for the Earl of Northumberland's insistence on the marriage. Books of parenting advice (yes, they existed even then) recommended never forcing a marriage where the "fancie is not pleased" (Sim, 2011). Contrary to modern belief, women of the Tudor time period did not all wed as child brides. On average women were about 26 years old when they got married, and the average age for men upon their first wedding was around 28 year old (Cressy, 1997). While people were expected to wed 'suitable' mates to please and/or aid their families, it was considered foolish to make a couple who didn't at least like each other marry. Similar to the arranged marriages that still occur today in some cultures, it was hoped the couple would fall in love and most of the time they did. If marriages *had* to be made for dynastic or economic reasons then the couple usually did everything they could to fall in love with each other, if for no other reason than in to relieve their families' worries. If a couple met and fell in love, then their families would usually let them wed provided they were not *too* unequal in sociocultural or economic status. What Northumberland did to his son was unusual.

If Cavendish was correct and it was the king who pushed Anne and Percy apart, then Henry VIII was even more in the wrong than Northumberland. Supposedly Anne never found out that Henry was the real source of her heartache. Like others, she blamed Wolsey for Northumberland's refusal of the marriage. Cavendish wrote that Anne swore "if it ever lay in her power, she would work the cardinal as much [similar] displeasure" (Ives, 2004). If Cavendish was right then the hand of fate would soon deal Anne the aces she needed to carry out her threat. Anne may have initially played her cards close to her chest in regards to the Cardinal, but it would turn out that she wasn't bluffing.

CHAPTER TWELVE

No one knows for sure when Henry fell in love with Anne. It may have happened as early as 1524, and it was certainly in full swing by 1527. When Henry first coerced Anne into a relationship, he still had a reputation of chivalry and "a lover of justice and goodness", but by the time he had Anne executed on May 19, 1536, he was considered the Mouldwarp, and "a tyrant more cruel than Nero" (Erickson, 1980). What happened?

There may be a medical explanation. A theory published in The Historical Journal postulates that Henry had a Kell positive blood type concurrent with McLeod syndrome, resulting in both his reproductive losses and his altered mental state after age forty (Whitley and Kramer, 2010). McLeod syndrome can only be manifested in people – thus far always men -- with a Kell positive blood type. Furthermore, a man can have both the K(K1) blood type effecting pregnancies and still express McLeod syndrome due to variant Kell antigen expression (Marsh et al, 1983). Usually the symptoms of McLeod syndrome begin to appear near the patient's fortieth birthday and grow increasingly worse over time. The disease has physical manifestations, but it is also accompanied by an erosion of mental stability. Over time, the patient becomes more irrational and erratic, to the point where he displays schizophrenia –like behaviors.

Therefore, if "Henry had developed McLeod syndrome, which would have begun to affect him around the age of forty, then the King's relationship with Anne can be used as a yardstick to measure his deteriorating mental stability. When his behavior toward her during their courtship is contrasted with his actions in the latter half of their relationship, a distinct shift in his personality becomes evident" (Kramer, 2012).

Frankly, the king was so egotistical that even his best personality was off-putting. When Henry first began pursuing Anne she did everything she could do to politely tell the king that she was uninterested in a liaison (Lindsey, 1995). She never boldly told him, "Swive off, varlet!" because that would have meant the political and economic destruction of her and her entire family. When her polite rebuffs didn't seem to be working on her would-be swain, Anne packed her bags and fled to Hever in the summer of 1526 (Starkey, 2009). She refused to return to court, even with her mother there to act as chaperone, no matter how much Henry whinged about it (Ives, 2004).

The King definitely whinged about it. He wrote to her, in the disbelieving shock of a man who had never been told no in his life, that he had "been told that the opinion in which I left you is totally changed, and that you would not come to court either with your mother, if you could, or in any other manner; which report, if true, I cannot sufficiently marvel at, because I am sure that I have since never done anything to offend you, and it seems a very poor return for the great love which I bear you to keep me at a distance both from the speech and the person of the woman that I esteem most in the world: and if you love me with as much affection as I hope you do, I am sure that the distance of our two persons would be a little irksome to you, though this does not belong so much to the mistress as to the servant" (Phillips, 2009). I find in astounding that anyone can accuse Anne of being "come-hither" when her letters to the king can be so clearly inferred to have said "go away".

It can also be inferred that before she left court she had allowed him to hope that she viewed him with "as much affection" as he did her. Why did he think this way? Isn't it evidence that she was a coquette who led him on? Not really. She didn't have any other *choice* than to politely accept his attentions. She was constrained by court etiquette and sociopolitical judiciousness to be very nice to the king. Is she to blame that his ego made him assume a polite no was an enthusiastic yes? Manifestly, Henry had no understanding that when a woman runs away from you as far as she can go and gently tells you she doesn't like in you 'that way' and she just wants to be friends it indicates a lack of interest on the lady's part.

Henry's belief in his own appeal would not allow him to comprehend her rejection. He wrote to Anne, moaning that:

> "On turning over in my mind the contents of your last letters, I have put myself into great agony, not knowing how to interpret them, whether to my disadvantage, **as you show in some places**, or to my advantage, **as I understand them in some others**, beseeching you earnestly to let me know expressly your whole mind as to the love between us two. It is absolutely necessary for me to obtain this answer, having been for **above a year** stricken with the dart of love, and not yet sure whether I shall fail of finding a place in your heart and affection, which last point has prevented me for some time past from calling you my mistress" (Phillips, 2009).

Despite the fact that Anne took care to "show" Henry she had no interest in being his inamorata, the king believed he could "understand" that she really did love him back for more than a year. It is obvious that Henry interpreted her expediently polite rejections to mean that she really did love him back (Lindsey, 1995). How frustrating would that be for a woman? She cannot use plain language to tell a man she isn't interested, but her stalker will continue to take anything less than plain language as a "maybe" or a "yes".

The king swore to Anne that if she would "give up yourself body and heart to me … I promise you that not only the name shall be given you, but also that I will take you for my only mistress, casting off all others besides you out of my thoughts and affections, and serve you only" (Phillips, 2009:3). Anne must have turned him down, because Henry plaintively wrote to her again. In that letter he told her that although "it is not fitting for a gentleman to take his lady in the place of a servant, yet, **complying with your desire, I willingly grant it you**, if thereby you can find yourself less uncomfortable in the place chosen by yourself, than you have been in that which I gave you" (Phillips, 2009). Anne's response to this promise is not known for certain, since her letters to him weren't kept, but based on Henry's reply she must have written to him that she was the King's loyal servant *only* and *uncomfortable* being called his mistress. How much clearer could she have been?

Henry complained in one of his missives that Anne didn't write him back, sulking that "it has not pleased you to remember the promise you made me when I was last with you that it, to hear good news from you, and to have an answer to my last letter; yet it seems to me that it belongs to a true servant (seeing that otherwise he can know nothing) to inquire the health of his mistress, and to acquit myself of the duty of a true servant, I send you this letter, beseeching you to apprise me of your welfare, which I pray to God may continue as long as I desire mine own" (Phillips, 2009:5). Her lack of response to his letter is the early renaissance equivalent to not returning a phone call. It is so blatantly a brush off that it is hard to understand why Henry didn't see it that way. It is also hard to understand how or why any historian has been able to interpret the lack of response as the ploy of a woman playing hard to get. If she had played any harder to get she would have had to beat Henry over the head with a stick. "The argument that she must have been plotting to entice Henry in order to gain the crown ignores too many facts clearly written in Henry's own hand" (Kramer, 2012).

    Rather than just accept the fact that Anne did not want to be his lover, Henry wrote to her that **if he just knew for certain** she didn't love him then he would "do no other than mourn my ill-fortune, and by degrees abate my great folly" (Phillips, 2009:14-15). However, no matter how many times she said no, and no matter how she phrased her rejection, Henry could NOT be certain she was *really* saying no.

    There are historians who are as convinced of the king's irresistibly as Henry was himself, and just cannot believe Anne was *really* saying no. Victorian writer Paul Friedmann explained that "Anne kept her royal adorer at an even greater distance than the rest of her admirers. She had good reason to do so, for the position which Henry offered her had nothing very tempting to an ambitions and clever girl … it cannot be considered an act of great virtue that Anne showed no eagerness to become the king's mistress" (1884). Alison Weir claims that Anne "often failed to reply to the King's letters, probably deliberately, for everything she did, or omitted to do, in relation to Henry was calculated to increase his ardour (2007). David Starkey writes that Anne's coolness toward Henry was because she had "guessed" she was "beyond Henry' power to give up" (2009).

What was it, exactly, that was Anne supposed to do in order to prove that she sincerely did not want to be involved with Henry? Apparently just saying no, running away, and refusing to have sex with the king is somehow not convincing.

Henry didn't give up; he simply changed his plan of attack. It seems that in his mind she was only saying no to the position of mistress. She surely could not have been saying no to him, in all his pulchritudinous majesty. Henry upped the ante by offering Anne marriage and matching crown. It should be noted that, "there is nothing to show that the plan to make Anne his queen had come from Anne" (Bernard, 2010). The king himself appears to be the one who came up with the idea. It was not that when faced with "a seductive would-be mistress who was refusing to submit without the ultimate guarantee of marriage, Henry duly crumbled" (Matusiak, 2013). Nor was it true that "Anne Boleyn's denial of her sexual favours to the king may have encouraged him finally to unravel the conjugal knot that bound him … [making him] as weak as he was as he was foolish" (Matusiak, 2013).

Henry had *already* been making plans to divorce Katherina and marry another noblewoman for the political alliance and potential heirs *before* he began harassing Anne Boleyn. He stopped having sex with Katherina altogether in 1524, and there is evidence he and Wolsey were plotting the dissolution of the marriage in 1525 (Scarisbrick, 1970). The news of Henry's intent to divorce Katherina didn't become public until later in 1527, but it had been in the works prior to the first indication of the king's obsession with Anne. Even in the spring of 1527, Wolsey thought of

Henry's divorce as a way to get the king to marry a French princess (Ripley and Dana, 1883). No one suspected that Henry wanted to make Anne anything but his chatelaine.

What about Anne? What did she want? In the face of such implacable pursuit by the most powerful man in England, what was left for her to do but try to maintain some of her moral integrity as her price for acquiescing to his demands?

When the king started talking marriage it was no doubt clear to Anne that Henry was never going to let her go. No one, no matter how much he loved her, would agree to marry her as long as Henry wanted her. She was either going to wed the king or stay single for the rest of her life. The universal condemnation for an unmarried woman who wasn't a nun made the choice of spinsterhood a very bitter pill to swallow. If she wanted security and a family and a place in society, she was going to have to marry her stalker.

Anne sent Henry a customary gift on New Year's Day, probably in 1527, that was of great import. It was a pendant of a ship with a diamond being "tossed about", and there was a small figure of a woman on board. Henry, no stranger to leaping to conclusions that best suited himself and familiar with romantic symbology, easily understood the gift to mean that Anne was seeking his protection (Ives, 2004). She had finally, after a long chase, given in. To this day her pragmatic bow to the reality of her situation has been taken as a sign she wanted Henry all along.

Notwithstanding her capitulation, there is no other indication she 'chose' Henry. Thomas Wyatt, another of Anne's many admirers, wrote a poem about her:

> Whoso list to hunt, I know where is an hind,
> But as for me, alas, I may no more.
> The vain travail hath wearied me so sore,
> I am of them that farthest cometh behind.
> Yet may I by no means my wearied mind
> Draw from the deer, but as she fleeth afore
> Fainting I follow. I leave off therefore,
> Sithens in a net I seek to hold the wind.
> Who list her hunt, I put him out of doubt,
> As well as I may spend his time in vain.
> And graven with diamonds in letters plain
> There is written, her fair neck round about:
> Noli me tangere, for Caesar's I am,
> And wild for to hold, though I seem tame.

The sonnet reveals that Wyatt had sought her love without success, but had to give up pursuit because she was now exclusively Henry's prey (Lindsey, 1995). Like any woman, Anne's only defense was in flight. Like anything hunted, sometimes flight was not enough to prevent capture.

Henry was as happy as a clam. He wrote her, gushing that: "The demonstrations of your affection are such, the beautiful mottoes of the letter so cordially expressed, that they oblige me for ever to honour, love, and serve you sincerely, beseeching you to continue in the same firm and constant purpose, assuring you that, on my part, I will surpass it rather than make it reciprocal, if loyalty of heart and a desire to please you can accomplish this" (Phillips, 2009:11). It apparently never crossed his mind that she had surrendered to the inevitable, rather than succumbed to his charms.

Now would come Anne's most controversial decision; her seeming refusal to consummate her relationship with Henry for several years.

It doesn't seem to occur to very many people that this was probably as much Henry's decision as hers. Henry had genuinely convinced himself that his marriage to Katherina had been a false one, cursed by God (Scarisbrick, 1970). Henry was deeply committed to the view of himself as 'noble'. He could persuade himself that he was in the right, even when faced with a quantity of hypocritical speciousness that would choke a horse. He honestly seems to have thought that the Pope, and even Katherina, would accept his rationales without a fuss. Possibly he thought that Katherina, the wife who had always made him her first priority, would be saddened but the idea she would fight it tooth and nail didn't seem to occur to him. Henry seemed frankly shocked when Katherina flatly refused to believe any of his theological sophistry and instead used everything she could, including the power of her nephew Charles V, to block the nullity suit (Starkey, 2003:204).

As for Anne, she seems to have been sincerely religious and felt she had a moral responsibility to remain a virgin until marriage. I cannot help but think, however, that if she had really loved Henry she would have allowed him to have sex with her. To be formally pre-contracted to marry was usually all it took to get the sociocultural blessing to consummate the relationship. No one judged contracted couples who made love. They were as good as married. Moreover, disputes about the legitimacy of any children she and Henry had prior to his annulment could be resolved later, as they had been for the children of John of Gaunt and Kathrine Swynford. John of Gaunt, who was the third surviving son of Edward III, and Swynford had three sons and a daughter. When John of Gaunt married Swynford, their children were declared legitimate by an Act of Parliament during the reign of Richard II and given the surname Beaufort (Bevan, 1994:4). Thus, there was a clear precedent to follow if children had predated the wedding. Henry VIII was the descendant of one of John of Gaunt's previously-bastard sons; the king's paternal grandmother, Margaret Beaufort, was the granddaughter of Sywnford's son John.

One historian even goes so far as to wonder why Henry didn't just go ahead and rape Anne, since she was clearly asking for it by holding out for all those years. John Matusiak wrote he cannot believe that simply taking Anne by force or coersion "was not an option, given the indirect pressure that could so surely have been applied on Anne by means of her father, Thomas Boleyn, and her uncle, the Duke of Norfolk … she had but one ace to play and the king should have trumped it decisively. In brief, Henry should either have had her and left her or simply left her and had done" (2013). Perhaps Henry's was reluctant to rape Anne because he viewed rape as repugnant and/or sinful? Just a thought.

Then there is the fact that Henry was heavily emotionally invested in the idea of himself as a hero, not a villain. He wanted to be seen as a reluctant man with no other moral choice than to ask for the annulment. In November of 1528 he gave a speech to his courtiers and London's upper-crust wherein he explained his decision to annul his marriage to Katherina was an unavoidable tragedy, declaring that "if the marriage might be good, I would surely choose her above all women" (Ives, 2004:97). He expected the public to see him as a man who was clearly trying to do the right thing to alleviate the "sores" and "pangs" of his worried conscience (Scarisbrick, 1970:217). Surely no one would suspect that he also wanted to get rid of an old, unfertile wife and replace her with a prettier fertile one? The public was not impressed with his explanations. The people of London apparently did not see a king afflicted with a moral dilemma; instead they saw a man who wanted to dump Katherina for the hotter, younger Anne Boleyn. Henry did not take the public rejection well. The popular "support for [Queen Katherina] and the poor reception by the notables of his speech" (Ives, 2004:98) sent him scurrying to Anne for comfort.

Even if it was only Anne who wished to delay consummation, one could hardly blame her. Nothing Henry did suggested that sleeping with him prior to wedlock was a good idea. Moreover, she had reason to question his sincerity in the early years of their relationship.

During the summer of 1528 one of Anne's maids contracted the 'sweating sickness', an extremely virulent disease that most often resulted in death. In response, the king ordered Anne to stay at Hever Castle, in case she had already become infected but wasn't showing symptoms yet, while he *fled to the countryside with Katherina* (Lindsey, 1995). He not only abandoned Anne, he took with him the spouse from whom he was supposedly separated. He could not have made clearer his respect and deference for Katherina's position as wife. This was unlikely to have inspired Anne's loins to ache for him.

Henry wrote Anne a letter to reassure her that although he was leaving her behind while he skedaddled away with his wife to a safer place, he was really worried about Anne's health and loved her to bits. The King wrote that the "uneasiness my doubts about your health gave me, disturbed and alarmed me exceedingly, and I should not have had any quiet without hearing certain tidings" (Phillips, 2009:25). It can be argued that Henry needed to take this prudent course with his own health as the king, but there was no real reason for Katherina to accompany him when he made his getaway. The queen could have been ordered to flee to another castle or manor with little comment. The king could have likewise sent Anne away to a safer place, even if he could not have taken her with him.

Nevertheless, when Anne became ill with the dreaded disease the king was obviously distraught. He even went so far as to wish that he could bear half of her illness (Phillips, 2009:22). He also sent one of his personal physicians to attend her. While it is all well and good that he would have given up half of his heath for Anne's recovery, the fact of the matter is that he had run away with his wife. There is, sadly, no evidence of what Anne thought about the contrast between his romantic words and his unromantic behavior. It's hard to imagine she was thrilled by his actions, though.

Doubtlessly, Henry and Anne didn't expect to have to wait five years before they would have sex. Neither of them was prepared for the ferocity of Katherina's resistance. The queen waged a public relations battle as well as using Charles V to block the nullity suit in the Holy See. With popular opinion on her side, Katherina kept Henry on the ropes. She knew him well enough to know he would hate being seen as the bad guy. Katherina also used every legal and theological argument she could to burn Henry's flimsy case against their marriage to the ground. She had many loyal friends at court who reported Henry's every plan to her so she could construct quick counterattacks (Starkey, 2003). Nor was Katherina letting anyone forget who was queen. Her regal dignity was so steadfast that Henry became petulant. The King sent her a message speculating that she must not love him, because she showed "no pensiveness in her countenance, nor in her apparel nor behavior" (Lindsey, 1995).

I won't go into great detail about Henry's protracted and miserable attempt to end his marriage; there are entire books written by excellent historians that are devoted to that topic. Rather, I will focus on the public perception of Anne's role, and how she became the scapegoat for all of Henry's worst cruelties.

For years the king had Anne live at court with Katherina. Katherina was still officially the queen, and at the same time Anne was being treated as Henry's de facto wife (Ives, 2004). He spent most of his leisure hours with Anne and had her with him at ceremonial events, but he also continued to make court appearances and eat the occasional family meal with Katherina. Henry "appears to have been trying desperately to have both his beloved, Anne, without really losing the ersatz mothering of his wife, Katherina, the woman who had been taking care of him so long … he tried to woo Anne, fight the Vatican, keep Katherina happy, and maintain the facade that he was only getting an annulment because he absolutely *had* to do it, all at the same time. It must have been mentally and emotionally exhausting" (Kramer, 2012). Meanwhile, Anne was left to take all the blame for his attempts to leave Katherina. For her part, Katherina acted as though Anne was invisible and did not exist.

Anne was also blamed for the fact Henry was acting like a love-struck mooncalf. He was the laughingstock of Europe (Ives, 2004). Some of the populace of Europe wondered why Henry was putting up with Anne's resistance. Like the modern scholar John Matusiak, they thought since Anne "had but one ace to play" that "the king should have trumped it decisively" by taking her to bed with or without her protests. Many people simply assumed that the king and Anne were already lovers, and regarded Anne as nothing but a "goggle-eyed whore" who had enslaved Henry with her cunning nethers.

Like Jezebel and Cleopatra before her it was assumed that she was using artful and deviant sexual skills to subjugate a powerful man. The idea that a man could genuinely love a woman and value her mind as well as her body apparently stretches the imagination past belief. Like Ahab and Mark Antony, Henry VIII was ridiculed for his preposterous adoration of a mere woman. Others also noticed Anne's likeness to Jezebel. Princess Mary's confessor, William Peto, compared Henry and Anne to Ahab and Jezebel in one of his sermons in spite of the fact that the king and his love were sitting in the congregation to hear it (Wilson, 2003).

Anne initially dealt with the domestic mess she was embroiled in with calm good manners. She used her opportunities to subtly advocate for Reformation writings and leaders, encouraging Henry to read reformist literature and persuading him as to the wisdom of Reformist teachings. She was able to get Henry to read a pamphlet by the exiled reformer Simon Fish, called *The Supplication of Beggars*, which was an overt attack on the clerical abuses of the Catholic Church (Scarisbrick, 1970). One of the central ideas espoused in the work was that the Church harmed the kingdom because it made money from tithes and rents but gave nothing back to the treasury (Wilson, 2003). These thought-provoking attacks on the Church appealed to the king, so he pardoned Simon Fish and had him brought back to England (Ives, 2004:134). Anne also coaxed her fiancé into reading Tyndale's *Obedience of a Christian Man*, which argued that the king should not take orders from anyone, including the Pope (Wilson, 2003).

Nothing says "trollop" like a woman debating theology and encouraging religious growth in her boyfriend! I wonder why this aspect of Anne and

Henry's relationship is ignored in favor of speculation about the raunchy details of their love life? Could it be that it interferes with the narrative that Anne was a scheming harlot intent on a throne?

CHAPTER THIRTEEN

Before Henry lost his heart to Anne Boleyn, he had spent some time enamored of her sister Mary Boleyn Carey.

There is no record of Mary being a wit like her brother and sister, but neither is there any indication that she was stupid. She was pretty and sweet-tempered, an ideal woman in her day. Yet time and time again Mary would be cast as second banana to Anne. When they went to France with Henry's sister Mary, it was Anne who was asked to stay in the French queen's retinue afterwards. A second son (albeit a nephew of the Duke of Somerset on his mother's side and from an old established Lancashire family on his father's side) was considered good enough for Mary to wed, but Anne was recalled from France to potentially become the bride of the future earl of Ormonde. Mary was Henry VIII's mistress, but Anne was the one whom Henry fell elbow over teakettle in love with. Mary was eclipsed by Anne even in her own family. Anne and George were close friends, and Mary was always at least slightly an outsider in the glimmering clique that embraced them. What was it like to be Mary, the one who always stood in her younger sister's shadow even when her sister was only twelve?

Although never a queen herself, Mary Boleyn has been erroneously and viciously slut shamed even more than Anne simply because of her relationship to a queen. Mary was slut shamed in an attempt to denigrate Anne. Without her ties to a queen Mary would have been allowed to drift into obscurity without being remembered as one of the biggest sluts in history. Thus, in her own way, Mary has been slut shamed for a crown and deserves and honorable mention.

Why is Mary remembered as a "great and infamous whore" (Weir, 2011)? That tag has stuck because she is rumored to have been the lover of both the king of France and the king of England, and because of spurious accusations that she had sex with other French courtiers.

First, let me take a moment to address the supposed affair she had with Francis I. To start with, the "evidence" of her affair is ridiculously scant and if it were on any other topic it would have been taken with a grain of salt. There are only three pieces of "evidence" (Ridgway, 2011):

One accusation was written in Rodolfo Pio the Bishop of Faenza's letter to Prothonotary Ambrogio on the 10th March 1536 (LP x.450): "Francis said also that they are committing more follies than ever in England, and are saying and printing all the ill they can against the Pope and the Church; that "that woman" pretended to have miscarried of a son, not being really with child, and, to keep up the deceit, would allow no one to attend on her but her sister, whom the French king knew here in France 'per una grandissima ribalda et infame sopre tutte.'"

The second accusation was by Nicholas Sander in his 1585 book *Rise and Growth of the English Schism*: "Soon afterwards she appeared at the French court where she was called the English Mare, because of her shameless behaviour; and then the royal mule, when she became acquainted with the King of France."

The third and final accusation was by Lord Herbert of Cherbury in his book written in 1649 entitled *Life and Raigne of King Henry the Eighth*, in which he quotes William Rastall, the author of a biography of Sir Thomas More written around 1557. Rastall wrote that while in France Mary Boleyn "behav'd herself so licentiously, that she was vulgarly call'd the Hackney of England, till being adopted to that King's familiarity, she was termed his Mule."

As you can see, the only evidence of Mary had sex with Frances I *or anyone else at the French court*, which was given by a person **who was even alive at the same time as Mary Boleyn**, was in the letter by Rodolfo Pio, the Bishop of Faenza, who was writing about *an event that was supposed to have happened more than two decades prior*.

It beggars the mind to wonder why anyone, let alone a trained historian, would assume that a political and religious enemy of Anne Boleyn was telling the gospel truth about her sister. I know that historians are only human and the lure of the lurid tempts them as much as anyone else but frankly I would like to see a little more skepticism when it comes to gossip about the Boleyns. Furthermore, no historian believes that Anne Boleyn didn't miscarry in January of 1536. It is well known that Mary was not the only one to attend Anne in the birthing room. In fact, Mary had been banished from court. Why, then, is the final part of a sentence chock full of disproven information given so much credence? The need to slut shame Mary Boleyn has overridden academic prudence.

There are other reasons to be skeptical of the idea that Mary and Francis I had a relationship. Mary was only in France for six months, from the fall of 1514 to the spring of 1515. She would have been a well-born virgin in her mid-teens and thus would have been under intense chaperonage. Although older court noblewomen sometimes took lovers, an unmarried woman was expected to be a virgin (Rickman, 2008:203). It was a "show me the hymen" school of social mores. If the French king had deflowered Mary, the young daughter of one of Henry's friends and an important ambassador, it would have raised some dust vis-à-vis diplomacy. It would have been news. Big news. At the very least the Francis would have had to have given Mary a nice gift for her dowry or made a present to her father.

Let's also not forget that Francis I became king in January 1515, but at no time in the *years* following his coronation was Mary Boleyn ever listed by a contemporary as one of his mistresses. Believe me, the French would have noticed. Watching Francis try to sleep with every woman in his court was a bit of a national pastime. It was only during the height of Anne Boleyn's unpopularity and demonization that Mary became the "great slut". Out of the blue people started claiming that Francis I had called her his "English Mare" because he had "ridden" her so much. Am I alone in thinking that gap in Mary's attendance at court and everyone's "memory" of her harlotries is suspicious?

It does seem a tad unfair that Mary Boleyn has become renowned as round-heeled based only on hearsay and innuendo spread twenty years after the supposed events and written by people who despised and feared the Boleyn family. She did, however, appear to have had an affair with Henry VIII.

Mary Boleyn was recalled home from the French court of Claude and Francis in 1519, and married William Carey on February 4, 1520. There is nothing recorded by her contemporaries to indicate that she was anything other than a maiden (although once betrothed she and Carey could have sealed the deal with very little social approbation). Her short time in Henry's court had been long enough to catch the king's eye.

It is likely that king Henry VIII was having an affair with Anne's sister Mary by the Shrovetide pageant of 1522. No one is sure when the relationship began, but it is most likely that the romance didn't occur until after she married William Carey on Feburary 4, 1520. Within a year or so after that there are some signs that Mary was being wooed by Henry – such as his appointment of Thomas Gardiner to Tynmouth Priory after she asked him to -- but it isn't until 1522 that Mary's husband started becoming the "beneficiary of a spate of royal grants" (Ives, 2004). These grants continued until 1525, coincidently the same year Henry raised Thomas Boleyn to the status of Viscount Rochford.

Presents to Mary as well as to her husband and father, one of Henry's signature marks of courtship, began to pile up. Carey, who was already one of Henry's companions, was made the keeper of New Hall in Essex and became bailiff for several other manors. Thomas Boleyn, who had been an important figure at court and in the king's favor for almost two decades, additionally became the treasurer of Henry's household. Many historians suggest that Mary began sleeping with the king in the summer of 1522, but it is not assured. One of the things that suggest the king's relationship to Mary started around that time and continued off and on for a few years is the fact that Henry, ever the courteous cuckholder and liberal lover, became exceedingly openhanded with Mary's male kin. He gave Carey generous royal grants between 1522 and 1526, as well as making Thomas Boleyn Knight of the Garter in 1523 and Viscount Rochford on June 18, 1525. Even George Boleyn, Mary's younger brother, came into his share of the spotlight. George was given a country mansion, Grimston Manor, in 1524 and in 1525 he got a coveted position as a gentleman of the Privy Chamber.

Amy Licence, in her richly researched book *The Six Wives & Many Mistresses of Henry VIII*, meticulously compiled the evidence of how, when, and where Mary and Henry began their affair. According to Licence, Mary's relationship with the king was probably based on fortuity and fun, rather than a protracted romance, with Mary being merely, "a diversion for the king, who probably took his pleasure with her when circumstances presented an opportunity. She was not established in her own lodgings at court in proximity to the king … nor was she listed as playing any further role in the court ceremony of these years" (Licence, 2014). At its most basic level, Mary and Henry were friends with benefits.

But were they also parents?

Speculation has long abounded that Mary Carey's two children, Catherine and Henry, were the fruit of seeds planted by Henry VIII. Certainly, Catherine had a Tudor look about her, but William Carey was also descended from Edward III and what with noble inbreeding of cousins it is frankly more surprising that gentlefolk continued to look dissimilar to each other. Looks, in this case, cannot tell tales. Nonetheless, there is a chance on or both children *might* be his, in that "While her affair with the king lasted, Mary would have been sleeping with two men. Perhaps not equally … [but] William Carey would not have refrained from sleeping with his wife because she was having an affair with Henry … Carey would have been Mary's everyday lover, while Henry was her lover for special occasions" (Licence, 2014). Although historians are reasonably certain that Mary and the king were lovers, there is very mixed support for the idea that either or both of Mary Boleyn Carey's children were fathered by Henry VIII. Her daughter Catherine was born in 1524 and her son Henry was born in the spring of 1526, so wouldn't the timing fit? Not necessarily. Henry may easily have been still bestowing grants to William Carey for turning a blind eye to the affair for years after the sex had stopped, so Henry's liaison with Mary may have ended in 1523 or earlier. Furthermore, once Mary had begun to "cohabit with William Carey, her children came in quick succession" (Ives, 2004). Some historians believe that Henry VIII was not the kind of guy who liked to share his mistresses with their husbands. In their opinion, the odds that he was still having sex Mary after she resumed married life with Carey are slim.

    Henry would have also been eager to prove his virility by taking credit for royal bastards. Some people have postulated that he couldn't claim Mary's children without exposing his hypocrisy about incestuous relationships, since having sex with two sisters who were living at the same time was even more "incest" than having married his brother's widow. I don't think that would have stopped Henry from claiming healthy babies as his, though. First, Mary's daughter and maybe even her son were probably born before Henry had serious designs on Anne Boleyn. Secondly, that cat was out of the bag already. Henry would later ask the Pope for a dispensation to marry Anne Boleyn that would count even in the case of "affinity arising from illicit intercourse in whatever degree, even the first" (Kelly, 2004). This is, historians agree, because of his sexual relationship with Mary Boleyn. He might as well have cried "I slept with my fiancée's sister" in town halls across his kingdom. Why would he have been squeamish about claiming the children but then gung-ho about asking for a very revealing dispensation?

    Mary's daughter, Catherine, was most likely conceived in 1523 and there is a good chance Henry was still visiting Mary's bedroom every now and again at that time. Mary's son was born March 4, 1525 and –

providing Henry had not ceased sleeping with Mary after she became pregnant the first time, as he had done with other lovers – may or may not be the king's offspring. The odds are against it, though. Not only is there Henry's aforementioned distaste for pregnant mistresses, the dates for little Henry Carey's conception look discouraging. The king was staying with the Carey's from approximately the end of March to the end of April in the spring of 1524. He had definitely returned to Windsor by April 23 of that year. Henry Carey would have been conceived at the end of May or the beginning of June, a few weeks after the king could have slept with Mary.

Other than Henry, there is no other evidence that Mary was unfaithful to William. When her husband died in 1528 Mary was left destitute. Fortunately, her sister Anne stepped up to become Catherine and Henry's patron and guardian. This did not mean that the children lost contact with their mother; it simply meant Anne became responsible for their upkeep and education.

Anne also talked Henry into giving succor to his former lover when Mary's husband William died from the sweating sickness. Her husband's death left Mary in great hardship with two small children to feed. As would any caring sister, Anne tried to help Mary. She wrote to Henry and begged him to financially assist the newly made widow. To please Anne, Henry promised Mary one hundred pounds a year and wrote to Thomas Boleyn insisting that he also support Mary. The assistance must have been welcome to the king's former flame, but the letter Henry sent to her with the money was doubtlessly less so. In the letter Henry chides Mary for her sinful past, as if he wasn't the one to abet her in fornication and adultery (Lindsey, 1995). The king's hypocrisy towards Mary may have bolstered

Anne's determination not to surrender her body to Henry outside of wedlock, lest he view her with the same disgust and leave her in penury like her sister.

Mary appears to have returned to court by January of 1532, and on October 7th she was one of the ladies who escorted Anne to Calais. There is no record of her being particularly noted by King Francis, her theoretical former lover. There is no rumor, no hint of scandal that connects Mary to anyone for the years of her widowhood. She faded quietly into the background, with no other ambition than to be content.

The next time Mary resurfaces in history it is once again because of her love-life. She secretly married William Stafford, a man who -- although a cousin of the king's – was a younger son with no land and no money and only a very minor position at court (Weir, 2011). Mary had fallen in love with Stafford, who was a dozen years her junior and handsome, in 1534. The dishonor and shame such a marriage (at the time and in context) would mean for her extended family did not dissuade Mary from wedding Stafford, but it did encourage her to keep her marriage secret until her advancing pregnancy gave the game away. All of Mary's kin were horrified and outraged by her behavior, and Anne would have had little choice but to banish her sister from court even if she hadn't been just as angry herself.

Mary and Stafford, cast out and facing poverty, were in a bind. Mary wrote to Henry's then Secretary, Thomas Cromwell, to beg for his assistance. Her letter, though, displays either a complete lack of tact or a bravado bordering on stupidity. In it she points out, "For well I might have had a greater man of birth and a higher, but I assure you I could never have had one that loved me so well … I had rather beg my bread with him than to be the greatest Queen in Christendom" (Schutte, 2014). Her tone, rather than being the fully abject apology it should have, was defensive of her marriage and it is hard to read the remark about not wanting to be queen as anything but an arrow aimed at Anne.

Nevertheless, it was Anne who helped her sister when all male relatives turned their faces from her. It was Anne who sent Mary some money and an expensive gold cup to help her establish a household when no one else would help her (Bramley, 2014).

Mary and Stafford lived in Calais, where Stafford worked for Lord and Lady Lisle until Henry married Anna of Cleves. After that they lived peaceably and in what seems to be relative comfort in Essex. Mary died on July 19, 1543. She was the last of the Boleyn children but not the last of her line. Her daughter and son would produce between them more than 20 children, most of who lived to adulthood. Mary's descendants, who include luminaries like Charles Darwin and Winston Churchill, have continued to thrive throughout the centuries. She is the ancestress of Queen Elizabeth II and of William Duke of Cambridge through his mother, Lady Diana Spencer (Hart, 2009). The bloodline of Mary Boleyn Carey Stafford sits on the throne of England.

Mary, as far as historical evidence suggests, shared her favors with three men in the course of her lifetime, two of whom were married to her. That is hardly promiscuity. So why is she a great and infamous whore? What did she do to deserve slut shaming? Was it just a way of trying to humiliate Anne Boleyn further?

Perhaps the real sluttiness of Mary Boleyn is the fact that she, in an age which demanded compliance of women, was noncompliant? She married for love in defiance of kinship and protocol. She chose happiness over wealth and fame. She rebelled, she was a troublemaker, and she considered her own needs to be important. She was, in short, her own person determined to live her own life. As a result, to this day she is remembered and frequently depicted as the slutty and slightly dim older sister of a famous queen, a "mare" to be "ridden" by any man.

CHAPTER FOURTEEN

Second only to the idea that Anne Boleyn was a trollop are the reports of her foul temper. Everyone knows Anne was a shrew, right? Wrong. It is only after Anne is living with Henry at court, reduced to a shadow wife and being called a "naughty paikie" (Fraser, 1992) in the streets, that she developed her reputation for being a virago.

Think about what Anne had been through. From the moment Henry decided she would honored with his intentions, Anne had to try to ward him off diplomatically, go into hiding, deal with a no-way-out decision to marry her stalker, and be responsible for charming the aforementioned stalker, manage relatives (the duke of Norfolk leaps to mind) and court members who treating her like a skank, as well as hear herself called vicious epithets by the populace who loved Katherina and blamed her for Henry's mistreatment of their beloved Queen. Not to mention that she was constantly on display and every word out of her mouth was subject to a conspiracy of misrepresentation and misinterpretation. Enemies were all around her and everyone hated her, yet none of it had been her idea. I don't know about you, but I would be a little cranky.

There are no reports of her having a vicious disposition before she was targeted by Henry. It is only after she was forced to be the king's next lady love that she is recorded as being anything other than charming. Both Queen Claude of France and Margaret of Austria thought Anne was wonderful. She had the men at court fawning over her, but there is no evidence she wasn't also popular with her fellow ladies-in-waiting. Henry Percy, the future Earl of Northumberland, fallen head over heels in love with her. The poet Thomas Wyatt had immortalized her in verse. Where was her mean-spirited hostility then?

Anne only started blowing up at people when she was trapped, waiting for the finalization of Henry's divorce. She only gained her reputation as a harridan after she had been pushed to the limits of what she could bear with acceptable feminine docility

One of the occasions when Anne is recorded as having lost her temper with the king happened on St. Andrew's Day, November 30, 1529. Henry had gone to have dinner with Katherina, who was still officially the queen and his wife. During dinner they fought. All of Henry's arguments were verbally ripped into pieces by the angry Katherina. The queen finished her decimation of his justifications for annulment by telling him that "for each doctor or lawyer who might decide in your favor and against me, I shall find a thousand to declare that the marriage is good and indissoluble" (Starkey, 2003). Flustered, Henry responded that he would "denounce the Pope" and "marry whom he pleased" (Starkey, 2003) before fleeing back to Anne in search of comfort. Anne, however, was in no mood to comfort him. Instead, she told him that he was a dunderhead to argue with Katherina, because the queen *always* won.

Anne then went on to accuse him of being so weak-willed that one day he would return to Katherina, abandoning Anne after having destroyed her reputation and any chance she had of marrying anyone else. She threw into Henry's face the fact that she would have probably born several children by now if he had left her alone and let her wed another nobleman. Anne, clearly at the end of her tether, cried "alas!" and bid "farewell to my time and youth spent to no purpose at all" (Starkey, 2003). This is not an entirely undeserved complaint.

Then in June of 1530, Anne found out that Katherina was still sewing Henry's shirts. Anne was incensed. Henry was promising her that they were very close to being able to legally marry, but at the same time his behavior demonstrated that the queen was his wife (Fraser, 1992). Anne was vexed with Henry and she made no secret of it. Henry ordered that his linens be taken to Anne from then on (Starkey, 2003). Anne promptly hired a seamstress to make his shirts. She didn't want to tie up her time, which could be spend in hunting, reading, or playing music, by making little stitches in fine cloth. She had just wanted to sever another of the apron strings that tied Henry to Katherina. Considering that Henry had been stringing her along for more than three years and she was nearing her 30th birthday, her ire doesn't seem unreasonable.

Yet another of the things everyone *knows* about Anne Boleyn is that she was vindictive, and she is the one who destroyed poor Cardinal Wolsey. Historians such as David Starkey credit the length of Wolsey's slow downfall to the time needed for Anne to "toughen up" Henry and convince him to strike against his former chancellor (2003). The trouble with that theory is that it is based on sheer conjecture of Anne's feelings and motivations and an assumption of Anne's unlimited power over the king. Undoubtedly Anne bore a grudge against Wolsey, and was probably happy when he fell from grace, but she was far from alone. Many, *many* people in Henry's court had a case of seething resentment against Wolsey. Some of Wolsey's foes included Thomas Boleyn, the earl of Northumberland, the duke of Norfolk, and the king's best friend and brother-in-law, the duke of Suffolk. All of these men were too powerful for the Cardinal to challenge directly, so it was Anne he publically blamed for Henry's growing disenchantment with him. Wolsey called Anne "the midnight crow" and was convinced that it was her influence, rather than his own overreaching behavior, that had lost him the king's favor (Ives, 2004:128).

Susan Bordo, author of *The Creation of Anne Boleyn*, points out that historical rhetoric regarding Anne's feelings toward her foes often "paint a portrait of Anne as an evil huntress worthy of Greek mythology – or perhaps a vampire novel: "Anne's first target was Wolsey," "Anne had Mary in her sights," "Anne had her own quarry too: Wolsey," "The hunting down of another of her old enemies offered some compensation," etc (2013). Like her reputation as a sneaky bimbo, her vindictiveness is at odds with both her proclivities toward Christian evangelicalism and known historical facts. Anne, because she was not meek and she was reported to retaliate verbally when under enough stress, has born the weight of an entire court's worth of vendettas on her shoulders.

More likely it was several nobles, using Anne as a spearhead and rallying point for their alliance, who were egging the king on to destroy Wolsey. Moreover, the Cardinal did not nosedive toward the chopping block in haste; he drifted toward his end with lots of ups and downs. Late in September of 1529 the King decided, possibly with Anne's encouragement and certainly with the support of her faction, that Wolsey didn't really want the annulment now that he knew Anne would replace Katherina. Henry therefore ordered Wolsey to hand over the Great Seal as punishment (Scarisbrick, 1970). In October, the Cardinal was found guilty of *praemunire*, or supporting Papal authority instead of the King, which would cost Wolsey his head

(Ives, 2004). Wolsey did everything he could to please the King, including bribing all those who might help him with lavish gifts of money. "Cardinal Wolsey, in a wise yet assuredly painful move, signed over the title of his splendid manor, York Place, to the King in February of 1530. This pleased the King so greatly that he granted his former Chancellor a full pardon, and restored him to his former position as the Archbishop of York" (Kramer, 2012).

Wolsey, probably motivated by his hatred for "the midnight crow", responded to his pardon by stupidly offering his secret support to Katherina. The Cardinal thus committed treason by "advising foreign powers on the best tactics to use against his sovereign", and attempting to "foment unrest in England", in an attempt to "coerce Henry into leaving Anne" (Starkey, 2003). Wolsey was also caught red handed sending coded messages via a subordinate to Henry's diplomatic enemies and Henry had Wolsey arrested for treason on November 4, 1530. One of the men sent to arrest Wolsey was Henry Percy, Earl of Northumberland and Anne's former boyfriend. Why is Percy never recorded as "vindictive" like Anne, when he had as much reason as Anne to hate the Cardinal?

It seems obvious that Wolsey's treasonous activities are the source of Henry's ire, but Anne would get the blame there too. The ambassador from Spain, Eustace Chapuys, claimed that Anne threatened to leave the king if he did not arrest the Cardinal forthwith (Starkey, 2003). This is often taken historically as gospel, in spite of the fact Chapuys hated Anne's guts and could stretch the truth like taffy. He was a loyal friend to Katherina and his letters often refer to Anne as "the concubine" and "that whore" (Bordo, 2013). I have to question if a man as demanding of loyalty as Henry VIII needed Anne's bullying to be angry at Wolsey's betrayal.

Wolsey died a natural death on the trip back to London, on November 29, 1530 (Starkey, 2003). Henry subsequently changed the name of York Place to Whitehall and gave it to Anne (Lindsey, 1995:81). Even though Henry had already been "gifted" York Place and the decision was his, Anne would (of course) get credit for the posthumous insult to Wolsey.

It was shortly after the death of Wolsey that Anne began to openly fight with Katherina's supporters. Prior to the Christmas of 1530 both Katherina and Anne did their best to pretend the other was not at court. That yuletide, however, Katherina lost her temper and accused Henry of wanting a divorce so that he could marry his little brown tart, using theology as a meager cover story (Starkey, 2003). The king was finally had the high ground in an argument. He insisted that he *was not* having a sexual relationship Anne. His would-be future wife was not some sleazy tramp. It is probably that "Henry believed that if he was not physically committing adultery with Anne, then he was blameless; the idea of an "emotional affair" was not something people thought of in those days. It is even possible that he was now as emotionally invested in Anne's chastity as Anne was herself. Anne's virginity was his proof that his desire for an annulment from Katherina was wholly motivated by a sincere wish to do God's will in accordance with the text of Leviticus, rather than by prurient carnal urges" (Kramer, 2012).

Not only did the king quarrel with Katherina, shortly thereafter he did something that caused Anne to go ballistic. No one knows why the couple fought that January of 1531, but it apparently sparked Anne to the heights of rage. She even ended her relationship with Henry, probably sick of waiting on a dithering king who had his wife at court while Anne had to endure being called a home-wrecking whore by almost everyone in Europe. Anne was sincere, too. Henry had to go to Anne's relatives and beg them to get (via familial coercion) Anne to forgive him (Erickson, 1980). Henry, the king of England, had to grovel.

This was doubtlessly another reason for people to despise Anne. She was proving herself to be a very bad woman in the context of the Tudor ideal. Rather than being mild-mannered and following a man in all things, she fought back and had a mind of her own, Proud and independent and smart, Anne repeatedly violated the sociocultural rules of femininity. In contrast, Katherina was seen as the living embodiment of womanly virtue. This seems ludicrous, when the queen was clearly as strong and smart as Anne, but Katherina had always been careful to look like she was meek and following Henry, even when she was leading him around by the nose. Any subtlety Anne had in that area was long gone after three years of dawdling and tension. Thus, most people in London were on Katherina's side as the "good wife" and were vehement in their condemnation of Anne as the "bad slut".

Not long after, Chapuys reported that Anne had told to one of Katherina's ladies in waiting that she wished "all Spaniards were at the bottom of the sea" (Ives, 2004). Katherina was the "daughter of Spain", so the insult was unambiguous. Anne was further claimed to have said that she would rather see Katherina "hanged than have to confess that she was her Queen and mistress" (Ives, 2004). How rude, right? Possibly. Note how any mention of the things Katherina's ladies might have said to Anne to provoke were left out of the ambassador's report. What are the odds that Anne sailed up to Katherina's faction out of nowhere and started insulting the queen? Nevertheless, this encounter is typically used to indicate how hot-headed and mean Anne was.

Henry seems to have been delighted by Anne's anger. Perhaps he thought Anne's rage was a mark of her love for him. However, while Anne could be openly rude about the queen and fear no reprisals from Henry, the king continued to support Katherina's status with other members of his court. Anne could vent her frustration, but nothing would change. Any modern reader can see why Anne's fury increased in response to the whole situation.

One of Anne's biggest foes, Thomas More, found himself in a situation much like hers had been; just saying no was not a deterrent to a determined Henry. After Wolsey's death Henry needed a new Chancellor and he chose More, a renowned humanist scholar and friend, for the job. More tried desperately to turn down the position (Scarisbrick, 1970). If nothing else, More knew his loyalty to the Catholic Church would get him into trouble. Henry knew More disagreed with him about the nullity suit and the Reformation, and he promised More that he would never "molest his conscience" by making More fight on behalf of the annulment (Bernard, 2007). All Henry asked was that More remain quiet about his own ideology and support the king with tactful silence. More would keep his promise to Henry, even when he was placing his head on the king's chopping block.

The king turned forty on June 28, 1531. As postulated by the Kell/McLeod theory, his "behavior and mental stability began to deteriorate shortly thereafter, securing him a place in the popular imagination as a brutal despot, and radically altering the course of English history" (Kramer, 2012). Shortly after his birthday the King forced Katherina from court and demanded she go to live at one of Wolsey's former estates. Their daughter Mary was also banished to Richmond. Sadly, Katherina would never see her beloved husband and child again (Porter, 2007). It was the first time Henry had ever done anything deliberately cruel to his first wife, and the first time he had been anything other than a loving father toward his daughter.

The king also began to push harder for national and international recognition of Anne as his future queen. On September 1, 1532 he invested Anne with the title of Marquess of Pembroke, which she would be able to pass on to the "heirs male of her body" whether or not they were legitimate (Lindsey, 1995). Henry also demanded that Katherina give Anne the royal jewels. Of course, Katherina and her supporters believed that Henry only demanded the jewelry because that greedy bitch made him do it. The queen bitterly protested that her gems were going to adorn the "scandal of Christendom" (Starkey, 2003). There is no evidence that Anne was the one who wanted the jewelry, however. It is much more likely that Henry, now enraged with Katherina for defying him so long, was punishing his first wife.

Henry also wanted the jewels to decorate Anne when he took her to high level peace talks with the French in Calais. Hearing that Anne was being treated as if she were already queen must have hurt Katherina, but she may have been mollified when she learned that all the French women who had enough rank to formally "receive" Anne, including Marguerite d'Angouleme, were either mysteriously indisposed or adamantly refused to socialize with her (Lindsey, 1995).

Anne's embarrassment may have been because of Francis I's own political desires, however, rather than a condemnation of Anne. Francis was "angling for a match between his son … and the pope's niece Catherine de Medici – hardly the moment to appear to give public endorsement to Anne's position" (Ives,

2004). A few months later the duke of Norfolk would meet with Marguerite d'Angouleme and reported to Anne that she "was as affectionate to your highness as if she were your own sister, and likewise the queen … My opinion is that she is your good and assured friend" (Ives, 2004).

Then again, there were doubtlessly noble women who resented Anne. The fixed nature of marriage was one of the few things that women could count on. That a wife could be cast off in favor of a mistress was doubtlessly abhorrent to many of them. Rudely refusing to see Anne was the only way they could express their disapproval. Needless to say, no one was rude to the man who had created the entire mess. Henry was powerful in a way his paramour was not, and he could not be insulted even by proxy. Things were not all bleak for Anne at Calais, however. On Henry's insistence she was able to formally meet the king of France as though she were already England's queen.

Anne was an impressively regal figure, and it was shortly after the talks at Calais that Henry decided to marry her, with the benefit of clergy, despite the fact that the Pope had not yet granted his request for an annulment. Evidently, the King had tired of waiting for the Holy See. There is solid evidence to suggest that Henry and Anne were married in a small, secret ceremony in Dover on November 14, 1532, shortly after they returned from Calais (Starkey, 2003).

The wedding was, of course, top secret. After all, there were many who would see it as bigamous. Nevertheless, Katherina and her faction found out about it. Less than two weeks after Henry and Anne's semi-secret wedding, Katherina sent a letter to Chapuys to let him know what she had heard. She wrote:

> "I have received fresh injuries. I am separated from my lord, and he has married another woman without obtaining a divorce; and this last act has been done while the suit is still pending, in defiance of him who has the power of God upon earth. I cover these lines with my tears as I write. I confide in you as my friend. Help me to bear the cross of my tribulation. Write to the Emperor. Bid him to insist that judgment be pronounced. The next Parliament, I am told, will decide if I or my daughter will suffer martyrdom. I hope God will accept it as an act of merit by us, as we shall suffer for the sake of the truth." (Froude, 1891:)

    Katherina was, understandably for a woman of her character, willing to die rather than be told that she had been an incestuous concubine for the decades of her marriage to Henry. Less understandably, she was also willing to gamble with the life of her only surviving child. She seems to have feared Mary's loss of legitimacy even more than the loss of Mary's head. Without a doubt Katherina loved her daughter, but her top priority appears to have been to establishing the validity of her marriage to Henry and keeping her daughter in the line of succession.

    When Anne arrived back in London, a married woman as far as she was concerned, she busied herself with outfitting her household to reflect her new standing as the king's wife (Starkey, 2003). Henry and Anne were so eager to be seen as man and wife that they had yet another small wedding on January 25, 1533. This wedding was much less clandestine than the one in Dover. Anne's father and her uncle, who have frequently been portrayed as fellow-schemers in Anne's plans to get a crown from the besotted King, were in reality dismayed by the marriage (Froude, 1891:230). The political situation was too delicate for their comfort and that they feared retribution from both English Catholics and papal armies. If Anne had any such fears she never showed them. She was determined that she be known as Henry's wife. Perhaps Anne's eagerness was because was beginning to suspect she was pregnant? Just a few weeks later Anne was hinting to the court that she was with child (Ives, 2004).

As Anne became increasingly certain that she was pregnant, the king's annulment became more urgent. Henry wanted Anne to be recognized as queen before his son and heir (of course the baby was boy!) arrived. Deciding enough was enough, Henry appointed Thomas Cranmer as the Archbishop of Canterbury at the end of March (Ives, 2004:164). Cranmer would now be the man who would judge if Henry's first marriage should be annulled, not the Pope.

The tide had turned in Anne's favor. If her baby was a son it would spare the country the civil war that might come if a woman inherited Henry's throne. Moreover, it would be uncontestable proof that God approved of Henry and Anne's union. In April of 1533 on of Katherina's loyal supporters wrote to the Emperor that he "feared the Pope had sent, or might send, absolution to the King" (Froude, 1891).

It was around this time that Chapuys began to report that the King, once so "naturally kind and generous," had changed so much that he "did not seem to be the same man" (Froude, 1891). The ambassador, to no one's surprise, attributed Henry's behavioral changes to Anne having "so perverted him" (Froude, 1891) with her influence. However, if the King had McLeod syndrome, it was the disease, not his new wife, which was causing his personality change (Kramer, 2012).

On May 23, 1533, Cranmer ruled that the marriage between Katherina of Aragon and Henry was "null and void" (Scarisbrick, 1970). Nine days later, on June 1, 1533, Anne Boleyn was anointed and crowned queen by Cranmer himself.

CHAPTER FIFTEEN

The marriage between Henry and Anne has been historically thought to have been tumultuous, but that may have been an exaggeration by those who disliked Anne or those using hindsight based on her execution. Much of the evidence that Henry and Anne battled comes from Chapuys, who was far from impartial. For example, Chapuys wrote that just prior to Anne going into confinement to await the birth of her child, she and Henry had a fight over his infidelity. According to the ambassador, Henry advised her to "shut her eyes, and endure as her betters had done" and warned her that he "could humble her again in a moment" (Starkey, 2003). If true, this was grossly out of character for the king, if for no other reason than because such a kerfuffle was believed to endanger the life of his progeny. Medical wisdom of the time would have demanded that the queen's anger should have been met with attempts at appeasement, since emotional upset in gravid women was thought to be capable of causing fetal death and miscarriage (Cressy, 1997).

The birth of a son would have secured Anne even from the enmity of Chapuys. Unfortunately for the queen, on September 7, 1533 she gave birth to a daughter. Her first and only surviving child, this newborn girl would eventually become one of England's most revered monarchs, Elizabeth I. Notwithstanding her glorious future, Elizabeth's arrival was a serious disappointment to both Henry and Anne. Henry seemed to take the birth of a daughter with better spirits than Anne could manage. The king made the best of things, and focused on the idea that a hearty baby girl meant that hearty brothers would soon join her. Speculation that the King could not sire healthy babes had been a persistent rumor. A close friend of the Duke of Norfolk, a man named De Gambaro, wrote to the Duke that Anne's expected "child would be weak, owing to his father's condition" (Froude, 1891). Elizabeth's glowing health would have pleased Henry because they refuted the accusations about his virility.

A few months later Henry seemed to be proven correct in his prediction of future children with Anne. The new queen was known to be pregnant again by February of 1534, when Chapuys wrote to inform Charles V of the matter and again when Chapuys mentions the Queen's "condition" at the end of July. Further evidence of this pregnancy appears in a letter from George Taylor written to Lady Lisle in April of that same year describing Anne as having "a goodly belly" (Dewhurst, 1984). At the end of September of 1534 Chapuys again mentioned Anne's possible pregnancy, but this time reporting that Henry suspected his wife was not actually with child (Dewhurst, 1984). What happened to the baby? Some historians assume that the baby was either stillborn or died shortly after the birth, and the royal couple never made a formal announcement about their loss because the infant was another girl (Fraser, 1994). There is also the possibility that if the fetus miscarried before Anne felt it move, or "quicken," the fetus would be assumed to have not yet been given a soul, and would require neither baptism, name, nor burial rites (Hull, 1996). This kind of loss was usually not announced.

A few months later, in June of 1535, William Kingston again wrote to Lord Lisle that Anne was in possession of "as fair a belly as I have ever seen,"

(Dewhurst, 1984). Since no miscarriage or birth was ever recorded some scholars think this letter was misdated, and was actually written in 1534. That is, however, a big assumption. What is known for certain is that the lack of a successful pregnancy was eroding Anne's power at court to her faction's increasing distress.

It was around this time that the king began behaving with extreme ruthlessness. When he was younger Henry ordered executions only as a last recourse. In 1535, he started ordering executions with frightening regularity. One of the clearest signs of Henry's increasing violence was the execution of three Carthusian priests and a Bridgettine monk on May 4, 1535 (Starkey, 2003:523; Bernard, 2007:167-168). Their only 'crime' was their steadfast belief that the Pope was the Holy Father and head of the Church, which was now treason in England. A few weeks later, on June 22, Henry ordered the beheading of Bishop John Fisher. The king then had Thomas More beheaded on July 6. It should surprise no one to learn that Anne Boleyn was blamed for this bloodbath.

Katherina, the former queen who had suffered so much and had received so little from Henry in return, died on January 7, 1536. The fact that Katherina passed away without seeing her only child one more time was tragic, but at least her closest friend, Maria de Salinas, managed to be at her side. Maria, hearing that the Queen's end was near, ignored direct orders from the king rushed to be with Katherina. Maria had come to England with Katherina in 1501, and made a good marriage to William Willoughby, the 11th Baron of Willoughby de Eresby. Maria, who was a brave and loyal friend, sped sixty miles in freezing weather on horseback to reach Katherina before it was too late (Lindsey, 1995). At some point in her journey Maria was thrown off her horse. A resourceful woman, Maria turned this accident to her advantage and used the stains on her dress to convince Katherina's de facto jailer that she had "lost" the papers giving her permission to see the former queen (Lindsey, 1995). The jailor fell for it. Once Maria was inside, she went to Katherina's room and locked the door, flatly refusing to come out again. Afraid to bodily remove Lady Willoughby, Katherina's keepers allowed her to remain.

When the news that Katherina had died reached the court, Anne and Henry were not tactful. The king shouted, "God be praised that we are free from all suspicion of war," which was true but inappropriate (Starkey, 2003:549). Anne and Henry spent the next day rejoicing. They celebrated with feasts, dancing, and jousting. They gave every appearance that they were jubilant about Katherina's death (Lipscomb, 2009:52-53).

Although people once again blamed Anne for Henry's festivities, it was she rather than Henry who would eventually show any sorrow about Katherina's death or any remorse about how Katherina had been treated (Starkey, 2003:551). Furthermore, after Katherina's death Anne attempted to reconcile with the king's daughter Mary. As would be expected, she was rebuffed by the princess, who blamed Anne for everything her mother had suffered. Even though the queen was probably offended by Mary's rejection, Anne tried to apprise Mary of how much danger she was placing herself in by defying Henry. Rather than acting like the vindictive battle-ax she is accused of being, Anne tried to warn her step-daughter that she would be in a perilous position if the queen's baby was the son Henry wanted. Anne wrote a letter to her aunt, Mrs. Anne Shelton and the letter was "accidently" left for Mary to find. In the letter Anne told Mrs Shelton:

"My pleasure is that you seek to go no further to move the Lady Mary towards the King's grace, other than as he himself directed in his own words to her. What I have done myself has been more for charity than because the King or I care what course she takes, or whether she will change or not change her purpose. When I shall have a son, as soon I look to have, I know what then will come to her. Remembering the word of God, that we should do good to our enemies, I have wished to give her notice before the time, because by my daily experience I know the wisdom of the King to be such that he will not value her repentance or the cessation of her madness and unnatural obstinacy when she has no longer power to choose. She would acknowledge her errors and evil conscience by the law of God and the King if blind affection had not so sealed her eyes that she will not see but what she pleases. Mrs. Shelton, I beseech you, trouble not yourself to turn her from any of her wilful ways, for to me she can do neither good nor ill. Do your own duty towards her, following the King's commandment, as I am assured that you do and will do, and you shall find me your good lady, whatever comes." (Froude, 1891:388)

For people in the Tudor era, forty was generally considered to be the start of 'old age' (Lipscomb, 2009). Henry was now forty-four, but he still insisted on jousting with young men. On January 24, ironically during one of the tournaments he held to celebrate Katherina's death, Henry was unhorsed. The King was unconscious for more than two hours (Lipscomb, 2009). Just a few days after Henry's accident, on

January 29, Anne spontaneously aborted a male fetus. Anne was probably in the second trimester of the pregnancy. In spite of continued speculation to the contrary, there is no evidence that the fetus was deformed (Ives, 2004).

Henry later visited Anne in her chamber and sadly commented, "I see that God will not give me male children" (Ives, 2004). This understandably upset Anne, who told him that she had lost the baby because his fall from his horse had scared her so badly, and because he had broken her heart by loving other women (Lipscomb, 2009). Either shock or heartbreak was considered a good explanation for a miscarriage in this era, and there is no reason Henry wouldn't have accepted this assertion (Cressy, 1997). The king was "much grieved" and possibly ashamed that his behavior had caused Anne to miscarry, so he stayed with the queen for a while in order to comfort her (Walker, 2002).

Was her miscarriage the reason Henry killed Anne in May? Some historians think that Henry may have already been debating getting rid of Anne (Starkey, 2003:551). Charles V had begun to extend a diplomatic olive branch toward England after Katherina's death The Emperor made it crystal clear that if Henry would set Anne aside and make a "fit" marriage, there would be a complete reconciliation between their realms (Froude, 1891). Nevertheless, Henry didn't take the bait. On the contrary, he continued to vigorously fight to have Anne recognized as queen by Charles V mere weeks before her death (Ives, 2004).

Other historians agree with Greg Walker, who argues that Anne's downfall was not due to her miscarriages but rather to some hasty words she said to Henry Norris at the end of April (Walker, 2002). Anne wasn't the sharp-tongued ogress she is made out to be, but she was human therefore capable of speaking without thinking it through. One day the queen spoke hastily and it may have cost her life. Anne asked Henry Norris, who was engaged to her cousin Madge Shelton, when he planned to wed. Norris hedged that he would wait just a bit longer, which irked Anne. In her anger she told him he was looking for "dead men's shoes, for if ought came to the King but good, you would look to have me" (Walker, 2002:21). It was treason to even think about the death of the King, let alone to talk about whom his queen might marry after his demise, and Anne quickly realized she had put her foot in her mouth to her kneecap. She demanded that Norris go to her chaplain, John Skyp, and swear she was faithful to the King, or "a good woman" (Lindsey, 1995). Anne's enemies made sure that the news, on which they placed the worst possible interpretation, quickly reached the King's ears.

The theory that her conversation with Norris led to her execution has widespread support among historians. Anne's enemies were looking for any opportunity to dispose of her, and may have transmuted her hasty comment into her death warrant. One of those enemies was Thomas Cromwell, a former friend and the king's current Chancellor of the Exchequer. Cromwell and Anne were fighting over the fate of the smaller monasteries Henry's dissolution was targeting. Cromwell, motivated by either the hatred of Catholicism or by the desire to plump up the treasury, wanted to destroy every last monastery and confiscate their riches. In contrast, Anne wanted the smaller monasteries left intact so that they could produce scholars who would in turn spread the word of God throughout England (Starkey, 2003).

Cromwell knew Anne was a formidable obstacle in the way of his plans, which probably included a chance to fill his own coffers with a share of the expropriated monastic goods. Working under the timeless assumption that "the enemy of my enemy is my friend," Cromwell joined the Catholic faction in destroying Anne Boleyn.

Mark Smeaton, one of the queen's musicians, was arrested on the last day of April. He was a commoner, subject legally to torture, and was subsequently the only man to confess to having had sexual intercourse with Anne. There were rumors in London that Smeaton's confession was obtained after he had been "grievously racked" (Ives, 2004). Smeaton never recanted his confession. However, it is easy to understand why a man would rather die a quick death by beheading than to be tortured again; thus his testimony remains questionable.

The next day the King questioned Henry Norris after the May Day tournament. The King apparently offered Norris a full pardon in exchange for his confession, but Norris steadfastly maintained his innocence (Lipscomb, 2009). Norris was a groom of the stool and had been one of Henry's closest friends for more than two decades. If Henry had merely been determined to destroy his wife he didn't need to murder one of his most loyal friends to do it. Norris' death is senseless unless Henry VIII genuinely believed Norris to be guilty. If Henry had McLeod syndrome it could have cause a delusional paranoia that, when given even the smallest doubt about Anne, would cause Henry to develop an irrational but profound hatred of her. It is almost certain that her enemies fed and strengthened the King's growing suspicions of her. Seemingly convinced that Anne had slept with several men and had plotted to do away with him, Henry had her arrested on May 2.

Other men were besides Smeaton and Norris were then accused of adultery with the queen, among them

Sir Francis Weston, William Brereton and Anne's own brother George Boleyn. With a grand total of five presumed lovers, including the incestuous relationship with her sibling, all of Europe seemed prepared to believe any calumny of Anne.

Chapuys recorded that "On the evening of the day on which the Concubine was sent to the Tower, the Duke of Richmond went to his father to ask his blessing, according to the English custom. The King said, in tears, that he, and his sister the Princess, ought to thank God for having escaped the hands of that woman, who had planned to poison them" (Froude, 1891). He also seemed to believe that Anne had betrayed him with more than a hundred men (Lindsey, 1995). The tales of Anne's sexual excesses grew exponentially, and soon the Imperial ambassador to the French court reported that the King had actually caught Anne in bed with the royal organist (Froude, 1891). On May 13, John Husee, a friend of Lord and Lady Lisle, wrote them with the latest news from London about Anne's trial. To Lady Lisle he wrote,

"Madame, I think verily if all the books and chronicles were totally revolved and to the uttermost persecuted and tried, which against women has been penned, contrived, and written since Adam and Eve, those same were, I think, verily nothing in comparison of that which hath been done and committed by Anne the Queen, which though I presume be not all things as it is now rumored, yet that which hath been by her confessed, and other offenders with her, by her own alluring, procurement, and instigation, is so abominable and detestable, that I am ashamed that any good woman should give ear thereunto. I pray God give her grace to repent while she now liveth. I think not the contrary but she and all they shall suffer." (Froude, 1891)

Husee likewise sent a letter to Lord Lisle, declaring "Here are so many tales I cannot tell what to write. Some say young Weston shall scape, and some that none shall die but the Queen and her brother; others that Wyatt and Mr. Page are as like to suffer as the rest. If any escape, it will be young Weston, for whom importunate suit is made" (Froude, 1891).

A Spanish tale had Anne hiding Smeaton in the sweets closet of her antechamber, to be brought out for sexual dalliance by her attendant whenever she used the code of asking for marmalade (Ives, 2004). The French ambassador's assistant claimed that when courtiers had to tell Henry that when he went to bed at night Anne already had "her toy boys [mignons] already lined up. Her brother is by no means last in the queue. Norris and [Smeaton] would not deny that they have spent many nights with her without having to persuade her, for she herself urged them on and invited them with presents and caresses" (Ives, 2004).

Why were the King and his court so willing to believe such insane tales about Anne? It would have been almost impossible for Anne to find the time and privacy to have sex with one man, let alone dozens. Where did this drivel come from?

It may have boiled down to beliefs about witchcraft.

For the Tudors, witches were undeniably real. Witches were men or women who worshiped the devil and who would do terrible things for no other reason than the enjoyment of doing evil. Witches were also thought to have extreme and depraved sexual desires (Warnicke, 1991:192-193). Rumors about Anne Boleyn had already suggested that Henry had been "seduced by witchcraft" (Starkey, 2003:551). Cardinal Pole, in one of his many recorded condemnations of Henry's divorce, wrote that Anne was a "Jezebel and a sorceress" (Denny, 2007). Accusing her of being in league with the Devil was more than a mere hyperbolic statement for Tudors.

If Henry thought his wife was a witch then he would believe any accusation made against her -- no matter how unlikely or vile. Furthermore, the "belief in witches would also encourage others, both noblemen and commoners, to be willing to entertain the notion that Anne wanted to poison her step-children, had indulged in wanton carnality with a variety of lovers, and had even enjoyed an incestuous affair with her brother. Everyone "knew" witches did these sorts of things" (Warnicke, 1991:4). People employed the circular reasoning that if Anne was a witch, then she must have done these things, and if she had done these things, then she must be a witch. As is usual with public opinion, there was an assumption that she would not have been accused of such awful behavior unless she had done something to arouse suspicion. Anne's enemies must have rejoiced in this perfect catch 22 that assured her destruction" (Kramer, 2012).

In reality, evidence of Anne's adultery was fairly non-existent, consisting almost entirely of Mark Smeaton's forced confession. Cromwell tried to explain away the lack of proof by claiming that the facts were so bad "that a good part had not even been given in evidence at the trial" (Ives, 2004).

Anne was shocked and devastated by her arrest. She was transported to the Tower from Greenwich in broad daylight so that everyone could witness her humiliation. When Henry's counselors, some of who had been her friends, had brought her into the Tower and handed her over to her jailor, Master Kingston, she went to her knees before them swearing her innocence and begging them to plead with Henry on her behalf (Ives, 2004). History has a fairly good record of the things Anne said while she was in custody, since her Kingston reported every word she said to Cromwell.

Anne, still somewhat composed, asked Kingston, "shall I go in to a dungeon?", to which he replied that she would be given the rooms she had stayed in during her coronation. This appears to have broken Anne, who cried out, "It is too good for me. Jesu, have mercy on me!" Kingston said that Anne subsequently "kneeled down weeping a great pace, and in the same sorrow fell into great laughing". He told Cromwell that Anne fell prey to that same combination of laughter and weeping "many times" during the time she was incarcerated (Ives, 2004).

Many people have interpreted Anne's laughter as hysteria, a manifestation of her emotional trauma. Susan Bordo, however, argues that Anne's laughter had an additional component: "Anne also laughed – in the same conversation with Kingston – when he told her that "even the King's poorest subject hath justice". It's hard to read that laughter as anything other than mocking Kingston's naivety about the King's "justice". Similarly, Anne's laughter over being housed in her coronation room can be read as a reaction to the bizarre, bitter irony of her situation" (Bordo, 2013).

Unlike the lute player Mark Smeaton, the other men with whom Anne was accused of adultery were of too noble lineage to be tortured. Without torture, no more "confessions" were forthcoming. Edward Baynton, who had served as Anne's vice-chamberlain and had now turned firmly against her in her hour of need, was so worried that the lack of evidence would "touch the King's honour" that he "recommended a trawl through Anne's ladies" for information (Starkey, 2003).

Anne Boleyn has frequently been portrayed as cunning, as befitting a temptress who played Henry VIII like a cheap fiddle in order to snag a crown. In contrast, her *actual* behavior was often not the kind indicating a duplicitous ability to manipulate people to her best advantage. Anne was often too frank for her own good. That was unquestionably the case when she was imprisoned in the Tower. She went over, out loud and at length and in front of hostile witnesses, any possible thing she might have said or done to cause Henry's suspicions. It was Anne, the supposed wily serpent in the Tudor garden, who gave Cromwell most of his paltry ammunition against her by her stupidly forthright comments.

In all honesty, Anne's entire career had been a long series of telling truths when she should have been lying, flattering, or conniving. Did she soft-soap and bribe her powerful relatives, so they would be at least semi-loyal? No, she allegedly treated the duke of Norfolk "worse than a dog" (Mackay, 2014); she was apparently more affected by the fact he was a horrible man than she was by his title and potential usefulness. Did she toady up to Cromwell, and keep him in the dark about her plans with sweet-talk? No. She challenged him openly and it cost her dearly. During her incarceration, Cromwell "took care to block access to the King" (Starkey, 2003), barring anyone of power who was sympathetic to the queen. Did she devote herself to fawning over the king and buttering him up for even more advantages? No. She was the only person in all of England who would call him on his shenanigans.

Cunning is perhaps not the best word to describe her.

Anne was smart and gifted with fortitude, though. Chapuys, a man who detested her, wrote that when her actual trial came the queen denied all charges and "gave to each a plausible answer" (Denny, 2007). Thomas Wriothesley reported that she defended "herself with her words so clearlie, as thoughe she had never bene faultie to the same" (Warnicke, 1991). Her clear words did her no good. Since it was a kangaroo court of the worst sort, a guilty verdict was preordained and swift. With rock-solid composure Anne's only response was to tell the court that she was prepared for death and was only sorry that so many innocent men were condemned to die as well.

The men were executed on May 17, 1536. What Anne must have felt at the death of her brother and courtiers must be left to the grim imagination. More obvious was her feelings at Mark Smeaton's death. When she heard that Smeaton, the only one of the accused to have pleaded guilty, had died without recanting his confession she said, "Did he not acquit me of the infamy he has laid on me? Alas, I fear his soul will suffer for it!" (Froude, 1891:430).

Anne herself would be beheaded on May 19th, with as small an audience as possible. Kingston had warned Cromwell that the queen was likely to "declare herself to be a good woman", because Kingston had witnessed her last sacrament and had heard her swear "as touching her innocency always to be clear" (Starkey, 2003). Knowing that Anne was innocent and might spill the beans, Cromwell delayed her beheading past the usual time of execution to discourage crowds. This provoked Anne, and she told Kingston that she had hoped to have been dead before noon. Kingston, also aware that she was innocent and that he was aiding and abetting in a legal murder, tried to soothe her by promising her that she would feel very little pain.

Upon hearing this cold comfort, Anne's sardonic sense of humor arose even in the face of death. She told Kingston: "I heard say the executioner was very good, and I have a little neck", after which she began "laughing heartily" (Denny, 2007). Kingston would report that Anne had "much joy and pleasure in [her] death" (Starkey, 2003). I think it is safe to say that Anne's gallows humor was completely beyond Kingston's grasp.

Finally, Anne was escorted to the scaffold. In spite of Kingston and Cromwell's attempts at stealth, there was a crowd of about a thousand people, including the King's son Henry Fitzroy and Thomas Cromwell (Ives, 2005). Did Cromwell feel victorious that he had manipulated Henry into destroying the queen before she could cause Cromwell to lose his comfy place next to power? If so, karma was swift because Henry would have Cromwell's head on the block just a few years later on July 28, 1540.

As was customary, Anne got to make a farewell speech which said in part, "I am come hither to accuse no man, nor to speak of that whereof I am accused and condemned to die …if any person should meddle in my cause, I require them to judge the best. And thus I take my leave of the world and of you all, and I heartily desire you all to pray for me." Although this speech looks very humble, and almost an admission of guilt to the modern mind, for the sixteenth century it was a "boldly" done refutation of the crimes (Ives, 2005). Anyone listening to her would have heard the subtext of her innocence ringing as clearly as a bell. Even ambassador Chapuys, whose animosity toward and loathing of Anne is well-documented, became convinced that she was innocent (Starkey, 2003:578).

Calmly, Anne Boleyn allowed her weeping attendants to help her put her long hair up into a cap so it wouldn't impede the sword. She then knelt and one of her ladies in waiting tied a blindfold around her eyes. While Anne was still in the act of commending her soul to Christ, her head was cleanly severed from her body. Her ladies in waiting, unaided by anyone else, wrapped the dead queen's body in cloth and carried it to the chapel of St. Peter. There the body was stripped of its clothing and "placed in an elm chest which had contained bow-staves ... There, near her brother, Anne Boleyn was buried" (Ives, 2005).

Henry was engaged to his third wife, Jane Seymour, less than twenty-four hours after Anne's death and he remarried eleven days later.

CHAPTER SIXTEEN

In modern discourse Anne Boleyn continues to be either pilloried as a whore or upheld as an angel, but it is the ever-popular slut shaming of Henry's second wife that I am addressing.

Anne Boleyn is, in the opinion of many, "the most controversial woman in English history. She is shaped by preoccupations with the mystery of female power, described as a witch, bitch, temptress, cold opportunist … a woman whose power is feared, her gender mistrusted" (Delahunty, 2013). She has been castigated as "a whore, a home wrecker, [and] a soulless schemer" (Lindsey, 1996). In novels and plays, on television and in the movies, Anne Boleyn continues to slink about as the ultimate femme fatale. Even today history buffs online comment that Anne was "a piece of work" who "deserved to die" because she poisoned Henry's first queen, calling Anne a "sociopath", "cruel and crazy", a "wack-job", a "horrible person" who "stole someone's husband", and "sly" … all before declaring Anne did things she patently and provably did not do.

In her book *The Creation of Anne Boleyn*, Susan Bordo talks about how many media representations of Anne, "inevitably led to recycling the image of Anne Boleyn as the seductive, scheming Other Woman. That's the classic soapy element of the story, after all: sexpot steals husband from mousy, menopausal first wife. [Michael Hirst, the creator of the Showtime series The Tudors] says he never intended this, and attributes it less to the script than to "deep cultural projections." He had initially seen Anne ... as a victim of her father's ambitions, and believed he was writing the script to emphasize that. He was surprised when "critics started to trot this line out: 'here she is, just a manipulative bitch.' Well, actually I hadn't written it like that. But they couldn't get out of the stereotypes that had been handed down to them and that's what they thought they were seeing on the screen. It didn't matter what they were actually seeing. They had already decided that Anne Boleyn was this Other Woman, this manipulative bitch" (Bordo, 2012).

Philippa Gregory's best-selling novel *The Other Boleyn Girl* reheats the image of a slutty Anne Boleyn and serves it afresh. In the book -- which has the majority of its dates and larger history correct and is a well-written story -- Gregory portrays Anne as a scheming man-eater willing (even enthusiastic) to have sex with her own brother in her climb to power. The Anne of *The Other Boleyn Girl* is a sociopath, unable to love anyone but herself and happy to trample family and friends under her ball-crushing feet. While it makes for compelling reading, it is very inaccurate history.

Even some post-Victorian academic historians have jumped on the slut shaming bandwagon. In 2010 historical biographer G. W. Bernard wrote a book about Anne Boleyn in which he said, "it remains my own hunch that Anne had indeed committed adultery with Norris, probably with Smeaton, possibly with Weston, and was then the victim of the most appalling bad luck" of having her actions come to light (Bernard, 2010). This led to tabloids and newspapers trumpeting headlines such as, "Anne Boleyn DID have an affair with her brother: The poem that 'proves' the adultery of Henry VIII's queen" (Hull, 2010). Unfortunately for Bernard, nothing was proven.

The biggest flaw in Bernard's theory is that most of the dates during which Anne had been accused of having affairs can still be concretely disproved almost five centuries after the fact. On her blog, "The Anne Boleyn Files", historian and author Claire Ridgway compiled all the evidence against Anne to give an outline of the dates in which Anne supposedly had affairs:

6th and 12th October 1533 – Anne and Henry Norris at Westminster
16th and 27th November 1533 – Anne and William Brereton at Greenwich
3rd and 8th December 1533 – Anne and William Brereton at Hampton Court
12th April 1534 – Anne and Mark Smeaton at Westminster (date for Anne procuring Smeaton)
12th and 19th May 1534 – Anne and Mark Smeaton at Greenwich
8th and 20th May 1534 – Anne and Sir Francis Weston at Westminster
6th and 20th June 1534 – Anne and Sir Francis Weston at Greenwich
26th April 1535 – Anne and Mark Smeaton at Westminster
31st October 1535 – Anne and some of the men compassed the King's death at Westminster
2nd and 5th November 1535 – Anne and her brother George Boleyn, Lord Rochford at Westminster
27th November 1535 – Anne gave gifts to the men at Westminster
22nd and 29th December 1535 – Anne and her brother George Boleyn, Lord Rochford, at Eltham Palace

    8th January 1536 – Anne compassed the King's death with Rochford, Norris, Weston and Brereton at Greenwich

    Ridgway then explained how historians have debunked roughly 75% of these claims:

    6th and 12th October 1533 – Anne had not yet been "churched" after Elizabeth's birth and the court was not at Westminster at all; it was in Greenwich at the time.

    3rd and 8th December 1533 – Once again, Anne was not physically present for her own adultery. She was in Greenwich, not Hampton Court.

    13th and 19th May 1535 – Mark Smeaton may have been at Greenwich on the 19th May, but Anne was definitely in Richmond.

    April, May and June 1534 – Anne was not only heavily pregnant those months, she was in Hampton Court when she was supposed to be seducing men in Greenwich.

    31st October 1535 – Why would Anne kill the king when Catherine of Aragon was still alive? Anne would have gotten the chop and Mary would have undoubtedly gotten the throne.

    27th November 1535 – Again, Anne was pregnant and not even in Westminster at the time. She was at Windsor on that date.

    22nd and 29th December 1535 – she was already pregnant, so why seduce her brother?

    8th January 1536 -- How could Anne be plotting the King's death at Greenwich when she was actually at Eltham Palace?

    Apparently these facts don't count when contrasted to Bernard's "hunch".

Bearing the historical facts in mind, what *exactly* did Anne do to be slut shamed for the next five centuries? She refused to date a married man until she knew he was getting a divorce. She refused to have sex with her fiancée until he put a ring on her finger. She gave birth to a daughter and had two miscarriages (perhaps three). All the evidence shows she was innocent of the adultery and incest of which she was accused. What on earth did she do that was oh-so-slutty?

Like any good slut shaming narrative, what she did is not as important as the cultural motif she can be shoehorned into. Any of her actions that flat-out contradict her supposed harlotry are ignored or dismissed. She refused to date a married king? Well, since Henry VIII didn't reward his mistresses as handsomely as did other royals, "it cannot be considered an act of great virtue that Anne showed no eagerness to become the king's mistress" (Friedmann, 1884). Remained chaste? She was just keeping Henry entangled in her guileful web. Got her head chopped off? It's implicitly her fault for "miscarrying of her savior" (Lipscomb, 2009); if she had given Henry a son then he wouldn't have *had* to look for a reason to kill her. Sluts, as everyone knows, get what's coming to them.

Even *Henry's* actions were her fault. Inasmuch as Henry "frequently made a public fool of himself in his fervor for Anne and his love for her" (Norton, 2011), Anne has been blamed for "making" the king into a mooncalf. Much of the hatred of Anne Boleyn in her own time stems from the fact that a "love-struck middle-aged man was an unsettling sight. When that ageing man was a king … the uneasiness grew, for here was an all-powerful being in thrall to a woman … the obvious way to absolve that feeling of unseemliness in the spectator was to blame Anne". (Dunn, 2007).

Everyone blamed Anne. Katherina blamed Anne for Henry's desire for a divorce. Wolsey blamed Anne for his political and economic losses, not the king and certainly not his own actions. Chapuys blamed Anne for the schism between Catholicism and England, not the actions of the Holy See that had inspired an entire reform movement throughout Europe. Princess Mary blamed Anne for the king's emotional cruelty toward his once pampered eldest child. A large chunk of the population blamed her for Henry's lusts. It must have been very hard for the English when Anne was dead, because she took the ultimate scapegoat with her to the grave.

Anne's true crimes were not those of sexual impropriety, but those of gender inversion. She was too "masculine" to be a good girl. A man -- a *king* no less -- fell in love with her and acted "feminine" in his adoration, which had to have been her fault somehow. She was too smart to be discounted, and she was determined to bring about religious reform that would flout the existing conventions. Like other evangelical women she was outspoken about her religious opinions. She made a mockery of the status quo.

Anne Boleyn is a slut because she had a vagina and a strong will.

Historically, women who express themselves or "attempt to declare their own agency ... have been shamed into silence" (de la Torre, 2014). History is still repeating itself. Slut shaming is a tool to silence women as much as it is a way of policing their sexual activity. Women who speak out, women who invade what is considered to be a "masculine" sphere, are often punished with slut shaming that has no more bearing on their work than leprechauns have with polar bears.

Iris Classon, a well-respected Swedish programmer who had chronicled her entry into software engineering, discovered this phenomenon first hand when she was profiled in one of Europe's leading computer science magazines, *ComputerSweden* (Frick, 2012). The article initially garnered a lot of attention from the Swedish developer community at large. However, a vociferous minority of misogynistic trolls were extremely unhappy that a woman developer had been featured. These trolls used the online comments section of the article to call into question Classon's qualifications and experience based solely on her gender. At first, the trolls contented themselves to the (unfortunately) typical sneers mocking the idea that she could have been hired for any reason other than because she was a woman. However, when other programmers -- male programmers -- defended Classon and pointed out that their hiring experiences were similar the comments quickly became darker and nastier. Classon later blogged about the fact that it took little more than an hour before the magazine had to 'close' the comment feed and after three hours "all offensive comments are deleted, my images removed, and the video removed on one article … [and] The title of the article is changed not to indicate my (sic) gender."

Classon's personal and professional accounts also became bombarded with the shamefully standard rape-and-death threats against her. ComputerSweden's response to the incident was to write a rather milquetoast editorial about the need for more women in the developer community, and how regrettable it was that they had to close the comment feed (Lindqvist, 2012). However, the editorial failed to mention the magazine's decision to remove Classon's identity from the original article and failed to address or condemn the continuing harassment Classon was still suffering.

Meanwhile, the attacks on Classon steadily became more personal and more invasive. Classon recorded some of the episodes on her now shuttered blog:

08:30 am– My husband leaves for work. First time I don't go with him- I got a few things to take care of at home before I head to work

08:35 am – Phone call from a number I don't recognize. Breathing on the other end. Person hangs up after a 10 seconds. I get a weird feeling. I go to my computer to look up the number.

08:38 am – My phone plings. It's an MMS with a video. The video is of a man masturbating, video is shot from the hipbone down to mid-thigh. It's a white male, overweight, small chubby hands, no dirt under his nails and he is circumcised. He is aroused, breaths heavily, but has a problem with his erection. The video is recorded just a few minutes before it was sent.

08:42 am – SMS: "Are you kind of horny? Maybe craving a big hard cock..?" Text is in Swedish

08:43 am – SMS: "Or maybe just some arousing phonesex? With video call?" Text is in Swedish

09:03 am - I text back: "Fuck of. I'm on my way to the police right now, with information from your phone carrier Telia and meta data from the video. I'm married, so the answer is no, and don't you fucking think that you have the right to do this you fucking idiot. Do you really think you can be anonymous when you send a video through sms? As soon as I have your address the police will knock on your door and hand over an Idiot of The Year diploma to you. Congratulations. No you keep wanking of, but do it on your own. "

09:20 am – phone rings, a different number (turns out to be another phone carrier, Comviq). Following conversation takes place.

Him : "I want to fuck your pussy, I'm going to…" – he is making his voice hoarser and darker, breathing heavily but also sounding nervous

Me: "Look dude, if you want to talk to me you got to speak up. I can't hear a shit because of the whole breathing thing you got going on"

He pauses. Complete silence for a few seconds. Then repeats what he said, word for word, louder. I can better hear his voice.

Me: "Really? You can't talk louder? I'm telling you I really can't hear what you are saying. Turn it up" He repeats, loudly this time, sounds nervous as hell and not that aroused anymore. His voice cracks mid-sentence and he hangs up. He doesn't call back.

Despite Clausson's determination to fight, it eventually became too much for her and in November of 2014 she began the process of "410ing", which is computer programming community code for "infosuicide" wherein a person deletes and/or lets go defunct their online presence. She has, at least for now, closed her blog, shut down her twitter account, stepped away from the software developer community github and is trying to pull the tentacles of Facebook off her virtual skin. She has decided to run silent, existing only as an anonymous user. This is disturbing for the greater developer community. One self-identified man blogged about what a shame it is that:

"this amazing woman who once was so excited and enthusiastic to be part of this "community" is leaving it. She's had enough, can't do it anymore. She is going to leave behind her github account, so that code she wrote will still be available for people, but she is leaving. The hundreds of people who supported her and told her to hang in there and tried to assure her that **not everyone**

is like that just couldn't compete. This is devastating to me for several reasons: we're losing all the amazing knowledge and wisdom and insight she provided while documenting her journey to become a programmer. We're losing the future potential of her work, and the many things she may have done which are now not going to be done. We're also losing an amazing role-model for women in technology, which we desperately need more of. For me, though, I think the thing that makes this all really hurt, is the fact that I have to pause and think, even for just a little bit, when I want to tell my girls that there is nothing they can't do. Because while it is true, they **can** do anything, are there things that are going to become too painful and damaging when they do them well that I will regret having supported them?"

Iris Classon's one crime which inspired her harassment and eventual silencing? She had a vagina but could develop computer code.

The larger "gamer" community is another perceived male space where women enter at their peril. While many gamer communities are sources of vital social support and friendship, women frequently suffer harassment at the hands of a few vitriolic members (Stuart, 2013). In spite of the fact that women make up 47% of online gamers (Galarneau, 2014), they are still viewed as outsiders in a masculine virtual world. The screen captures (photo recording as evidence) on the blog *Fat, Ugly or Slutty*, where gamer women can share stories of harassment, are disturbing as they are ridiculous. The name-calling is exacerbated a thousand fold when self-identified female players are winning a game. For example, women and girls routinely receive messages such as:

"your nans [nan is] dead bcz [because] I face fucked her"

"slutty bitch"

"ima rip your neck open and fuck the gaping hole ald [and] finish off in your eyes"

"stupid slut"

"lol its hard to hear with all the fat in your ears .... Block me now fat bitch ... forgot your fat you can do that with you fat cause youre fat"

"whore"

"bitch"

In one case a woman reported, "Got this message while playing Mass Effect 3. He didn't take kindly to my asking for more teamwork. Oh, and he didn't like that I got the high score. Oops." The message? "yeah your mad cunt I don't need you to carry me with all that dick your suckin. YOUS JUST A FAT VIRGIN HOE ohh and get blocked ☺"

It's the smiley face at the end that really makes it piquant, no?

The gamer community was further deluged with misogynistic screeching during the #gamergate debacle in 2014. In theory, #gamergate is a group of loosely affiliated individuals concerned about the ethics in video game journalism. In reality, it is a hate group that is as sincerely devoted to ethics in game journalism as the Ku Klux Klan is to family values (Allaway, 2014). As a collective #gamergate has systematically targeted women who work in the video game industry with terrorist threats in an effort to drive away those they see as responsible for the slowly evolving inclusiveness of women in the gaming industry. In reality, the fact that about half of all video game players are girls or women has been driving the push toward less male-centric video concepts. This organic change has nevertheless "led a section of male players who identify as "core gamers" in the classic sense – own next-generation consoles, play online multiplayer shoot-'em-ups, wouldn't touch brightly-coloured mobile games like Candy Crush with a barge pole – to feel like their club is being picked on" (Stuart, 2014).

The small group of self-styled "core gamers" were particularly angry about Anita Sarkeesian, a feminist pop culture critic who dissected sexism in video games on her blog Feminist Frequency. Sarkeesian attempted to raise $6000 to fund a series of videos entitled Tropes vs. Women in Video Games, which would be an exploration of the negative way women are portrayed in most video games. Sarkeesian received a tidal wave of hate speech in retaliation for her 'assault' on 'real gamers', including such pithy phrases as "tits or back to the kitchen, bitch" and "fuck off prude" (Watercutter, 2012). The anger turned into seething bitterness when Sarkeesian's project exceeded its funding goal due to widespread support among the majority of gamers.

This festering resent toward women messing up 'pure' video game culture went from a simmer to a boil when Eron Gjoni, the ex-boyfriend of games developer Zoe Quinn, "published a revenge blog listing men she had allegedly cheated on him with, including games journalists and industry insiders. It was alleged that an affair with Nathan Grayson, a journalist at the website Kotaku, had led to favourable critical treatment of her game" (Stuart, 2014). Now those that considered themselves core gamers had a clear target that they could go after while masking their misogyny with the righteous indignation of outrage over the lack of ethics in journalism. Slut shaming in the form of rape and death threats rained down upon Zoe Quinn, especially via Twitter. Conservative actor and fellow core gamer

Adam Baldwin proposed #gamergate as the hashtag to distinguish tweets about the topic, and a movement was born.

Zoe Quinn was compelled to leave her home and go into hiding after seeing her "address posted online and terrifyingly plausible plans to cripple her laid out with cold-blooded straightforwardness" (Hern, 2014). Although it was quickly established that Nathan Grayson had never reviewed her game and had never written about her once they had started a relationship, the attacks on Quinn continued, exposing the idea that #gamergate was about ethics in game journalism as the smokescreen it was. Even after it was proven that Quinn and Grayson had *not* committed any ethical violations and Quinn was clearly in fear of her life, #gamergate militant Adam Baldwin still sent out tweets linking to videos that provided nude pictures of Quinn and her home address (Hern, 2014).

Furthermore, in spite of the continued insistence of #gamergate that its motives were to promote ethics in game journalism, analysis of the data revealed that the targets of #gamergate were women who had the audacity to be part of gamer culture rather game journalists (Wofford, 2014). While Nathan Grayson and his editor received some negative comments, the overwhelming majority of insulting tweets and feedback were aimed at women who had nothing to do with theoretical or actual ethical malfeasance. Leigh Alexander is one of the few game journalists to have been targeted and her only 'crime' was to be critical of #gamergate. Brianna Wu, a games developer who disagreed with #gamergate but who has never been accused of ethical infractions, has received venomous rape and death threats in such frequency that she and her husband had to flee their home for their own safety (Hart, 2014).

Anita Sarkeesian also came under renewed attacks by the emboldened members of #gamergate, requiring her and her family to go underground due threats claiming she would be raped and murdered (Campbell, 2014). Sarkeesian also had to cancel a speech she was scheduled to give at Utah State University when "members of the university administration received an email warning that a shooting massacre would be carried out at the event. And under Utah law, she was told, the campus police could not prevent people with weapons from entering her talk. "This will be the deadliest school shooting in American history, and I'm giving you a chance to stop it," said the email, which bore the moniker Marc Lépine, the name of a man who killed 14 women in a mass shooting in Montreal in 1989 before taking his own life" (Wingfield, 2014).

Many male gaming luminaries made concerted efforts to push back against the misogyny directed at the women in the gaming community. However, "the men who supported Quinn and Sarkeesian, such as Phil Fish or Tim Schafer, sustained no small measure of attempted intimidation for their trouble ... often bound up with gender politics. Men will find themselves struck by accusations of feminization, "white knighting," taunts about their genitalia, and so forth; their detractors see men's association with an apostate woman as especially damning" (Cross, 2014). The onslaught of gender-biased verbal abuse suffered by men who stood up against #gamergate regarding the harassment of women indicates that one of the deepest motivations of the semi-political movement is to punish anyone they see as a feminist. It is an attempt to drive women and their allies out of the gaming community, or at least make them afraid to suggest any reformation or gender parity.

In this narrative, women who try to change things are sluts because they are not performing women's gender roles 'correctly'. They are active, rather than passive. They are talking back to those who see themselves as authoritarian representatives of culture. Slut shaming – and the attendant rape and death threats that are embedded in gender policing – is used as a method of silencing women who seek to be agents of change. It often works. The blitzkrieg endured by outspoken women in the gaming industry has resulted in the fact that several female game developers have become "unwilling to comment, citing concern for their safety" (Wos, 2014) on #gamergate. Female developers' receive letters "from young girls who dream of being game developers, but are terrified of the environment they see" (Wu, 2014) who are thus discouraged from entering the industry. Rape and death threats against current women in gaming preemptively silence women who would have been involved in game development in the future.

How can words be so damning as to drive women away from careers and compel them to silence? You can judge for yourself. To demonstrate how exhausting the constant barrage of anti-feminist and anti-women gamers' hostility can be, Anita Sarkeesian published just *one* week of threatening tweets she receives as a sample of the kind of harassment she faces. Among the 157 tweets were "fuck you mother fucker slut birch female ass hoe slut" and "you annoying fuckign cunt" and "you can qritcue the games … With your slut cunt" and "I hope you get raped by 4 men with 8 inch cocks" and "imam kill u and rape u" and "im going to come to your house and violently rape you in front of your family". There were also many tweets advising Sarkeesian to kill herself, sometimes in specific ways that recalled the way other victims of slut shaming had committed suicide, such as drinking bleach. The hatred rolling off the comments was palpable. Inasmuch as the need to make friends is a hard-wired into the human brain as the need for food, this kind of abuse takes an immense emotional/psychological toll on the receiver (Samarrai, 2013).

Although almost all of the tweets that Sarkeesian got that week were variations of the theme "fuck you, you stupid bitch/whore, you should be raped", several of the attacks were from men/boys enraged by what they saw as Sarkeesian playing the "victim card". Those tweets included those saying, "you criticize gamers for "threatening you" 1v1 me gta [Grand Theft Auto the video game] u be the prostiture and I'll be the guy that runs you over you attention whore", "please shut the fuck up but wait you'll make a article about how I threatened you and act like I'm Satan well bitch u r", and "So what! People get angry and make a threat in game and 1 hour later their the nicest person in the world! Stop lying to the media!" and "keep on scamming your followers threats are a part of gaming, always has been. Stop trying to victimize yourself for money!" and the all caps glory of "FUCKING CUNT WHORE STOP TRYING TO PLAY VICTIM YOU'RE FUCKING STUPID!!!!!". There are even accusations that Sarkeesian had set up dummy accounts to send herself threatening messages in an attempt to make #gamergate look bad. The irony that the tweeters were victimizing her in the same messages they were using to claim she was not victimized and had made-up the attacks herself escaped them.

Tellingly, several of the tweets were directed at feminism in general as well as Sarkeesian. Some of the comments included, "I hope every feminist has their head severed from their shoulders", "fucking bitch you don't deserve rights feminist need to good to jail for existing #MeninistTwitter" and "get the fuck out you feminist cunt" and "your feminazi shit is a waste of time" and "Just kill yourself dumb whore, stop feeding the media with all this fake feminist propaganda". Clearly the idea of women wanting and/or achieving equality is a source of profound social angst and fear for insecure males, inciting their anger against it.

Commenters also seemed incensed that Sarkeesian would consider rape and death threats toxic to the gaming environment or sexist in any way. Tweets on this topic included "Stop. You do not understand about gaming, Death Threats are made daily, as well as rape threats. guess what? It's not only women!" as well as "Death threats and rape threats are in the culture of gaming … Have you ever played an Online game? Get used to it …" and "it's a normal. It's part of gaming, stop being such as pussy or I'll rape you". It seems to be beyond their comprehension that using feminine terms to denigrate is sexism and encourages the continued entrenchment of sexist behavior (Glick and Fiske, 1997) or that these kinds of "jokes" or wordplay *normalize* rape and sexism. Almost 1/3 of college age men don't understand that forcing a woman they know to have sex IS the same thing as rape (Edwards et al., 2014). Rape jokes and casual rape threats make rapists think they are normal, or in the majority. It presents rape as 'just one of those things'. Rape is already so normalized that rape threats are the status quo, and complaints about rape threats are therefore transgressive actions to be punished.

Anne Boleyn and #gamergate may seem to be completely unrelated, but beneath the surface there are still strong cultural links between the Protestant-leaning queen and men who seek slut shame women into silence and compliance. Anne Boleyn was hated and continues to be slut shamed centuries after her death because she was a woman who made her opinions known, who was a driving force for cultural change, and who did not quietly accept traditional male authority. The women targeted by #gamergate, or who are otherwise driven out of the fields of technology, are assailed for the same reasons Anne Boleyn and other reformist women were hated by the establishment; they are trying to alter a male-centered environment. Those women were and are slut shamed to remind them that they are bad girls. They are punished for their audacity. They are humiliated to stop their attempts to use their agency. Their dismantled reputations and lives serve as a warning and a reminder to all women of what can happen if she challenges male privilege.

As one of the men and/or boys attacking Anita Sarkeesian tweeted, "We're not going to stop until no one will openly admit to being feminist".

CHAPTER SEVENTEEN

Anne Boleyn isn't the only one of Henry VIII's queens to be slut shamed for perpetuity. Katheryn Howard, his fifth wife, has been maligned as a scarlet woman for almost five hundred years by laymen and historians. What makes her such a filthy harlot? No more and no less than that she had two boyfriends before marrying Henry VIII, one of whom she slept with, and an unconsummated flirtation with a courtier after she had wed the king.

Seriously. That's the entirety of her so-called sordid behavior.

Katheryn was one of many children born to the obscure and scrounging younger brother of the Duke of Norfolk, Edmund Howard, and his first wife, Jocasta Culpepper (Smith, 2009:39-42). Unfortunately, her mother died when Katheryn was young. Katheryn was then sent to live her step-grandmother, Agnes Howard, the dowager duchess of Norfolk and the second wife of the duke of Norfolk's father. Agnes Howard had a large household, and many of the major and minor noble families sent the younger daughters there to act as ladies-in-waiting in order to fine tune their social skills. There were so many young women and girls in the household that there was actually a dormitory, called the Maidens' Chamber, where they all slept. Agnes had the door to this dormitory locked each night in order to preserve the theoretical chastity -- or at least the marriageability -- of her wards (Starkey, 2003:644-646). However, many of the dowager duchess's teen ladies-in-waiting, like heterosexual young women throughout the centuries, were more interested in having a boyfriend than they were in preserving their virtue.

Katheryn had been largely neglected in her childhood, but post-pubescence she found that she -- like her cousin Anne Boleyn -- possessed an allure that rendered her especially desirable to men. Women who are imbued with this inherent sensuousness are usually blamed for the attention they attract. Garnering too much male notice marks a woman as a doxy who is no better than she should be.

Even in modern times women are considered the gatekeepers of morality, but it was a much stronger responsibility in Katheryn's day. Inasmuch as women are the ones required to have self-control and keep suitors at bay, women who "give in" to wooing males are ergo bad women. They have failed in their gender-based duty to keep male sexuality in check. Women who either encourage or enjoy the sexual attention of men are still frequently conceptualized as jezebels out to lure men to their moral doom. For Katheryn, the rewards must have outweighed the moral censure. Doubtlessly starved for affection and attention, Katheryn discovered that she could gain both endearments and pleasure by being flirtatious and indulging in some physical romance with her swains. She has been consistently depicted as a slattern and a mattress-back for her choices.

She must have been incredibly charming, since her suitors always seemed to fall elbow over teakettle in love with her. Katheryn's first boyfriend was her music teacher, Henry Manox. Manox was an adult male of undetermined age, whereas Katheryn was somewhere between 10 and 15 years old. Thus, to the modern reader, it is more reasonable to describe Katheryn's first "boyfriend" as a sexual predator and pedophile. However, the understanding of the age of consent and adulthood was different in the 16th century; if Katheryn were 15 years old – which is the most likely date – then Manox would have considered her grownup enough to woo.

His relationship with Katheryn did not work out well for the smitten Manox. He later freely admitted that he was in love with Katheryn, and he claimed she returned his interest. When others told him there was no way for him to win with a woman born so much higher than he was, the music teacher bragged that he had once had Katheryn, "by the cunt, and I know it among hundreds" (Starkey, 2003:669). However, outside of allowing him to fondle her genitalia, Katheryn didn't seem to be that into Manox. She told him point-blank that she would never marry him because as a Howard by birth she could count on a much better match (Lindsey, 1995:160). While she evidently enjoyed his embraces and his adoration of her, he was clearly not someone she was overly infatuated with. Their semi-romance ended abruptly when Agnes Howard caught Manox and Katheryn canoodling. Agnes was irked more than scandalized, and struck Katheryn for being foolish enough to risk her reputation with a nobody like Manox. The dowager duchess also forbade them to ever be alone together again (Starkey, 2003:646-647). The loss of Manox didn't seem to have any lasting effect on Katheryn. She moved on, and did not look back.

Katheryn soon caught the attention of Francis Dereham. He was a more respectable suitor, and although he wasn't wealthy he was gentleman of reasonable means (Starkey, 2003:647). Like Manox, Dereham appears to have fallen in love with Katheryn. Witnesses would later report that Dereham had repeatedly begged her to marry him, but Katheryn was unwilling to commit. She liked him, but thought she could do better in the long run. (Lindsey, 1995:162). Although she wasn't madly in love with Dereham, she fancied him enough to have sex with him. Moreover, her enthusiasm for continuing their liaison indicates she found sex to be pleasurable. Imagine! A woman having sex for fun rather than True Love! Katheryn didn't seem to worry that an unexpected pregnancy would force her to the altar, since she would later claim that she knew how to "meddle with a man and yet conceive no child" (Loades, 2009:116). She wanted to have sex, but not marriage or babies from it.

    Katheryn was far from alone in her notions. Several of the 'maidens' in the Maidens' Chamber enjoyed having lovers. The young women who shared the dormitory bribed the dowager's maid to bring them the key to their door. With a copy of the purloined key, they opened their door at night and allowed their suitors to visit. The various boyfriends would bring alcoholic beverages, "strawberries, apples and other things to make good cheer" with, and would "commonly banquet and be merry there till two or three of the clock in the morning" (Starkey, 2003:647).

    Manox was rancorously jealous. He had boasted that Katheryn had promised to let him be the one to 'deflower' her, and said that "from the liberties the young lady has allowed me, I doubt not of being able to effect my purpose" (Lindsey, 1995:161). Manox, however, failed to convince Katheryn to have sex with him. He was enraged and sulky that Katheryn had actually chosen someone else to "get" the maidenhead he felt was his. In an attempt to stop Dereham's visits to Katheryn, Manox slipped a note to Agnes Howard warning her about the shenanigans in the Maidens' Chamber. The dowager duchess, now informed "of their misrule", fussed at her young ladies-in-waiting, but she was much less concerned about the sex than she was that eating rich foods late at night would negatively affect the beauty of her charges (Starkey, 2004). Agnes Howard took further measures to keep the unmarried women out of bounds, but the idea that people in their teens and early 20s wanted to have sex with one another just wasn't that shocking.

While in the dowager duchess' manor, Katheryn was never taught to connect severely negative consequences with sex. Nor was she wise enough to understand that the permissiveness allowed to a woman of no importance in Agnes Howard's household would be forbidden to a married woman or a woman of higher rank. When she later married Henry VIII, she failed to see that actions taken lightly by a girl of little note would be judged harshly when they were taken by a queen.

This is not to imply that Katheryn was stupid. Although she is often portrayed as a dimwit, she was intelligent enough to figure out a way to sneak the letter incriminating her and Dereham out of Agnes Howard's room so that Dereham could make a copy of it. Once they had a copy of the letter, it didn't take Dereham and Katheryn long to figure out that Manox was the culprit behind it. Instead of getting Katheryn back, Manox became the recipient of her disgust and anger, while Dereham accosted the music master and called him a "knave" (Starkey, 2003). Meanwhile, the nocturnal visits between the young men and their sweethearts continued in spite of the increased security measures.

Katheryn apparently enjoyed her affair with Dereham during its duration, but she left him without a backward glance when she had a chance to get to court in the winter of 1539. When her lovesick beau tried to remind her they were as good as engaged, having called each other husband and wife, Katheryn let him know that for her part she never considered them contracted to wed. She was thrilled to leave the Dowager's household and become one of ladies in waiting for the new queen, Anna of Cleves. When questioned later, Katheryn declared that she had never promised to marry Dereham and that everyone "that knew me, and kept my company, know how glad and desirous I was to come to the court" (Starkey, 2003:648). Dereham may have seen a future with Katheryn, but she saw him only as a friend with benefits.

    An engaging coquette, Katheryn took to court life like a duck to water. What she lacked in formal education she made up for in flirtatiousness and likeability. She soon became as popular in Henry's court as she had been in Agnes Howard's household. One of her conquests was Thomas Culpepper. He was a well-known skirt chaser and one of Henry's favorite courtiers. It is also likely that Culpepper was a rapist and a murderer. He, or someone else who coincidently had the same name and was also in Henry's good graces, sexually assaulted the wife of a park-keeper. Culpepper was such a contemptible craven that had some of his friends and hangers-on hold the woman down while he raped her. When other men tried to come to her aid, Culpepper stabbed one of her would be rescuers to death. Culpeper was arrested for his crimes, but since he was a pet of the king he was granted a royal pardon and was never punished for either the rape or the murder (Lindsey, 1995:168). In spite of these offences, his popularity at court remained unaltered. His fellow courtiers and the ladies in waiting were unaware of his crimes, or more likely they did not care. The woman he raped and the man he killed were both commoners, and not quite human to many members of the upper crust at the time.

The romance between Katheryn and Culpepper cooled off abruptly in early 1540. When a fellow courtier told Katheryn that he had heard that she and Culpepper were engaged, she shrugged it off, telling him, "If you heard such a report you heard more than I do know" (Starkey, 2003:649). The most probable cause for the sudden estrangement between Katheryn and Culpepper was that she had attracted the notice of the king. She was probably thrilled to have caught the king's eye, but if she had not been then her uncle, the duke of Norfolk, would doubtlessly have ordered that she make herself available for Henry. The king had become serious about her by April of 1540, and was most likely besotted with her at least a few weeks before that, so the timing fits her withdrawal from Culpepper. Katheryn was not the type to have missed the opportunity to become a royal favorite, and Culpepper would have been a hindrance to her goal to keep the king interested in her.

It is likely that part of Henry's intense infatuation with Katheryn was subconsciously based on the fact she resembled his first queen in her youth. Both the newlywed Katharina of Aragon and Katheryn Howard were diminutive and plump, and both of them made it their mission in life to indulge Henry's whims. Katheryn must have had Henry firmly by the nostalgia the minute she fluttered her eyelashes at him. Someone informed Agnes Howard that Henry fell in love with Katheryn, "the first time that ever his Grace saw her" (Smith, 2009:95). For her part, Katheryn was extremely good at making suitors believe she loved them as much as they loved her.

For the duke of Norfolk and his Catholic allies at court, Henry's interest in Katheryn was heaven sent. Norfolk spoke of his young niece to the King in glowing terms, in spite of the fact the duke had ignored her most of her life and hardly knew her at all. The once burdensome orphan now had feasts held in her honor. Rather than having to make do for clothes, Katheryn now received stylish new garments for court from Agnes Howard (Starkey, 2003:650). The young woman was carefully groomed, being told "how to behave" and "in what short to entertain the king's highness and how often" (Scarisbrick, 1970:429). There is a good likelihood that she was also coached on what to say about Cromwell in order to hasten his fall and execution, since the duke was one of Cromwell's most bitter enemies. The odds are good that Katheryn was overjoyed to be of such importance to her powerful uncle and the king.

Nor was the fact that Henry VIII was married to Anna of Cleves at the time an obstacle. The court was filled with rumors of the king's unhappiness, and switching wives had become something of a royal habit. Soon plans were afoot for Henry's marriage to be annulled and have Anna become his "sister".

Unlike Katheryn, who didn't need to be in love to be in a relationship, the King was a romantic to his bones. Once Henry was in love, he was determined to make Katheryn the new queen of England. The fact that this was an idiotic political move, one which would potentially alienate his Germanic allies and would certainly forward Norfolk's agenda, did not matter one whit to the king. Henry was acting with the same reckless determination to wed his true love as he did when he was a younger and healthier man. In his mind he still saw himself as the dashing young king who rescued and married his destitute widowed sister-in-law, Katherina of Aragon. He was the man who "loved where he did marry" (Erickson, 1980). He would have the bride he wanted come hell or high water. When it came to marriage, the king was a perfect storm of romantic feeling, narcissism, and stubbornness.

The nuptials of Henry and Katheryn Howard were held quietly on July 28, 1540, the same day Thomas Cromwell was beheaded. It had been less than eight months since the king had married Anna of Cleves. Two weddings in one year was quite an accomplishment, even for Henry VIII. The king was forty-nine years old, but consummating his marriage to Katheryn was not a worry. His bride, who was probably in her late teens or maybe early twenties, made him feel young again and his lust for her overcame the erectile dysfunction that had plagued him since his early forties. His marriage coincided with a terrible drought killing crops and cattle and leaving peasants to starve, but Henry was too happy to care (Starkey, 2003:650). The lack of rain ensured sunny days for hunting and starry nights for feasting, dancing, and making love. For that short summer, Henry could fancy himself a young and virile man again, and that was all he cared to know.

In spite of his age and infirmaries, Katheryn was probably enthusiastically willing to marry the King. However, when she said "I do" it is likely that what she really meant was "I do want to be the queen". Her wedding was not a love match. Marrying Henry would have been her way out of obscurity and into prestige. Instead of being nobody she would be somebody. Everyone who had ignored her as an unimportant girl would suddenly respect her as valuable.

Henry, though, firmly believed Katheryn was as in love with him as he was with her.

Energized by bliss, Henry could not do enough to show his affection to his new bride. He called Katheryn his "rose without a thorn" and boasted to his courtiers that she was a "jewel" (Lindsey, 1995:164). Naturally blessed with the ability to make people happy when she wanted to, Katheryn was wise enough to submit to Henry in all things and agree with his every word. She was showered with gifts in return for her docility. The King was deeply enchanted, and gave her a motto that reflected her easy acquiescence: "no other wish save his" (Smith, 2009:138). Katheryn had a great deal of motivation to please her husband, which Henry saw as a delightfully feminine trait and was convinced it was a sign of her overwhelming love for him. The French ambassador wrote that Henry was so enamored of Katheryn that "he cannot treat her well enough" (Starkey, 2003:651). Undoubtedly the king showered her with material goods.

To show his affection, Henry bought Katheryn a warehouse worth of beautiful and expensive gowns, gloves, shoes and headdresses. He practically smothered her in gemstones and jewelry, including one incredible necklace with 29 rubies, 116 pearls, and a gold pendant holding a large diamond, a large ruby and a long baroque pearl hanging on the end, and another necklace with 33 diamonds, 60 rubies, and a border of pearls (Starkey, 2003:651). He also gave her earrings, bracelets, rings, and furs. The girl who had grown up as a neglected and poor dependent relation was now rolling in loot and adulation.

Katheryn has often been blamed for the fact Henry spent so much money on her. Because the king's gifts were bountiful, Katheryn has been seen as greedy or grasping. Notwithstanding the image of the young queen as covetous, historical facts indicate that she was as generous as she was acquisitive. Yes, Katheryn clearly loved to receive expensive presents from her enchanted husband, but she gave just as lavishly to old friends and relations. She gave her supporters and dependents gifts of money as well as positions in her household. She also asked Henry to give them jobs as well. This behavior was considered to be an essential part of good breeding in the Tudor era (Starkey, 2003:661). Those who were given positions of authority were expected to do their very best to secure the fortunes of other members of their extended kin networks. Katheryn seemed more than willing to help those who came to her for a handout. All evidence indicates that she never gloated or held her rags-to-riches affluence over those who had been less fortunate. She may not have fallen in love easily, but there is plenty of evidence that she was open-hearted in other ways.

She was also incredibly gracious to Anna of Cleves. The fact the two ladies were going to meet eventually at court must have caused masters of etiquette to be nearly fainting with terror. The earl of Essex, who was the man responsible for matters of deportment within the royal household, must have had kittens when he had to arrange the meeting between a former queen and the former lady-in-waiting who supplanted her. There was no precedent for such an occasion, so the poor man had to wing it, (Starkey, 2003:652). Katheryn had once waited on Anna of Cleves as a lowly member of her household, and now the young girl had usurped Anna's husband and the crown. How would Anna treat her successor to the throne? How would the present queen treat her former queen? If either woman behaved in a petty, jealous, or rude manner there would be a huge scandal. The whole court must have been biting its collective nails to see what would happen.

Happily, all worries were unnecessary because both women were wonderfully free of pettiness. When Anna of Cleves came to meet the new queen in early January of 1541 the former queen went down on her knees in respect before Katheryn, showing "as much reverence and punctilious ceremony as if she herself were the most insignificant damsel at court" (Starkey, 2003:653). Katheryn graciously responded by pleading with Anna to stand and then bent over backwards to extend every courtesy imaginable to the previous queen. They had dinner together with Henry and then stayed to dance with each other after Henry went to bed (Lindsey, 2003:165). Katheryn and Anna seem to have been of similar dispositions, in that they wanted to experience fun and to give enjoyment to others.

The new queen also used her influence over Henry to mitigate his blood-lust. Katheryn kindly petitioned for Henry's mercy on behalf of both commoners and courtiers alike. She asked the King to stop the execution of a low-born spinning-woman named Helen Page, and also pleaded for the life of a courtier named John Wallop, both times with success (Lindsey, 1995:167). When Henry threw the famous English poet, Thomas Wyatt, into the Tower for the iniquitous crime of having formerly received Cromwell's patronage, Katheryn begged Henry to free him as well (Starkey, 2003:659). To oblige his pretty young wife, Henry released Wyatt. Is Katheryn remembered for her mercy and intervention to deflect Henry's wrath? No. She is remembered as the hussy who cuckolded the king. Nothing else a woman does, no matter how good, can overcome slut shaming.

Katheryn was not the avaricious chippie people make her out to be, but she wasn't a saint either. Despite of her usually jolly temperament, she was as capable of getting into a snit as any other human being. Famously, she fought with Henry's eldest daughter, Mary.

It is not surprising that Katheryn and Mary didn't get along. They were oil and water at best, or fire and a powder keg at worst. Katheryn was devoted to frivolity and apparently considered her religion (when she considered it at all) to be something she had to do but not anything she had to worry about (Starkey, 2003:654-655). Mary was of a serious, even dour, mindset and devoted to Catholicism. She saw her religion as the guiding star in her life. Mary had good reason to cling to her faith; she had suffered unbearable emotional abuse at the hands of her father, had been torn away from her beloved mother, and had been declared a bastard. Mary would furthermore have been extremely biased against Katheryn since the new queen had supplanted what Mary saw as the king's lawful wife. Mary had come to love Anna of Cleves during their brief acquaintance, and her step-mother had been pushed aside so that the king could marry Anne Boleyn's sexually alluring cousin. This almost certainly reopened Mary's emotional wounds regarding her parents' acrimonious separation. It was probably Mary's loyalty to Anna of Cleves that caused the first battle between herself and the new queen.

No one knows exactly what happened between Mary and Katheryn. The historical record just vaguely mentions that Mary did not treat the newest queen with the "same respect" as she had treated Jane Seymour and Anna of Cleves (Lindsey, 1995:166). Undoubtedly it was hard for Mary to treat a younger, lower-born, frivolous woman as her superior in rank. This attitude, which Mary must not have hidden well, offended Katheryn. The young queen threatened to have some of Mary's personal ladies-in-waiting sent away. The threat of losing even more allies and people close to her must have upset Mary greatly, because she quickly "found means to conciliate" her stepmother (Whitelock, 2010:112). Katheryn, who was too good-natured to be vindictive, allowed the ladies to remain in Mary's household. The queen also displayed her lack of maliciousness when she encouraged Henry to allow his eldest daughter to come back to court full time. Even to her enemies, Katheryn was undeniably kind.

Katheryn made a credible attempt to be a good to Henry's children. She made large gifts to Mary, hoping to win her affection. There may have been a dual motive with Mary, since Henry's eldest daughter was a significant political figure and many at court still looked to her as the hope of restoring Catholicism to England. Norfolk, as Katheryn's uncle, may have even pressured the queen to be nice to Mary. However, Katheryn also gave gifts to Elizabeth, and there was no reason for her to be nice to a girl who had such a cloud hanging over her parentage. In fact, it might have been in Katheryn's best interest to disassociate herself to Anne Boleyn's child. Katheryn was more kind than cunning, though, and was generous to her youngest step-daughter. It was mostly because of Katheryn's efforts to unite the siblings as a family that Mary, Elizabeth, and Prince Edward all exchanged New Year's gifts with one another in 1543 (Starkey, 2003:660). Unfortunately, Katheryn wasn't able to enjoy that success because Henry had executed her almost a year earlier.

The queen was sometimes foolish in her generosity. For example, she appointed many of her friends from Agnes Howard's household to serve her at court. These friends were well aware that Katheryn had a former lover, and it would have been wiser of Katheryn to have those young women married off or sent away to houses in the country. Worse, she was imprudent enough to have Dereham himself appointed to her household as her private secretary (Lindsey, 1995:167). It was especially problematic to have Dereham around. The man was an idiot. The dunderhead actually bragged to people at court about being in the queen's favor, and was so imbecilic that he claimed that if the King were to die "I am sure I might marry her" (Smith, 2009:148). This was, by imagining the death of the king, treason. Dereham was a liability and Katheryn should have taken steps to remove him. A word in Norfolk's ear, and Dereham would have doubtlessly been pushing up daisies. Alas for Katheryn, she was not of a Machiavellian mindset.

Although stupid in hindsight, Katheryn's patronage of the people from her less-than-chaste past was not as preposterous as it seems. For one thing, it was expected of her. The queen was under tremendous pressure from the dowager duchess and other noble relatives to give Dereham a place at court because he was a relative and ally of the Howard family (Starkey, 2003:661). She probably also thought that Dereham would not be suicidal enough to admit he once shared her bed. If anyone, including Dereham, had ratted her out for her past then they would have also lost their cozy place at court. People who told tales would have fallen as hard as Katheryn herself.

The only truly asinine thing Katheryn did was flirt with Thomas Culpepper.

CHAPTER EIGHTEEN

Katheryn and Culpepper probably began their illicit relationship in the late winter or early spring of 1541. At first it was light coquetry, acceptable to the ears of others and possible to pass off as gallantry. As the affair intensified, they wanted privacy to indulge in sexually-laden flirtation. Their so-called affair mainly consisted of these trysts. Doubtlessly it would have resulted in hanky-panky sooner or later. Culpepper certainly thought so, since he admitted that he had "intended and meant to do ill with the queen, and that in likewise the queen so minded to do with him" (Lindsey, 1995:176). Nevertheless, their romance was discovered before it reached that stage. Katheryn and Culpepper swore that their romance had "not passed beyond words" (Smith, 1982:199) even after they had both been sentenced to death. Thus, they were executed for *lust* rather than for physical adultery. Unhappily for Katheryn, lust was enough to be treason.

Why would she risk her life for the mere thrill of an illicit romance, without even the benefit of sexual gratification? Katheryn may have been more motivated by the excitement of intrigue than from love, or even sexual desire. Culpepper would later testify that Katheryn loved him, while Katheryn herself refuted it (Lindsey, 1995:176). It is likely she indulged in the semi-affair for fun rather than a grand passion. In spite of her sweet words and promises to Culpepper, he meant no more to her than Manox and Dereham had. Culpepper was convinced that Katheryn was enamored of him, but Katheryn seems to have given Culpepper the style and not the substance of her affections.

If she wasn't in love, why did Kathcryn, who was occasionally silly but seldom stupid, risk everything to flirt with Culpepper? He was handsome, dashing, and charming, as many sociopaths are, so she probably did fancy him, but there is no evidence she was infatuated with him -- let alone in love. Perhaps Katheryn simply didn't understand how much she had to lose? The queen had never been taught anything other than flirtation and fashion. She may not have understood that what she was doing was treason even if she and Culpepper had never had sex. She had been getting way with breaking rules her entire life, thanks to her popularity, so it may not have occurred to her that it was impossible to continue with her assignations with Culpepper without being discovered. Perhaps she reasoned that since anyone complicit with her liaison with Culpepper would be in as much trouble as herself, she was safe from anyone tattling on her. Then there was the environment around her. Henry's court was full of intrigues, immorality, and infidelity so outrageous that it beggars the imagination. If no one else had to die for their extramarital shenanigans, why should she? Finally, she might have thought she only needed to be discreet for a little time, since her unhealthy husband was libel to kick the bucket before too long.

One of Katheryn's biggest mistakes was to trust one of her ladies-in-waiting, Lady Rochford, the widow of George Boleyn. Why would Katheryn place her faith in Jane Boleyn, when Lady Rochford had been instrumental in the deaths of her husband and Anne Boleyn? Even if Jane had not cooperated with Cromwell from mendacity or malice, she was still not someone with quick wits or discretion. It is possible that the queen didn't think of Lady Rochford in context with the Boleyn's downfall, since Katheryn was a young girl far from London when Anne and George were executed. All that seemed to matter to Katheryn was that Lady Rochford was eager to help her meet with Culpepper.

Another mystery is why Lady Rochford was willing to put her life in jeopardy to aid the queen's illicit amour. Jane Boleyn would be executed for treason, just like Katheryn and Culpepper, should the dalliance be discovered. Did Rochford think that she could escape by turning informant, as she had with her late husband? Or did Jane just not think that far ahead in her efforts to make the queen happy?

Whatever motivated the Queen, Lady Rochford, and Culpepper, it was a brainless thing to do. Henry was a very dangerous man, and they all should have remembered that "the king's wrath is death" (Smith, 2009:64). Just that May, Henry had ordered the beheading the elderly Countess of Salisbury, Margaret Pole, the godmother of his eldest daughter and his mother's first cousin (Fraser, 1992:342). Her execution was politically moronic and completely unnecessary. Her threat to Henry's throne or kingdom was nonexistent. Moreover, she was the only leverage he had over her rebellious son, Cardinal Reginald Pole. By killing the Countess, the king ended any power he might have had over Cardinal Pole. To make the matter of Margaret Pole's death even worse, there was an inexperienced youth filling in for the headsman that day, and the beheading became butchery. The innocent countess was struck several times around her head and shoulders before she finally died (Fraser, 1992:342-343).

A rumor, entirely unconfirmed, has grown up around the circumstances of Margaret Pole's gruesome death. The story recounts how the Countess, crying out that she was not a traitor and would not willingly be treated as one, fought with those trying to kill her and told her executioners that if he wanted to cut off her head "he must get it as he could" (Lindsey, 1995:172). This is probably more of a legend meant to acknowledge the strength of character Margaret Pole possessed than anything truthful, but it seems a fitting epitaph for the Countess of Salisbury, whom Henry's councilors called "rather a strong and constant man than a woman" (Lindsey, 1995:172).

Doom struck Katheryn in November of 1541. Although she had no personal enemies, her powerful uncle had multitudes who wanted to discredit her to get to him. They discovered she had previously had sex with Francis Dereham (Lindsey, 1995:174). Thomas Cranmer, the Archbishop of Canterbury, wrote Henry a letter detailing the shocking allegations against the queen and left it in a pew for the king to find. Henry was initially incensed at the allegations, insisting Katheryn was maligned and that the rumors were "rather a forged matter than of truth" (Starkey, 2003:668). Henry demanded an investigation in order to clear is beloved queen's good name. This terrified the tattletales. What if Henry decided that they were spreading calumny against the queen and their lives should be forfeit because of it? Cranmer and the others were now strongly motivated to prove Katheryn's guilt; their lives may have depended on ending hers.

Happily for Katheryn's accusers and unhappily for Katheryn herself, evidence in the form of sworn statements from all parties was not hard to obtain. Katheryn's former boyfriends, her current amour, and her supposed friend Lady Rochford all turned on her like jackals.

The king appointed four men to scrutinize the queen's past. The investigators first went after Manox,

Katheryn's former music instructor. He confessed that Katheryn had allowed him to touch her genitals, provided that he would then ask for nothing else. He swore under oath that he and Katheryn had never had sex, even when he was questioned repeatedly, and possibly even tortured. (Lindsey, 2003:175). If the search had stopped with Manox, the queen might have been safe, since her virginity – if not her maidenly modesty – was intact.

Regrettably for the queen, Dereham was interrogated next. Rather than protecting the young woman he had once claimed to love, Dereham confessed to having had sex with Katheryn. Even if Dereham hadn't squealed like a stool pigeon, other witnesses who had lived with Katheryn in the maidens' chamber would have cooked her goose. Several testified they had heard Dereham and Katheryn having sex, with one woman describing the "puffing and blowing" between the couple (Starkey, 2003:670). However, Dereham could have argued that he and Katheryn had never gone beyond heavy petting, no matter what other people in the maiden's chamber might have heard, since it was so dark at night in Tudor bedrooms that no one was likely to have actually *seen* them having sex. The only person who claimed to actually have *seen* anything could only testify that she had witnessed Dereham lift Katheryn's dress and look at her body (Starkey, 2003:670). Of course, it may have been torture, rather than a lack of chivalry, that inspired Dereham to give the details of his relationship with Katheryn (Starkey, 2003:674). However, by admitting that he had taken the queen's virginity, poor Dereham condemned himself to a grisly death.

When the news of Katheryn's prior relationships with Manox and Dereham was reported to Henry, the king wept and raged so violently that his ministers feared for his sanity -- which was already tenuous (Smith, 1982:198). The king was prostrated with grief that his young bride had not been a virgin. Henry grabbed a sword and waved it around, claiming the queen would never have "such delight in her lechery as she should have pain and torture in her death", but he also cried with such abandon it was considered "strange in [one of] his courage" (Smith, 1982:198). He plumbed the depths of self-pity, and bemoaned his luck at getting "such ill-conditioned wives" (Scarisbrick, 1970:432). He even tried to blame his council for his decision to marry Katheryn, because he didn't want to admit he had made a mistake. The only way the king would be able to soothe his wounded feelings was by ordering his young wife's death. Henry, as he had done to other wives, left Katheryn without a farewell or hint of the coming storm. (Starkey, 2003:671). He returned to Whitehall in London while Katheryn remained unawares at Hampton.

Things would quickly get worse for Katheryn. The fact she had given Dereham the post as her private secretary made the investigators suspicious that Katheryn had continued her affair with him after she was married. Dereham, desperate to prove that he had not resumed his romance with Katheryn, offered the information that "Culpepper had succeeded him in the Queen's affections" (Starkey, 2003:674). This was much worse that Katheryn's lack of virginity. Any dalliance Katheryn had indulged in as queen was high treason, and death for treason included being hanged, drawn and quartered.

Culpepper and Lady Rochford were too well-born to be tortured, but they were just as forthcoming as Dereham had been under questioning. They also tried desperately to save themselves to save by blaming Katheryn for everything. Culpepper insisted that

Katheryn had pursued him so vigorously he had no choice but to meet her. Lady Rochford also vowed that she was only a lowly servant of the queen, forced against her will to abet Katheryn in her immoral acts, which is probably malarkey considering that Rochford acted eagerly on the couple's behalf during the course of the intrigue (Lindsey, 1995:171, 176). Rochford furthermore insisted that Culpepper and Katheryn must have engaged in sex as well as flirtation, "considering all the things that she hath heard and seen between them." (Lindsey, 1995:176).

In the end, Katheryn showed no more scruples in blaming others for her own behavior than they had shown for her. The queen accused Manox and Dereham of taking advantage of her and said that Culpepper and Rochford had coerced her (Lindsey, 1995:175-176). She also insisted that she had not been pre-contracted to Dereham (Smith, 1982:199). This was folly, since a precontract with Dereham would nullify her marriage to the Henry, leaving her an adulterer and a bigamist but not a traitor. Katheryn didn't seem to understand this, though. Although she was smart, or at least smarter than she is given credit for, she was ignorant of the law and had no one to explain it to her. Her better educated friends and relatives, all of whom had been happy to use her connections to benefit themselves, couldn't be bothered to help her. They wanted as much distance between Katheryn and themselves as possible, lest Henry's ax throw a shadow on their necks as well.

Even without Katheryn's agreement, Henry could have accepted Dereham's assertion that they had been precontracted, which would have made her Dereham's common-law wife. Their engagement would have made pre-marital intercourse socially permissible (Smith, 1982:196). There were others who could testify that Dereham and Katheryn called each other 'husband' and 'wife' openly during their time in the Dowager Duchess' household (Strickland and Strickland, 1851:286). A pre-contract would have meant that she had never legally wed Henry, and therefore could not have committed treason. Furthermore, a precontract would have freed the king to find another wife. Katheryn could have been given to Dereham and sent from the court in penury and disgrace, or she could have been consigned to a nunnery. Either of these options would have been a serious punishment for such a gregarious young woman. Henry could have easily spared his sweet-natured wife the death penalty. Yet the king was uninterested in mercy, or even justice. Katheryn had made a fool of him, and he wanted her to pay for it with her life. He also wanted her lovers dead as well.

On November 22, Katheryn's title was stripped from her by the Privy Council and she was indicted for "having lead an abominable, base, carnal, voluptuous, and vicious life" before marriage and acting "like a common harlot with diverse persons" while falsely "maintaining however the outward appearance of chastity and honesty" (Farquhar, 2001). In sum, Katheryn was accused of being a slut but not "looking" like a slut. This was, in the Tudor mind, particularly heinous. It put paid to the common myth that men could tell a woman was a virgin at a glance by her innocent demeanor and firm breasts. It reminded Tudor men that sluts could hide in plain sight and that they could 'trick' men into marrying them. Sluts were dangerous because they were women who could make men look like idiots.

Dereham's execution in December of 1541 was particularly macabre. Dereham was taken off to Tyburn on a cart, hanged until he was semi-conscious, revived until he was aware of what was happening to him, then disemboweled, beheaded, and his corpse was cut into four pieces (Starkey, 2003:680-681). He died a traitor's death even though he had committed no treason. His only crime was the fact he had sex with Katheryn, his de facto common-law wife, before she had even met her future husband. He was tortured to death because he had 'gotten' the Queen's maidenhead, rather than leaving it for Henry. The knowledge that Dereham had slept with Katheryn first rankled the King's heart until he could only be soothed by Dereham's ghastly death.

Culpepper was, irrationally, given an easier death. Thanks to his high status in society he was merely beheaded. It was a quick and easy death for the only man who had actually committed treason against the king. Nevertheless, there is some satisfaction in knowing that inasmuch as Culpepper was a rapist and murderer, his execution was at least mimicry of justice. With any luck, the woman that he had raped, and the family of his murder victim, were in the crowd to watch his execution.

Having executed Dereham and Culpepper, the king could concentrate his wrath on Katheryn and Lady Rochford. They were both condemned by an Act of Attainder on February 11, 1542 (Starkey, 2003:682). The king was also determined to punish several members of his former queen's family, including Norfolk, for having allowed him to marry 'used goods'.

In an attempt to save his own hide, Norfolk wrote Henry one of the most wretched and servile letters ever penned by a human hand. Moreover, the duke threw everyone else to the wolves. Norfolk's letter begged Henry not to consider him in the same light as his "ungracious mother-in-law", nor his "unhappy brother", nor his "lewd sister", and took pains to revile the "abominable deeds" of his niece, whom he had not hesitated to procure for the king like an old pimp when Henry had shown his interest (Starkey, 2003:681). Apparently the letter was sufficiently groveling, since the king pardoned Norfolk. Henry also spared the rest of the ex-queen's family. However, nothing could save Katheryn – not that anyone bothered to try.

If only Katheryn had been more ruthless and conniving! If she had been of a Machiavellian mindset, she could have had her uncle use his ducal powers to have Manox arrested and executed on false charges as soon as Henry had indicated she would be his next queen. She could have had the only person absolutely positive she was not a virgin, Dereham himself, quietly murdered or exiled. She could have preempted the rumors that could be spread about her past behavior by having Norfolk go to the King, before she married Henry, to complain she was being maligned in an attempt to injure *the family*, making any gossip about her seem to be a false attack by Howard enemies. Once Henry had imprisoned or executed anyone who 'slandered' the queen, it would have been too dangerous for others to accuse her of impropriety. She would have never risked a flirtation with Culpepper, or have been so foolish as to trust Lady Rochford. Sadly, nothing that Katheryn did was ever that well thought out. She lived in the moment, pursuing happiness and material goods, rather than accumulating power and forging her security.

Henry's fifth wife was beheaded February 13, 1542. In spite of her youth, she made a "most Godly and Christian end" (Starkey, 2003:684). Katheryn had asked that the headsman's block be brought to her in her rooms, so that she could practice the correct position. Thankfully, she had a competent executioner and her death was quick.

Francis I of France, who was one of the most noted and notorious womanizers in the whole of Europe as well as a king, exclaimed without a hint of irony that the queen "hath done wondrous naughty" when told of

Katheryn's transgressions. He wrote Henry a condolence letter about the "lewd and naughty behavior" of the queen and assuring his fellow king that the "lightness of women cannot bend the honor of men". It seems not to have occurred to either Henry or Francis that their 'honor' was much more tainted than Katheryn's could ever be. Their extramarital sex lives didn't count. They were men; QED they couldn't be disgraceful sluts. They would never have to pay for the so-called crime of having had illicit sex.

For Katheryn, however, the butcher's bill had to be paid in full.

CHAPTER NINETEEN

Even those who are sympathetic to Katheryn Howard often describe her in terms that suggest a harlot. For example, David Starkey condescendingly explains that he can write about Katheryn's "promiscuity without disapproval", calling her a "woman with a past" but without intention of condemnation because "like many good-time girls, she was also warm, loving and good-natured" (Starkey, 2003:648 and 655). Lacey Baldwin Smith wrote that her life was "little more than a series of petty trivialities and wanton acts, punctuated by sordid politics", but nevertheless lamented that her life was cut so tragically short due to the backstairs politics that "transformed juvenile delinquency into high treason" (Smith, 2009:10). Both biographers have a genial attitude about the fallen queen, and they obviously view her as having been overly punished and victimized by forces beyond her control. Notwithstanding their sympathy, though, it is also clear they see her primarily as a sweet natured strumpet.

Others have been even less kind to the young queen. In fact, it could even be said that most "historians judge her by the same standards of behavior expected of an early modern Englishwoman, and, perhaps unwittingly, assume that because she broke the cardinal rule of chastity, she must have failed completely in adhering to expectations of femininity. Therefore, Katherine has often been depicted as stupid, promiscuous, foolish, greedy, and vain" (Kizewski, 2014). David Loades assures his readers that Katheryn Howard was a "wanton slut" who "certainly behaved like a whore both before and after her marriage" (Loades, 2009). It wasn't just her sexual ethics that were called into question. Alison Weir wrote that Henry's fifth bride was "a frivolous, empty-headed young girl who cared for little else by dancing and pretty clothes" (Weir, 2007). Sometimes Katheryn's sluttiness is excused upon these terms. Antonia Fraser described Katheryn as "a flighty young thing with an eye for a handsome young man ... pleasure loving ... the sort of girl who lost her head easily over a man, a girl who agreed generally with what men suggested" (Fraser, 1992).

Rarely have historians pointed out that her sexual history was not extreme. The depiction of Katheryn as a trollop is unfair. It is the result of the double standard that makes the sexuality of all women suspect. Her supposed adulterous affair, which was in actuality an unconsummated flirtation, should be looked at in context. She was a young woman in her late teens who was given very little choice about marrying Henry. Although he was a king, he was also an obese man more than thirty years older than her with malodorous leg wounds that wept gore and pus. Worse, the conventions of the time meant that her sex life with Henry would be particularly gruesome. People believed that sex in anything other than the missionary position was 1) a sin and 2) would breed weak children. Additionally, children were thought to be inconceivable if the woman did not achieve orgasm and "release her seed" too. That means that Katheryn Howard had to lie underneath a smelly old man a foot taller than she was and more than twice her weight during sex, and had to at least pretend to enjoy it to keep him happy with her. What if the damp bandages from his seeping leg ulcers touched her? What if he experienced trouble maintaining an erection (which had happened when he was married to Anne Boleyn) and it took repeated tries over long periods for him to finally be finished with her?

Her adulterous flirtation may not have been strictly moral, but few would argue that it was not *understandable*.

There is one way, however, in which Katheryn truly was the 'whore' she has been so frequently called. The second the King showed an interest in her, she and her family were willing to give Henry access to her body in exchange for financial gain, which is the very definition of prostitution. Once sold, the Queen's sexuality was supposed to stay in the service of her family and the man who bought her. It is the fact Katheryn wanted to have sex where the was no profit for her family, and in violation of her husband's right to the exclusive use of her reproductive capabilities, that lead to her death. She didn't want to marry Dereham, and she wasn't interested in Culpepper for his money. She simply liked them and wanted to be with because it was enjoyable to her. There was no great financial reward in it for her, or for her kin. She was punished with death because of the times she did *not* prostitute herself.

So what was the underlying reason for Katheryn's slut shaming and death? Again, it goes back to enjoyment. Katheryn had sex because she liked it, not because she was in love. This violates the cultural assumption that women only have sex because of a deep emotional connection with their partners.

The male courtiers of the Tudor era knew that having sex with a woman didn't mean they were in love with her. They also knew that there were women with whom one could have sex, or even love, but should never marry. Gentlemen of this time knew that they must wed a woman of the correct social standing, preferably with a large dowry to sweeten the deal. The fact that Katheryn, a woman, knew the same things appears to be what has shocked most historians. It is likely that the reason for her enduring reputation as an immoral minx is because she usurped the male prerogative of enjoying sex without love, and chose marriage without hearts-in-her-eyes idealism. It is likely that her ability to separate sex from love, and love from marriage, is what has gotten her decried as a hussy for centuries.

Even today there is still the persistent myth that women cannot *really* have casual sex without becoming emotionally attached. Culturally, men are constructed as lust-crazed beings that need little to no emotional fulfillment from intercourse. Men are the active agent in sexual relationships and are portrayed as having a harder time controlling their sexual impulses. Boys will be boys, and all that baloney. This perception has been used to rationalize men's *natural* lack of fidelity, giving men who are unfaithful more leeway for forgiveness. Men cannot be sluts because, even if they slept with the entire female population of Southern New Jersey (including the pets), then they were just doing what *normal* guys do. In contrast, women are purported to be *naturally* monogamous. Since women are the ones who can control their libido, they are the ones responsible for saying "no" to sex. Men just can't do that, apparently. Culture also insists that chicks are unhappy and unsatisfied with sexual liaisons that are not built on a foundation of emotional intimacy. This hearts-and-flowers view of women's eroticism makes any woman who enjoys sex outside of a committed relationship an *abnormal* woman. It means that promiscuous female behavior is a sign of deviance. A polyamorous woman who gets her some just because it feels good is being female *wrong*. She is a bad girl. She is a **slut**.

Usually biology is used as the rationale for this ideology, suggesting that because women release the hormone oxytocin during sex, they "start to feel more emotionally bonded to whomever triggered it" (Hassler, 2013). There is a belief that gender behavior is "evolutionarily hardwired. Where men seem to be engineered to sow their "wild oats," women have, at least historically, been focused on finding a stable mate and settling down to the business of making a family" (Hartwell- Walker, 2010). This ignores the fact there is every bit as much of an evolutionary reason for men to bond with their sex partners as there is for women (Marshall Cavendish reference, 2010). The larger culture is also willfully blind to the multiple and repeated studies that have shown that there is no substantial difference between men and women when it comes to having sex just for fun versus an attempt to "forge a stronger emotional bond" (Buss and Meston, 2009).

Almost every single thing that everyone *knows* about the "natural differences" between men and women has been thoroughly debunked as a myth (Fausto-Sterling, 1992). This is especially true when it comes to sex. The idea that women cannot wait to pair-bond with Mr. Right so they can start having the babies they so urgently desire is a social construct, not a fact (Fuentes, 2012). In reality, neither men nor women are "naturally" monogamous; for most people remaining faithful to one sexual partner for life is challenging (Weiss, 2013). Women are as motivated by lust as men are, as demonstrated in a study done by "sexologist Meredith Chivers shows that when it comes to desire, women are as visually stimulated and more easily turned on than men" (Callahan, 2013). Women are just as likely to cheat – or at least desire another sex partner – as men are.

Current gender ideologies denigrate men as well. It portrays all men as bestial sex fiends as way to justify the aberrant behavior of a few males. Feminists may be the ones accused of being man-hating radicals, but *we* aren't the ones who decided that all men are skirt-chasing lechers without a heart and/or conscious. That would be the anti-feminists who insist we are "feminizing" men when we give men credit for having more brains than balls. The characterization of feminists as harpies is more about political propaganda than any reality. Obviously, the accusations that we are viragos is simply to keep men and women who otherwise have goals and values in common with the feminist movement from self-identifying as feminists (McCabe, 2005:481). However, it is the feminism, not the broader culture, which gives men the benefit of the doubt when it comes to sexual self-control.

The feminist movement also insists that not all women are delicate emotional princesses who trade sex for valentines. That stereotype makes women merely the passive objects of male sexual aggression. It implies that the entire reason women have a vagina is to secure a relationship with a man in exchange for giving him a place to park his penis. Yes, it is generally understood women don't need to lie there and think of England during sex anymore, but they still aren't supposed to really enjoy sex outside of True Love. If they do, then they are total sluts.

In spite of all the evidence against it, we "hold tight to the fairy tale … We hold on with the help of evolutionary psychology, a discipline whose central sexual theory comparing women and men — a theory that is thinly supported — permeates our consciousness and calms our fears" (Bergner, 2013). It suits us culturally to believe women are naturally prone to fidelity and romance. Women can only be slut shamed if they have done something "normal" women would never do.

When we make the assumption that women typically don't have sex for pleasure without an emotional commitment, we have also implied that women who do have sex just for fun are atypical, deviant, and abnormal. There is, based on our cultural narrative, something *wrong* with her. Women like Katheryn Howard who have sex for orgasms rather than True Love are conceptualized as fundamentally flawed because they go against nature itself.

This provides yet another justification for slut shaming. It is okay to shame a slut because she is an aberration. She is a danger not only to society but to the very concept of what makes women "feminine". Slut shaming, in the context of defending the natural order, becomes almost heroic. Women who are anomalies must be punished in order to prevent their unorthodox behavior from spreading and overturning culture as we know it. Slut shaming arises from the fear that sluts are dangerous.

Although Katheryn Howard was executed for treason, her real crime was to believe her body and its pleasures were hers to do with as she chose. She had sex with one man, just *one*, other than the king, and that long before Henry's interest in her had become even a twinkle in his eye, but she has been denigrated as a "faithless slut" ever since (Smith, 1982:198). The fact that she enjoyed the attentions of a handsome and charming young man when her elderly husband was absent has branded her forever as scheming and adulterous. Men sought romance outside of their loveless marriages with impunity, but for the queen to do so was shocking, *because she was not a man*. It is the double-standard writ large on the historical page.

CHAPTER TWENTY

Jezebel practiced marital fidelity and did not persecute Hebrews. Cleopatra was not a seductress and did not sleep with multiple partners. Anne Boleyn didn't pursue Henry VIII or have six fingers or have sex with her own brother. Katheryn Howard was not promiscuous. These are all egregious lies spread to slut shame women who trespassed against gender norms. Yet of all the lies that continue to haunt famous queens the one about Catherine the Great of Russia having sex with a horse is perhaps the most far-fetched and egregious of all.

Catherine the Great did NOT have sex with a horse. She did not die because a horse fell on top of her during one of her sexual escapades with the animal. She did not have a special sling made so she could screw her horse in comfort. Everything about Catherine the Great and sex with a horse that you have ever heard is utter horseshit.

Most of what you may have heard about Catherine's sexual adventures with humans is poppycock as well. Yes, she had lovers and several of the men she dated were younger than she was, but she was mostly a serial monogamist. There is no evidence that there were scores of men who shared her bed or that she had them tested out on her maids of honor first, as was suggested by her enemies. The young men weren't "procured" for Catherine, either. The empress didn't *need* men procured for her. Some of her lovers were introduced to her in court, but they were not brought to court specifically to act as studs. Men were not coerced into sleeping with her, either. Even when Catherine had gotten older and wider, she was still plenty lovable in and of herself. The majority of her former lovers were loyal to her interests unto death did they part, even though she had ended the intimate aspects of her relationship with them. They would even work together in court to further her successful reign. Most of her lovers *loved* her.

Catherine the Great, Empress of Russia, was neither Russian nor born into a royal family. She came into the world on April 21, 1729 as the first child of a minor Prussian noble and was christened Sophie Friederike Auguste von Anhalt-Zerbst. Her father, Christian August, was the third son of the ruler of the Prussian principality know as Anhault-Zerbst. Her mother, Johanna Elisabeth of Holstein-Gottorp, was a younger daughter of another principality ruler. Although both of Sophie's grandfathers were titled as the "Prince" of their small slices of Prussian soil, they were singularly unimportant and merely members of a "swarm of obscure, penurious noblemen who cluttered the landscape and society of politically fragmented eighteenth-century Germany" (Massie, 2011). The newborn Sophie was as likely to become Empress of Russia as the illegitimate son of the duke of Normandy was likely to become king of England. Nevertheless, like William the Conqueror, Sophie von Anhalt-Zerbst would rise above her origins and turn herself into a legendary monarch.

Although Sophie's father was reportedly loving towards his daughter in a stern, distant way, her mother rejected her as a useless girl from the onset. In contrast, Johanna lavished affection Sophie's younger brother. Johanna's dismal parenting was compounded by her determination to rid her daughter of any hints of an individualistic spirit that might make Sophie less desirable on the marriage market. To that end Johanna savagely punished her daughter for showing anything less than perfect servility and silent obedience. As a result of her mother's lack of warmth, even when Sophie became Catherine the Great she would always seek the love and approval of those around her (Magdariaga, 1991). She usually succeeded, with most of even her most hardened court opponents eventually succumbing to her charm. Moreover, because of her mother's cruelty Catherine learned to appear docile and submissive regardless of her true opinions or thoughts -- which led her foes to continually underestimate her.

Many people who grow up with insufficient caregiving at home are incapable of cultivating the type of agreeable personality that guarantees friends, but Sophie had an ace up her emotional sleeve. Her governess, Elizabeth (Babet) Cardel, gave her the kindness and tenderness the young Sophie did not get from her own mother. Catherine never forgot the magnanimity of her teacher. She would later write that Babet had a "noble soul, a cultured mind, a heart of gold; she was gentle, patient, cheerful, just, consistent – in short, the kind of governess one would wish every child to have" (Massie, 2011). With Babet as her example, the child Sophie was able to form true bonds of emotional intimacy with her friends and lovers as the adult empress Catherine. The men who were allowed inside her body had usually first entered her heart.

Her mother constantly assured Sophie that she was ugly, but when she was thirteen her mother's brother began acting in a manner that strongly implied that she was not unattractive. Sophie's uncle, Prince Georg Ludwig of Holstein-Gottorp, was ten years older than she was and at first Sophie though Georg was merely an affectionate uncle. Babet was suspicious of his motives in spending so much time with his niece from the get go, but Sophie didn't take his gallantry seriously until he proposed marriage. Shocked, Sophie then rejected his company. However, since she was starved for love and attention it wasn't hard for Georg to convince her that she should become secretly engaged to him. Fortunately, their relationship didn't go beyond kissing (although that's enough to make a modern reader's skin crawl). Sophie's mother was aware of the whole thing, and only "voiced misgivings" (Alexander, 1988) about it when she was concerned that Georg would be unhappy when she took Sophie to Russia.

 As atrocious as Johanna's behavior toward her daughter was, she was capable of the most obsequious butt-kissing imaginable toward those who were her social superiors. Peter the Great's daughter Elizabeth had become Empress of Russia in 1741 after deposing the infant Tsar Ivan VI. Elizabeth had once been engaged to Johanna's older brother, who had died of smallpox before they could wed. Seizing the opportunity afforded by the empress's fond memories of her dead fiancée, Johanna wrote to congratulate Elizabeth when she came to power. After an exchange of portraits and much kowtowing on Johanna's part, she was invited to bring her daughter Sophie to the Russian court to meet the heir to the throne, Elizabeth's nephew the Grand Duke Peter von Holstein-Gottorp in 1744.

 Sophie had already been introduce to Peter, who was her maternal second cousin, four years prior while he was still living in Prussia. The children had become at least tentative friends, and young Sophie had hoped a marriage would be arranged between them since Peter was in line for the crown of Sweden. What Sophie didn't know was that Peter was even more emotionally isolated than she was and that he was being physically and psychologically abused by his tutor, Otto Brummer.

Some biographers theorize that this ill treatment left permanent scars on Peter's mind and heart: "The violence which Brummer constantly inflicted on him produced a pathetic, twisted child ... fearful, deceitful, antagonistic, boastful, cowardly, duplicitous, and cruel. He made friends only with the lowest of his servants, those whom he was allowed to strike. He tortured pet animals" (Massie, 2011).

Or did he?

Others historians defend Peter, claiming Catherine and her supporters blackened his name in retrospect: "For a lack of neutral observers or statesmen unaffected by Catherin's demand for loyalty after the coup, the derogatory portrait [of Peter] cannot be validated ... according to [a German officer at court] Peter was an energetic monarch, concerned with education, law, and the courts. Despite his consuming interest in military affairs, Peter consulted frequently with his advisors ... Caspar von Saldern, Peter's Holstein advisor and a close friend [decried] the "calumnies of his enemies and ... the false assertions contained in Catherin's manifestoes" ... Charles T. de Laveaux, the French commercial consul in St Petersburg [claimed that] Peter was intelligent; although he suffered "nervous irritability" and was impatient, he was generous and open" ... falsely represented "practically everywhere as an imbecile and a ridiculous figure because of the manifestoes of his treacherous wife" (Leonard, 1993).

Whatever would happen between them later, Sophie and Peter were initially allies. Although Peter told his bride-to-be that he was only marrying her to please the empress and that he loved another girl, he also assured her that he liked her and that he was glad to have someone to talk to in German. Catherine herself would later affirm that her fiancée did everything he could to help her adjust to the new life into which she had been thrust (Alexander, 1988). The worst thing Peter inflicted on his betrothed was that he bored her to tears with overlong monologues.

While at the Russian court, Johanna managed to offend everyone – including the empress Elizabeth. Quiet and sweet-tempered Sophie was much more warmly received. The future empress had "realized that people preferred to talk rather than to listen and to talk about themselves rather than anything else" (Massie, 2011), which made her generally and genuinely popular her whole life. Sophie had made such a good impression on Elizabeth that not even the earth-shaking rage the empress now felt toward Johanna induced her to call off the wedding between Sophie and Peter.

Sophie had to convert to the Orthodox Russian Church before she could marry the heir to the throne. This, happily, did not prove to be a difficulty for her. She was already something of a skeptic regarding dogma; she had vexed her Lutheran tutor to the utmost when she asked him how God's infinite goodness could be reconciled with the terrifying notion of the Last Judgment (Massie, 2011). From her earliest youth Sophie had noticed her own "inclination to yield only to gentleness and reason – and to resist all pressure" (Massie, 2011); theological bullying was something she would have rebelled against. Fortunately, she was taught the Orthodox faith by Archimandrite Simon Tordorsky. This gentle prelate was the perfect tutor because he used tactful reasoning rather than authoritative doctrine to instruct the future grand duchess. The lessons went so well that soon she was able to cheerfully assure her stanchly Protestant father that there was "hardly any difference" between Lutheranism and the doctrines of the Russian Church and that "she had already resolved to convert" (Dixon, 2010).

Convert she did on June 28, 1744 in the huge and ornate Chapel of the Annenhof Summer Palace. She would later confess that she had to memorize and recite the creed in Russian as though she were a "parrot" (Massie, 2011), since she wasn't fluent in the language yet. She entered the chapel as the Lutheran Sophie Friederike Auguste von Anhalt-Zerbst and left it Ekaterina Alekseevna (or Alexeyevna), member of the Orthodox faith and future empress Catherine the Great.

Catherine had already started winning the hearts of the Russian populace before she had actually gone through a formal conversion. Unlike Peter, who remained German to the soles of his Hessian boots, she whole-heartedly embraced Russian modes of living and the Russian language. When Catherine became ill (supposedly as a result of her enthusiasm for learning Russian) she called for Tordorsky, the Orthodox priest guiding her conversion, to comfort her. Catherine was either sincerely interested in the Orthodox Church or was smart enough to at least act as if she were. The empress Elizabeth, who was helping care for the ailing young girl with her own imperial hands, witnessed it. Elizabeth was devout, and Catherine's apparently similar devotion to the church brought tears of joy to her eyes. Catherine's piety was especially appealing in contrast to Peter, who dismissed the rites of the Orthodox religion as superstitious flimflam compared to the simple purity of Lutheranism.

At the time, Russia was considered a semi-Asiatic European backwater with less Enlightenment than a French latrine. Many Russians were aware of this and very sensitive to slights on their culture, so Catherine's gung-ho attitude about Russia was gratifying to them. Catherine, ever eager to please others and win their regard, threw off her Prussian heritage and robed herself anew in the glories of her adopted country. She became, at least in public, more Slavic than a matryoshka, the iconic nesting doll of Mother Russia. In fact, Catherine was a bit of a matryoshka herself. Regardless of her smiling façade, there were other Catherines – including the cutthroat aspirant and the astute politician – that she kept hidden inside herself. People were often unaware of her multiple abilities until it was too late for counteraction.

The day after her conversion the formal betrothal of the grand duke Peter and the newly renamed Catherine took place. This also occurred in church, the Kremlin's Assumption Cathedral, with ostentatious and imposing religious formality. Empress Elizabeth decreed that Catherine was henceforth to be known as Her Imperial Highness Grand Duchess Catherine of Russia (Alexander, 1988). Then the engagement rings, which had been provided by the empress, were placed on their fingers by Elizabeth herself. It's hard to accuse Elizabeth of taking liberties with her role in the relationship, since the marriage was only taking place because she wanted it to. Moreover, the rings were "real little monsters, both of them" (Massie, 2011) worth oodles of rubles and it seems fair that she should place such a valuable gift on their hands herself. As long as she was empress, Elizabeth owned them and their marriage and everyone knew it.

Empress Elizabeth had more control over Catherine's life than even her parents had ever had. Elizabeth could disinherit Peter and/or send Catherine packing in ignominy on a whim. For the next twenty years Catherine would have to work harder to please the empress than she would anyone else, including her husband Peter.

Elizabeth Petranova was, like all human beings, a mixture of laudable and lamentable attributes. She had a "natural kindliness expressing itself in a ready courtesy, and impulsive sympathy, which came straight from the heart … She was gentle, affable, and familiar with all who approached her, yet always with a due regard to her dignity, and her playful gaiety was without the slightest tinge of malice … One of her most engaging qualities was her fondness of young people, children especially … she was just, equitable, and a great peacemaker" (Bain, 1899). She could also be a high-handed, vain, jealous, spiteful and didactic bully. Elizabeth, after deposing Ivan VI, had the toddler ripped away from his parents, rendered an "unperson", and locked away in near-solitary confinement like an animal for the rest if his life (Madariaga, 1991). For her crown, she could be cruel – even to babies. Catherine would see plenty of both the sublime and the hellish parts of Elizabeth's personality while she lived in the empress's court.

The date of Catherine and Peter's marriage was set for the following summer, but the bride was anything other than excited about her impending nuptials. The thought of her wedding made her "melancholy" and she wrote that she "often burst into tears without really knowing why" (Dixon, 2010). Her mother wasn't helping things either. Johanna was bitter that Catherine now had precedence and was escorted into formal and social gatherings first. She never hesitated to take her petty resentment out on her daughter.

Catherine found some solace in trying to buy the love she wasn't getting from her mother. She had been given 30,000 rubles by the empresses as an engagement gift, and after sending back a large chunk of the money to Hamburg to provide medical care for her sick little brother, she use the rest of the largess to augment her meager wardrobe and to bestow a continual stream of presents to the courtiers around her (Alexander, 1988). The grand duchess had to buy her own dresses because her mother had appropriated the monies set aside for Catherine's wardrobe for herself. The extravagant presents were necessary for Catherine to make friends at court. There was already an entrenched Russian custom of "gifts" that would be considered outright bribes in other parts of Europe but were considered an expected social lubricant among the Slavs (Lovell et al., 2000). Intensely happy to make others happy, Catherine threw herself into the custom with gusto.

One of the many reasons she needed to buy new clothes was to attend Elizabeth's infamous "Metamorphoses" balls (Rounding, 2008). At these masquerades everyone was required to wear the clothing of the opposite gender. Elizabeth loved to show off her excellent legs by displaying them in men's hose and breeches, often choosing to ride her horse astride and in masculine attire, so she relished these transvestite dances. The empress would dress as a Cossack, or a French carpenter, or would pretend to be a Dutch sailor named "Mikhailova" (Ramet, 2002). Catherine, who was also attractive in men's attire, loved these dances as well. During her own reign Catherine maintained the cross-dressing tradition, occasionally pretending to be a young man so convincingly she was able to flirt with unsuspecting women of the court to her great amusement (O'Malley, 2006).

Not surprisingly, the young grand duchess got into debt of about 2000 rubles. The empress, piqued by Catherine's fresh beauty and ever-growing popularity, decided to use these debts to publically humiliate her. Catherine was dressed down while at the opera with her fiancée and mother. The bearer of the empress's wrath "made certain that Peter and everyone else within earshot could hear. Tears sprang to Catherine's eyes and, even as she wept, more humiliation was added. Peter, instead of consoling her, said that he agreed with his aunt and thought it appropriate that his betrothed had been reprimanded. Johanna then declared that as Catherine no longer consulted her as to how a daughter should behave, she "washed her hands" of the matter … [Afterwards, Catherine] worked hard to reingratiate herself with her patron. And Elizabeth, when her fit of jealousy subsided, relented and eventually forgot the incident" (Massie, 2011). Catherine, however, remembered it clearly and took the lessons to heart. She was ever after careful not to outshine the empress, lest Elizabeth's unpredictable temper be unleashed.

Johanna, more capricious and far less maternal than the empress, continued to be a thorn in her daughter's side. Not content to have just Elizabeth and most of the Russian court loathe her, Johanna also managed to pick a fight with Peter when he accidently knocked over one of her writing desks. Catherine, in a desperate attempt to bring peace, told her mother that she was sure Peter had bumped into the writing desk without intent. Her mother spent the rest of her time in Russia making sure her daughter regretted her defense of her erstwhile groom. The result of Johanna's vicious attack on Catherine and Peter was that the grand duke would henceforth hate his future mother-in-law. Peter and Johanna often tried to force Catherine to "pick sides", which brought the teenaged girl acute misery. She frequently tried to placate both by buying them the same kinds of gifts she showered on her newfound friends in court.

There was an upside to Johanna's vile behavior, though: Peter felt more warmth for his future wife. According to Catherine, the grand duke "could see that my mother often attacked and scolded me when she was unable to find fault with him. This placed me high in his estimation; he believed he could rely on me."

Unfortunately, the fragile affection between Catherine and her fiancé was shattered when Peter contracted smallpox. Inasmuch as Catherine had never had smallpox, she was kept far away from Peter, who lay on death's doorstep for several weeks. When Catherine saw him again in February of 1745 she was repulsed by his distorted and scarred appearance. Was this shallow of her, especially since Peter had never been good-looking in the first place and she had always been willing to marry him for a crown? Of *course* it was, but she was in her early teens and this kind of shallowness is imminently forgivable in someone so young, especially someone who had no choice to marry a boy who was now rendered grotesque.

Peter, having access to mirrors and more intelligence than he is often given credit for, was well aware of how bad he looked. When he met Sophia again after his illness he asked her if she could still recognize him. She "stammered" her congratulations on his recovery, but she clearly found him to be "hideous" (*Memoirs*, 2007). It is doubtful that Peter would not have known by her reaction that she thought he appeared ghastly. He probably never forgave her, because from that moment on Peter seemed to be disenchanted with Sophie and any burgeoning friendship or love he may have felt for her appears to have been greatly diminished.

It didn't help that the grand duke was emotionally still a child, preferring games to romance. Hurt by Catherine's consternation when she saw his pock-marked face, he took to actively avoiding her in the months leading up to their wedding. Catherine could tell that Peter was behaving oddly but was uncertain what to do about it. In an attempt at conciliation she sought him out, playing dolls and toy soldiers with her soon-to-be-groom (Alexander, 1988). Their relationship remained strained, however.

Elizabeth was warned by court physicians that Peter, although 17 years old, was too physically immature and unhealthy to be married, but the empress was determined to have the couple wed that summer no matter what. As a sexual enthusiast herself, Elizabeth assumed that -- the doctors' warnings of immaturity or not -- once Peter was put to bed with his pretty bride then nature would take its course and more heirs would be added to the Russian court. The empress failed to take into account her nephew's nervousness and delayed puberty, as well as the fact that the bride was utterly and completely clueless about any possible seduction techniques she could use to encourage the groom. Elizabeth herself had encountered no problems initiating herself into the joys of sex, and she couldn't fathom how anyone but a numbskull would be unable figure it out.

The impending wedding night was a source of increasing confusion and dread of the unknown for Catherine. She was so "innocent that she did not know how the two sexes physically differed. Not had she any idea what mysterious acts were performed when a woman lay down with a man. Who did what? How? She questioned her young Ladies, but they were as innocent as she …. No one had any specific information … Catherine said that in the morning she would ask her mother. She did so, but Johanna … refused to answer. Instead, she "severely scolded" her daughter for indecent curiosity" (Massie, 2011). It didn't occur to Catherine to ask the one woman most qualified to give her explanation and directions: the empress. Elizabeth's rank was just too great for Catherine to ask potentially impertinent questions.

The nuptials between the grand duke and duchess were postponed a few times due to the extravagance of the ceremony and the inclement weather, but finally on August 21, 1745 Catherine became Peter's lawfully wedded wife. Now, all they had to do was consummate their marriage and beget another heir. They were in their mid-to-late teens and full of hormones. Surely the consummation was a given, right?

Wrong.

After the newlywed grand duchess was put to bed, she was left alone for several hours to wait in anxious boredom for her bridegroom to show up. When he finally entered the room, he commented to Catherine on how "amused the servant would be to find us in bed together" (Rounding, 2008), rolled over, and went to sleep. Bewildered, Catherine did likewise. In her *Memoirs*, Catherine wrote that this was "the state in which things remained for nine consecutive years without the least change."

Did Catherine and Peter's marriage go unconsummated for almost a decade? Evidence favors Catherine's assertion. Her perpetual virginity was a widespread piece of gossip in the Russian court and there was never a hint that she had conceived. There was also the distinct possibility that the grand duke had phimosis, a condition wherein the foreskin is too small and erections are extremely painful. An agent of the French government wrote that Peter was "unable to have children because of an obstacle, which the Oriental peoples remedy by circumcision, but for which [Peter] thought there was no cure" (Farquhar, 2001). The patient often outgrows phimosis on his own by the time he is 21, and this may have been what Elizabeth's doctors were trying to convey when they told her Peter was too young to marry.

An alternative hypothesis is that Catherine later lied about the lack of sex to make her extramarital affairs understandable and sympathetic. Peter never fathered a child on any of the women he was known to have had been sexually intimate with later, so his infertility would explain how he and Catherine could have been sexually active with no resulting pregnancies. Circumstantial evidence doesn't favor this theory, though. Supposedly after the grand duke had already been married for seven years when his valet, a Frenchman named Bressan, was suborned at the behest of the empress to figure out a way to rid Peter of his virginity so that the future emperor would know how to make babies with his wife (Massie, 2011). Madame Groot, an attractive widow, was successfully requisitioned for this task.

Regardless of his newly unvirginal state, rumor had it that even after Peter was initiated into the art of love he still avoided Catherine's bed (Farquhar, 2001). Was this true? If so, was it Peter's revenge for Catherine's reaction a decade before to his smallpox scars? Or did Peter at least force himself to do his marital duty now and then?

CHAPTER TWENTY-ONE

Even if her union with Peter had been a sexy rollicking love-fest, Catherine had other things to make her miserable in the early days of her marriage. Burdened with a husband who brought his toy soldiers to bed and made her play armies with him instead of making love to her, she tried to turn for her mother for comfort. Her mother, still displaying the maternal instincts of Cruella DeVil towards puppies, did everything to she could to make her daughter's life unhappier. Johanna asked the empress to dismiss Catherine's best friend from court, left Russia without bothering to tell Catherine good-bye, and told her creditors that her daughter was now responsible for the debt of more than 120,000 rubles which Johanna had racked up (Massie, 2011).

Children, with a few exceptions, try to maintain a relationship with their parents. The only way Catherine could maintain the fiction of a loving mother was to find ways to excuse her mother's behavior. Catherine would later insist her mother had left without a warning "in order not to swell my grief" (Rounding, 2008) with a prolonged leave-taking and that the dismissal of her friend, Maria Zhukova, was the work of the empress Elizabeth. Surprisingly loyal for a woman who would later depose her husband, the grand duchess risked Elizabeth's wrath by using her own influence and funds to arrange Zhukova's marriage, support, and providing her with an estate far from the royal court; "Catherine stuck by her friends" (Alexander, 1988).

Initially, Catherine tried to stick by Peter as well. Although he bored and exhausted her with monologues on the military and confounded her by bringing toy armies into bed, she wanted him to like her. Thus, she indulged him as much as possible, and aided him on the numerous occasions when he got his foot stuck in his mouth. From her perspective, "on the whole, we lived happily, the Grand Duke and I" (Alexander, 1988). Although he clearly didn't feel romantically attached to her, Catherine still hoped to be his friend. In her *Memoirs*, Catherine remembered that:

"I was fully aware of his lack of interest and how little I was loved … fifteen days after the wedding he had again confided in me that he was in love with 'demoiselle Karr, the Empress's maid of honor … I endeavored to conquer my pride, to not be jealous at all of a man who did not love me, but the only way to not be jealous was to not love him … I resolved to show great consideration for the Grand Duke's confidence so that he would at least view me as someone he could trust, to who he could say everything without any consequences. I succeeded at this for a long time."

Trapped in a sexless marriage with a man she was increasingly growing estranged from, Catherine was emotionally, physically, and psychologically vulnerable for an affair. Sure enough, in the late summer of 1752 she was seduced by an experience and handsome womanizer named Sergei Saltykov. Whether or not Peter was also sharing her bed for something other than sleep is unknown, but Catherine and most of Europe assumed that Saltykov was the man responsible for the grand duchess's first three pregnancies. Although Catherine miscarried twice, on September 20, 1754 she gave birth to a son, the future Paul I of Russia. Peter never repudiated his wife or rejected his heir, in spite of the fact he was well aware that the boy was probably not his child.

Catherine, who suffered low spirits during her pregnancy and who had crippling post-partum depression afterwards, was separated from her child in a manner repellent to modern sensibility. Empress Elizabeth seized the newborn, not even giving Catherine a chance to hold him once, and took complete charge of his care and upbringing. Catherine was able to see her son only on rare occasions. By the spring of 1755 she had only seen her baby three times; she couldn't even ask about him lest it be "interpreted as casting doubt on the care the empress was taking of him" (Dixon, 2010). As a result of the isolation and depression it appears that she never bonded maternally with her firstborn.

Adding to her sorrows was that her relationship with Saltykov was also at an end. Even if he hadn't been sent away from court to serve as an ambassador, their romance was doomed by his fickleness. Once the challenge of seducing a virginal grand duchess was gone, Saltykov was uninterested in maintaining their affair. He may have broken her heart but Catherine seems to have forgiven him. She would later write about him with no harsher condemnation that he "knew how to conceal his faults, the greatest of which were a love of intrigue and lack of principles. These failings were not clear to me at the time" (Massie, 2011). When she became empress of Russia she was kind enough to make him the ambassador to France, and Saltykov continued to try to romance almost anything in a dress for the rest of his life.

As her relationship with Saltykov ended, Catherine was wooed by a sweet young Polish nobleman named Stanislas Poniatowski. Poniatowski wasn't as handsome as Saltykov, but he wasn't skirt-chaser either. He implied in his later writings that he had been a virgin when he fell in love with Catherine and began their affair (Massie, 2011). The Polish nobleman was affable, sophisticated, educated in the Enlightenment principles Catherine also embraced, spoke six languages, and was whole-heartedly devoted to the grand duchess. Edgar Saltus wrote that "Saltykov was a ladies' man. Poniatowski was a lady" (1920) but the implication that Catherine's new lover was effete because he was gentle and cultured is ridiculous.

Catherine became pregnant with Poniatowski's daughter in 1757 and when she started showing she stopped her public appearances as convention dictated. This vexed her husband, who preferred that Catherine deal with social occasions. With a complete lack of discretion, the annoyed grand duke grumbled, "God knows where my wife gets her pregnancies. I have no idea whether this child is mine and whether I ought to take responsibility for it" (Massie, 2011). However, Peter was unwilling to swear that he never had sex with his wife during the time of conception and so he was officially credited as the father. When Catherine gave birth, the empress Elizabeth once more took the child away to keep for herself. The baby, Anna, died when she was only 15 months old.

It was not long after her daughter's death that Catherine formally asked Elizabeth permission to leave the Russian court and return to Prussia permanently. Many historians believe that Catherine was bluffing. Nonetheless, I wonder if she weren't just sick and tired of Elizabeth's kidnappings and mind games. Catherine's longing to escape may have been partly a bluff but also sincere.

Catherine's marriage had gone from bad to hellish. Peter, who had fallen in love with Elizaveta Romanovna Vorontsova, had started treating Catherine horribly. Vorontsova egged the grand duke on and the other maids of honor had become rude and insubordinate toward Catherine under the influence of Peter and his mistress. Peter's clear preference and elevation of Vorontsova was also a blow to Catherine's pride, since Vorontsova was the exact opposite of the attractive, cultured, and erudite grand duchess. One eye-witness recorded that Vorontsova had a "broad, puffy, pock-marked face and fat, squat, shapeless figure" while another declared that she was "ugly, common, and stupid" (Massie, 2011). The French ambassador compared Vorontsova unfavorably to a "scullery maid of the lowliest kind" (Anisimov, 2004). One of Peter's close German friends said that Vorontsova "swore like a trooper, stank, and spat when she spoke" (Kaus, 1935). Catherine was humiliated by Peter's choice of paramour.

Empress Elizabeth, obviously, did not wait to see if Catherine was bluffing and took steps to soothe her niece-in-law's feelings. Peter saw that his aunt favored Catherine and followed suit in healing the breech between himself and his wife. Being Peter he did it oddly. He would hold intimate suppers for himself, Catherine, Vorontsova, and Poniatowski and would then leave with his mistress after encouraging his wife and her lover to enjoy themselves alone (Massie, 2011). This made Catherine unhappy because she knew there would be sociopolitical fallout from Peter's behavior. It was one thing to turn a discrete blind eye; it was quite another to host your wife and the man cuckolding you to dinner. When word of the private suppers got around, Elizabeth could see that her nephew was making himself a laughingstock. There was nothing else for it – Poniatowski had to leave court for good in 1758.

Catherine, although understanding what had to be, was heartbroken. She later wrote in a letter that "On the day of [Poniatowkski's] departure, I was more distressed than I can tell you. I don't think I ever cried so much in my life" (Massie, 2011).

Poniatowski became another example of how loyal Catherine was to her former lovers, how much she was willing to use her position as empress to aid them, and how it behooved them greatly to not piss her off or break ranks. On August 2, 1762 she wrote Poniatowski to tell him that she was "sending Count Keyserling off immediately as ambassador to Poland to make you king" (Madariaga, 1991). Catherine, as usual, met her goals. In 1767 Poniatowski became King of Poland. He did his best to be a good ruler, including creating Europe's first ministry of education in the hopes of providing universal schooling for all Poles (Radzilowski, 2007). However, when Poniatowski's policies veered away from Catherine's into what she considered dangerously democratic waters, Catherine joined forces with her Prussian allies and literally (not figuratively) wiped the nation of Poland off the map. Catherine believed an Enlightened autocrat was the best form of government and she had a zero tolerance policy for the radical American and French notions of liberty and democracy.

I can argue that Catherine wasn't a slut, but no one can successfully argue she wasn't a tyrant. A benevolent tyrant for the most part, but she was a tyrant nonetheless.

Catherine would not take another lover until 1761, when she became charmed by a war hero named Grigory Orlov (Montefiore, 2005). Orlov wasn't the brightest star in the sky but he was movie-star handsome and good tempered. He was one of five brothers, all of whom where strapping young men. Orlov's "towering physique, courage in battle, free-spending manner, and amorous exploits" (Alexander,

1988) had made him immensely popular with his fellow guardsmen. His brother Alexi was a more pugnacious and less sweet natured, but was both a renowned warrior and close confidant of Grigory's.

The affair between Orlov and Catherine was kept extremely discrete. Even some of her closest friends were unaware of their relationship. Peter had been growing increasingly belligerent, and Catherine didn't want to provoke him. The grand duke had also stopped any pretense of visiting her bed, so when Catherine became pregnant again she knew she had to keep her condition secret at all costs. She had no doubt become resigned to having her child taken away at birth, and the fact this baby would have to be smuggled out of the palace and cared for elsewhere wasn't that different from the empress's usual theft of Catherine's infants.

Catherine's pregnancy became even more problematic when Empress Elizabeth died on January 5, 1762. Peter was now the emperor of Russia, and Catherine's position was tenuous.

Was Catherine already planning to depose her husband? Or did Peter's unceasingly contemptuous treatment of his wife push her toward that goal? Did Peter's ham-handed leadership create enough tension that she decided to exploit it only after his rule began? Was Peter really such a bad ruler, or did Catherine just claim he was in hindsight to justify her actions?

German historian/journalist Elena Palmer has headed a recent charge to redeem Peter's legacy. She points out that Peter was "a courageous liberal – at least by Russian standards – who expounded religious freedom, abolished the country's secret police (revived upon Catherine's accession), criminalized the killing of serfs by landowners, required education for the children of aristocrats (with proof submitted to the senate), established technical schools for middle-and-lower-class children, and exempted nobles from obligatory state and military service established under Peter the Great. The latter move alone prompted parliament to propose erecting a solid-gold statue of Peter III, but he demurred with the observation that Russia had better uses for its gold" (Newton, 2014). How did the Russians go from wanting to build a solid gold statue of Peter to dethroning him in just a few short months? If Peter's reign, so exemplary from the modern perspective, was well done then how did Catherine gather the support to overthrow him?

It looks like, as ever, Peter was his own worst foe. First, he was a dyed-in-the-wool German who made no secret of his distaste for Russians or for his plans to install non-Russians in key governmental posts. He surrounded himself with German advisors. He arbitrarily gave Frederick of Prussia back all the land the Russian army had shed blood to conquer during the preceding seven years. He wanted a new war with Demark, which would have spent Russian lives solely to gain back a small slice of the duchy of Holstein. He wanted the Russian army to emulate the rigid discipline of the Prussian army and his guardsmen resented it bitterly. He enacted his new laws (which were awesome) with no thought toward sweetening the medicine when he forced the nobility (whose support he needed) to swallow it. His "policy changes left influential groups and individuals threatened, disgruntled, anxious" (Alexander, 1988). He offended Russians deeply when he "pulled faces and laughed out loud" (Neville, 2006) during the state funeral of Empress Elizabeth. He told the Orthodox Archbishop that the rites of the church were superstitions, and that they all had to shave their beards and denude their church of iconography. He also managed to insult powerful men personally, practically driving away influential political players away with a stick and into collusion with Catherine.

Even with all those blunders, it is nevertheless possible no coup would have occurred. Peter was, after all, the only grandson of Peter the Great. His adoration of Germany could have been forgiven; the English king George I also remained as German as sauerkraut and yet he reigned unmolested. Furthermore, Peter had been heir to the throne for almost 20 years. What could have toppled a man so entrenched in his position?

An embittered and insulted empress with intelligence, patience, immense political savvy, charisma, and an axe to grind, that's what.

Encouraged by his uncouth mistress, Peter had been treating Catherine worse daily. The envoy from Britain "wrote to London in March 1762 that the empress's influence was slight: not only was she disregarded in matters of state, but it private affairs, too", and the French ambassador also noted that Catherine was held "in utter contempt" by Peter (Anisimov, 2004). Peter was openly talking of shipping off Catherine to a convent so he could marry his mistress and make Vorontsova the new empress. The French *charge d'affairs* wrote that, "Peter III's barbarous, senseless ferocity made it seem quite possible that he intended to eliminate his wife" (Farquhar, 2014). Throughout the Russian court and in diplomatic circles, "rumors were rife that the Emperor wished to rid himself of his troublesome spouse, by prison or by poison" (Alexander, 1988). Baron Breteuil warned that although Catherine put on "a manly face" when dealing with her husband's abuse, it was "impossible not to suspect (for I know her passionate audacity) that, sooner or later, she will venture on some desperate step" (Bain, 1899).

If Catherine had not felt herself to have been in jeopardy, would she have still deposed him? To be honest, she probably would have done it anyway because she considered Peter to be an idiot who couldn't govern Russia as well as she could, but her husband certainly didn't do anything to inspire her to hesitate or change her mind.

Catherine had much to do before she could move against Peter. She had to woo and gather conspirators. She and her allies needed to plan a strategy. She had to win military support. On top of everything else, she had to give birth to Orlov's baby and keep it a secret.

The empress's third child was born on April 11, 1762. One of the greatest testaments to how Catherine's kindness and civility won her the loyalty and devotion of her servants is in the actions of her valet Vasily Shkurin. When the empress went into labor Shkurin *set fire to his own house* to create a distraction, luring Peter and his entourage from palace to see the conflagration while Catherine gave birth (Massie, 2011). Her newborn son, Alexis Gregorovich (the future Count Bobrinsky), was snuck out of the palace and placed in the care of Shkurin's wife. The child was raised with care and in safety, and he has living descendants in the present day.

At the end of the month, Peter drove the nail into his own political coffin by publically humiliating Catherine and then drunkenly ordering her arrest. Peter hosted a state dinner and called his empress "dura!" (fool) in front of everyone present. Catherine burst into tears from embarrassment and begged a nearby count to tell her something funny so she could recover. That same night a rumor swept through the courtiers that Peter had ordered Catherine's arrest, and had only been dissuaded from that course of action by his field marshal Prince Georg Ludwig of Holstein-Gottorp, who happened to be the empress's uncle (Alexander, 1988). (Yes, it was the same uncle that had proposed to her all those years ago.) Georg had strong motivations to preserve his niece, and as a German the field marshal had significant influence with Peter. Catherine was safe – for the moment. She was also enraged. Catherine would later write to a former lover that, "It was then that I began to listen to the proposals [to depose Peter] which people had been making to me since the death of the empress" (Massie, 2011). She was almost certainly "listening" prior to this incident, but it was probably the catalyst for her *active* plotting against Peter.

Catherine had many allies. Her lover and his brothers had been laying the groundwork for Catherine's support among the guardsmen and now the Orlovs began to assiduously structure and secure the military involvement in her coup. Nikita Panin, the man who was in charge of the heir to the throne, was also brought into the fold. Panin desired a more constitutional form of monarchy in Russia and thought that if Peter was deposed then Catherine would only be acting as regent for her son Paul until the boy came of age (Streeter, 2007). Catherine did not see any reason to tell Panin otherwise. Princess Dashkova, who was fanatically loyal to Catherine in spite of being the sister of Peter's mistress, worked tirelessly to build support for Catherine among the noble and/or powerful families of Russia. The empress was also funded by the anti-Prussian interests in Demark, Austria, and France, who funneled money into her hands to be spread around as bribes and rewards to those who backed her coup (Alexander, 1988). Once Catherine felt secure in her network of collaborators in the military and nobility, she was ready to make her move.

On June 28, 1762 (18 years to the day after her conversion to the Russian Orthodox Church) Catherine was awoken by Alexi Orlov's arrival at Peterhof palace in the early morning hours. She rushed to St.

Petersburg, where she went straight to the barracks of the Izmailovskii Guards. Colonel Kyril Razumovsky knelt before her, and then administered an oath of allegiance to Catherine II to his fellow guardsmen. The Semyonovsky guards quickly joined her cause as well. The troops escorted her as she rode to the Cathedral of Our Lady of Kazan on the Nevsky Prospekt, where the archbishop of Novgorod proclaimed her the ruler of Russia. Catherine then marched with crowds of her adherents to the Winter Palace, where Panin brought her son out to her and declare his allegiance. Princess Dashkova fell at Catherine's feet and cried out "Heaven be praised!" (Massie, 2011).

Peter, at his summer retreat of Oranienbaum, initially had no idea he had been deposed.

Dressed as an officer of the Preobrazhensky Guard, Catherine and her followers rode to Oranienbaum. When Peter III heard that Catherine was marching toward him with a large number of soldiers, he sent away everyone but Vorontsova (who would not abandon him) and wrote Catherine a letter of apology promising to share power with her. When he didn't get a prompt response, Peter wrote again to Catherine offering to abdicate if she would let him and Vorontsova flee to Holstein. Catherine sent him a message that she needed him to give her his abdication in writing before she would let him go. Either credulous enough to think Catherine would let him go or just desperate, Peter wrote his abdication. It promised in part that:

> "I, Peter, of my own free will hereby solemnly declare, not only to the whole Russian empire, but also to the whole world, that I forever renounce the throne of Russia to the end of my days. Nor will I ever seek to recover the same at any time or by

anybody's assistance, and I swear this before God." (Massie, 2011)

If Peter had been able to better hold himself together, it is unlikely Catherine would have taken his crown. The emperor had several advantages: "his armies in nearby Livonia, primed for the Danish war, could easily crush the guards. Then there was the fortress of Kronstadt, still under his control, which commanded the sea approaches to St. Petersburg itself ...[but instead of fighting back, Peter] wept, drank, and dithered" (Montefiore, 2005). Frederick of Prussia said that Peter had "allowed himself to be overthrown like a child being sent off to bed" (Lincoln, 1981).

Although Catherine would assure the Russian people that she "never had the intention or the desire to ascend the throne in this manner", she sent a letter to Poniatowski after the event stating that the coup had been carefully planned out in advance: "Everything was done ... under my own direction ... [T]hings had been more than mature for a fortnight" (Leonard, 1993). Like other rulers in history, such as Henry VII in England, she had taken a very shaky claim to the crown and put herself on the throne via a mixture of will-power, military might, and political maneuvering. It wasn't a very nice thing to do to her husband, but people don't survive at the epicenter of power by being nice.

Peter was separated from Vorontsova (it is hard to see this as anything but spite) and sent to Ropsha. It was there that Prince Bariatinsky, a good friend of the Orlov brothers, murdered the former emperor. It seems to have been done without Catherine's knowledge or explicit consent, since Alexi Orlov sent her a note swearing, "no one intended to do it so ... at dinner, he started quarreling and struggling with Prince Bariatinsky at the table. Before we could separate them,

[Peter] was dead. We ourselves know not what we did. But we are all equally guilty and deserve to die … Forgive us or quickly make an end of me … We have angered you and lost our souls forever" (Massie, 2011). Catherine, hoping to quell accusations and censure, proclaimed that Peter had died of hemorrhoid colic. Very, very few people in Europe believed her story.

Peter's funeral didn't exactly help quell the rumors of his murder. His throat was swathed in multiple folds of a cravat, preventing anyone from seeing if it had markings. His hat was too large, and pulled down to obscure his blackened and swollen face. His hands were encased in gloves, so no one could tell if there were defensive wounds. His coffin was kept in dimly lit chapel during the viewing, and guards surrounded it; people were not allowed to get to close or look too long.

Catherine quickly released a manifesto describing her hostile takeover as something she had done reluctantly to preserve the might of Mother Russia. It was, naturally, based on a mixture of fact and fiction and had been spun like a top. In spite of Catherine's efforts to justify her ascension and her husband's death, Peter's murder had stirred up a lot of hard feelings and not a few pockets of counter-rebellion. Beranger, the French charge d'affaires who had once favored Catherine, now reported that she had "opened a vast field of for discontentment and factions … In one case, the grandson of Peter I is deposed and put to death; in another, the grandson of Tsar Ivan languishes behind bars. A Princess of Anhalt-Zerbst usurps the crown beginning her reign as Regicide" (Leonard, 1993). Her reign, which would last for 34 years, was off to a bad start.

CHAPTER TWENTY-TWO

Historians remain divided on the topic of Catherine's rule. I won't wade into that debate since the point of this book is not to explore Catherine's political life. Tsarina or tyrant, my primary concern is her sexual history. What made Catherine the Great a great slut?

Some historians and biographers have been willing to exaggerate in order to make you think that she was as slutty as possible. The prurient fabrications include allegations that she, "changed her lover as every day; repudiated them without any cause; required services from them often far beyond their physical strength" (T.C.M., 1896). Catherine was accused of being an empress "who enumerated her victories and could not count her amours (Saltus, 1920). It has been said that when she was an elderly woman "the two Zubov brothers and their friend Saltyklov "took turns" with the Czarina "in an office so vast and so difficult to fill", we may suppose that she still had a taste for physical love" (Troyat, 1980). Some biographers have gone so far as to say that Catherine's "voracious libido even demanded the occasional orgy" (White, 2007).

She was supposed to go through men like a rabid wolf through a lamb pen. Historical rumor has it that when she saw a potential lover he "was first examined by Catherine's personal physician for signs of venereal disease. If pronounced healthy, he was then given a different kind of "physical"; his virility was tested by a lady in waiting appointed for that purpose (Wallace et al., 2008). The woman who served in this capacity was called Catherine's "l'Eprouveuse" (a titular form of eprouvette, a fixed mortar used to test the strength of gunpowder); if a man pleased the l'Eprouveuse in bed then she would tell the empress so that Catherine would know in advance if he would be worth her time (Farquhar, 2014).

Both Countess Praskovya Bruce (née Rumjantseva), and later Countess Anna Protasova, were rumored to have served as Catherine's l'Eprouveuse during her reign. This is almost certainly slander. Evidence suggests that, far from having "testers", the empress expressly forbid her ladies in waiting sleeping with the men she loved. Catherine ended her relationship with both her lover Rimsky-Korsakov and her best friend Countess Bruce when she found out and that they were seeing each other behind her back (Dixon, 2010). The other historical rumors of orgies and multiple lovers working as a tag-team to satisfy Catherine the Great's overwhelming eroticism are even *less* realistic that the idea she had a l'Eprouveuse.

The empress has also been accused of being "a lesbian who passed through history dripping with blood and exhaling the perfume of Eros" (Saltus, 1920). Perhaps the definition of lesbian has changed, but I don't think having sex with multiple men qualifies her. Were there women she had sex with? As far as anyone can tell, the answer is no. She had several close female friends, and bed sharing for sleep/warmth but not for sex was very common in this time for both men and women, so she probably did have them in her bed overnight. Certainly some of her female friends were almost obsessively devoted to her, but there is no indication that these relationships were romantic rather than platonic. Catherine's most transgressive 'lesbian' act was to frequently dress as a man and riding astride on horseback. She had excellent legs that were showcased in tights and liked to gallop across fields and over fences, so there are many other reasonable causes for her wardrobe and riding choices than covert homosexual yearnings.

The idea that Catherine was a lesbian seems to have sprung from the works of Charles Masson. After the death of the empress, Masson became a Frenchman and published his *Secret Memoirs on Russia*. Being composed of the most lurid gossip Masson had ever heard about Catherine the Great with a few smattering of facts, *Memoirs* was a hit. Aristocracy was wildly unpopular in France at this time, so no matter how far Masson went to defame Catherine, he had an audience willing to believe it. He declared that "At the end of her life, Catherine became so masculinized that she required women: her tribadism with Dashkova, Protasova, and Brantiska was known everywhere, and the last favorite only served to hold the candles" (Monter, 2012).

Catherine's theoretical lesbian love affairs found warm waters to spawn in when it came to the fetid minds of Victorian historians. Like any culture struggling with significant levels of sexual repression, the Victorians saw sex *everywhere*. It was the heyday of written pornography, often featuring lesbian interludes for the female fictional characters. It was also the wellspring of "nymphomania", the definition of which included women who masturbated. Only mentally ill women would touch their clitorises for the purpose of orgasm! Catherine the Great was a particular bugbear for Victorian men, and even medical professionals claimed she "violated all the laws of sexual psychology. She fell into Lesbian practices; she had fancies that could only emanate from the brain of a nymphomaniac … All of Catherine's life was dominated by sexuality" (T.C.M., 1896). With all the men and women she was supposedly bonking, one wonders how she ever found the time to rule Russia.

What, then, is the reality of Catherine the Great's sex life? We've already seen that Catherine had just three lovers (four if she consummated her marriage) prior to becoming the autocrat of Russia; how many more notches did she carve on her bedpost after she assumed the crown?

Grigory Orlov is the one lover who spans the time before and after Catherine took the throne. They were together for eleven years. For Catherine it was a monogamous relationship, but Orlov had a tendency to wander into strange beds. As long as the empress remained ignorant about Orlov's occasional forays into other women, they were very happy together.

One of the first things Catherine did after she became empress was to stop hiding her romance with Orlov. Even some of her closest allies had been unaware that Orlov was sharing her bed. Their liaison came as a great shock to her best friend Princess Dashkova, who had been entirely unsuspicious that Catherine had any lover, let alone a strapping young guardsman so far beneath her in rank. Orlov's rank did not remain far below Catherine's for long. She showered him with promotions, honors, and gifts. He was allowed to wear her miniature on his coat, as a badge of her regard (Sergeant, 1905). In every way he was marked as her beloved, her favorite.

The one thing Catherine would not give him was her hand in marriage. Panin, who had helped put her own the throne and remained her right hand for many years, bluntly told her that "The Empress can do as she pleases, but Madame Orlov can never be Empress of Russia" (Massie, 2011). Catherine agreed with him. It is doubtful that she would have wanted to marry Orlov in the first place. Why should she get rid of one husband and gain full control over her life and reign, only to replace him with a more dominating man? Husbands had too much control over their wives, even when their wives were empresses. Catherine obviously loved Orlov, but she loved the throne much more.

Orlov's near-emperor status received mixed reviews. To his credit, some said that his "sudden elevation has neither made him giddy nor ungrateful; and his present friends are the same satellites which attended his course when he moved in a humbler sphere" (Dixon, 2010). These people were in the minority, however. A large chunk of the court, especially those more nobly born, despised him as an upstart, a brute, and a braggart. Catherine's friend Princess Dashkova loathed Orlov, and he returned her less than tender regard.

Catherine would later write that Orlov would have "remained for ever, had he not been the first to tire" (Streeter, 2007). The empress would later claim that it was *after* she had sent Orlov away as the Russian representative to the Turkish peace talks that she discovered his infidelities, but the timing of her appointment of the handsome young horse guard Alexander Vasilchikov as a gentleman of the bedchamber suggests that she knew about Orlov's extracurricular love life before he left and had already selected his replacement. Since she abhorred personal conflict, she sent Orlov off on his mission so she could welcome Vasilchikov into her arms without having to deal with her former paramour's possible temper tantrum. When Orlov heard he had been replaced, he hurried back to St. Petersburg, but Catherine ordered that he go to his country estate instead. While he was there she sent him tracts of land and the serfs who worked the soil as a parting gift. When she was sure he wasn't going to make a scene, she allowed Orlov to return to her court in May of 1773, but they were just 'good friends' from then on.

Vasilchikov appears to have been Catherine's "rebound" guy. He was a hale and hearty twenty-eight year old athlete, and she was a mature woman of forty-three; their relationship seems to have been more physically than intellectually inspired. Catherine turned to philosophers and academics for mental stimulation, but her lover's inability to join her conversations left Catherine bored and depressed. After fifteen months the empress could tolerate her pretty but dimwitted paramour no more, and retired him with the gifts of lands, money, household goods, and an annual pension of 5000 rubles.

Catherine would soon replace him, but it is wrong to think that it was just her money and power that won Catherine the affection of men. She was in her mid-forties, and still a very appealing woman both in appearance and in personality. According to an "impartial observer" she was "of that stature which is requisite to perfect elegance of form in a lady. Her mouth is well proportioned, the chin round, the nose rather long; the forehead regular and open, her hands and arms round and white, her complexion not entirely clear, and her shape rather plump than meager; her neck and bosom high, and she bears her head with peculiar grace and dignity" (Sergeant, 1905). Casanova (yes, THAT Casanova) described Catherine as "sure to please with her sweetness, her affability, and her intelligence, of which she made very good use to appear to have no pretensions. If she really had none, her modesty must have been heroic, for she had every right to have them" (Casanova, 2007 ed.). When a man whose name is synonymous with amorous love finds a woman charming, it is probably safe to say he knows what he's talking about.

During the last half of her relationship with Vasilchikov, the empress had become enthralled with the man who would be remembered as the most important of her lovers: Grigory Potemkin. When she first knew him she dubbed Potemkin "l'esprit" (the wit) and it wasn't long before her passion for this intelligent courtier became earthier in tone. She wrote to a friend that, "I have drawn away from a certain good-natured but extremely dull character, who has immediately been replaced by one of the greatest, wittiest, and most original eccentrics of this iron century" (Montefiore, 2000). Potemkin was the one man in Catherine's life who ever came close to being her equal in determination and mind.

The two strongest factions in Catherine's court, the Orlovs and those who supported Panin and Grand Duke Paul, were equally upset by Potemkin's elevation to favorite. He had loyalties to neither group, yet had sky-rocketed to the position of de facto emperor in a matter of weeks. Neither Panin or Orlov needed to worry, though. Catherine did not cease to love those whom she saw as her friends. Years before she had warned Panin that, even though she loved him, he should not damage or "even try to damage my opinion of Prince Orlov … they [the Orlov borther's] are my friends, and I shan't part with them. Now there's a lesson for you" (Massie, 2011). Although she was typically a warm and devoted friend to her allies, she was an empress and would be obeyed.

Europe quickly threw itself into a tizzy over Catherine's switch of Potemkin for Vasilchikov. Not only was she taking lovers, she was doing so *like a man*; she may have preferred men that were her equals but it was patently obvious that she wouldn't suffer a cold bed when there were pretty men who would fill it during the interim. Those who resented women in general, hated Catherine in particular. She was *breaking all the rules*.

Frederick of Prussia in particular got his nose out of joint. He was misogynistic to his bones and he loathed strong women most of all. He had experienced a succession of extreme defeats at the hands of Empress Elizabeth's army from 1756-1760, and now he was even more embittered about the fact Catherine was expanding Russian influence and power in a way he had wanted to do for his country … but hadn't been able to. In his jealousy he penned the caustic sentence, "A woman is always a woman and, in feminine government, the cunt has more influence that a firm policy guided by straight reason" (Montefiore, 2000). When he heard the empress had replaced Vasilchikov with Potemkin the Prussian king seethed that, "It's a terrible business when the prick and the cunt decide the interests of Europe" (Montefiore, 2000).

As long as Potemkin lived he was the most powerful man in the Russian court. Until his death in 1791 he was Catherine's principal advisor and her most beloved statesmen. There were even rumors that the empress had married him in secret. Catherine loved and trusted him, but she must have gotten tired of having to battle him for supremacy in their relationship. As long as she was sleeping with him he could not separate his lover from his empress. Catherine loved her crown more than she ever loved another human being and would not tolerate any threats to her sovereignty. Thus, in 1776 she replaced him with a new favorite named Peter Zavadovsky. Potemkin remained in his official positions and retained his full political power, but Catherine no longer allowed him to share her bed. He could no longer mistake himself as emperor. Charles

Masson wrote that she was "indulgent in love, but implacable in politics: ambition was her ruling passion, yet she always made the lover subservient to the empress" (1801).

Zavadovsky was another handsome man who was better looking than he was well-read, but unlike Vasilchikov he had a nasty streak. Catherine tired of him quickly, gave him some presents, and sent him on his way.

Two more men would follow this pattern as she sought the physical comfort she couldn't let herself enjoy with Potemkin. Simon Zorich, know at court as "Adonis" (Montefiore) replaced Zavadovsky in 1777. Zorich was full of testosterone and bravado, and swore he'd "cut off the ears of the man" (Troyat, 1980) who dared to try to replace him in Catherine's affections. This possessiveness irked Catherine. Then Zorich made the mistake of threatening Potemkin. Tired of her overwrought cicisbeo, Catherine pensioned Zorich off and replaced him with twenty-four year old Ivan Rimsky-Korsakov.

Rimsky-Korsakov, whose grandson Nikolai Rimsky-Korsakov would become one of Russia's greatest composers, didn't last long. He was gorgeous, but he made the error of sleeping with Catherine's best friend. She dismissed him, but wasn't vindictive about it. Potemkin, in contrast, was enraged by both Rimsky-Korsakov's treatment of Catherine and his disgusting bragging about their affair and Rimsky-Korsakov found himself banished to Moscow by the irate statesman. Potemkin was allowed back into Catherine's bedroom for six months after the Adonis had cheated on her, and Catherine's friend did his best to console her and apply balm to her wounded pride (Montefiore, 2000).

In 1799 Catherine met Alexander Lanskoy, who was exactly what she needed. He was only twenty, but seemed sincerely enamored of the fifty-one year old empress. Those who knew him said that Lanskoy was a "model of kindness, humility, civility, modesty, and beauty" as well as "cheerful, honest, [and] gentle" (Farquhar, 2014). Catherine loved him and thought he would be the comfort of her old age.

    The empress was enchanted and content with Lanskoy, and these years were productive ones for Russia. Of course, it is universally known that a woman cannot have both good sex and a good policy so Potemkin is frequently given credit for any Slavic accomplishments at this time: "During her happy years with Lanskoy, Potemkin became a statesman – he changed the direction of Russian policy, annexed the Crimea, founded town, colonized deserts, built the Black Sea Fleet and reformed the Russian army" (Montefiore, 2000). One can only assume that Catherine, stupefied by orgasms, was unaware of and uninvolved in these activities. Granted, she summarily got up at 6:00 AM, washed her face with ice, drank several cups of coffee that were strong enough to bend the spoon if you tried to stir sugar in, and regularly worked ten-hour days (Gorbatov, 2006) --- but surely she could not maintain her renown work ethic while also having a functional and pleasing romantic relationship!

    It is also a traducement to suggest that there was no other reason for a young man to have sex with Catherine other than for money and influence. The loss of her youth did not sacrifice all of Catherine's charms. The French painter Vigee Lebrun said that although an older Catherine had become unfashionably plump she was still incredibly charming, with long white hair and a "noble" face, with "beautiful, very white hands" (Madariaga, 1991). Lanskoy certainly found her appealing, and all historical evidence suggests he was as in love with her as she was with him. He was beyond contestation devoted to the empress.

Sadly, the comely and beloved Lanskoy died of diphtheria on June 25, 1784. Catherine was utterly destroyed by the loss. She wrote to her friend, Baron Grimm, that she was "sunk in deepest sorrow, my happiness is over. I thought I too would die at the irreparable loss of my best friend I suffered just eight days ago … my room has become an empty cave in which I drag myself around like a shadow … I can neither eat nor sleep" (Madariaga, 1991). She dressed in black, as though she were a newly made widow, and would not begin to pay attention to suggestions that she should find another favorite until a year had passed.

Catherine was lonely, and after her mourning period for Lanskoy she "made do" with another hunky officer of the guards named Alexander Yermolov. He was thirty, so he wasn't quite as boyish as some of Catherine's previous favorites, and although he was ignorant he was of a good character. He turned out to be proud and stupid, however. He tried to create a rift between Potemkin and Catherine, inspiring Potemkin to call him a "cur" and a "monkey" to his face in full view of fellow courtiers. Stomping off with a wounded ego, Yermolov told Catherine that either Potemkin went or he would. In a move that surprised only Yermolov, his empress gave him 130,000 rubles and suggested he live abroad for at least five years (Massie, 2011). Catherine had replaced him with a newer, better guardsman by the following day.

Alexander Mamonov was in his mid-twenties, beautiful, delightful, intelligent and educated, fluent in both Italian and French, and had the ever-important ability to keep Catherine amused when they weren't in bed as well as when they were in it. Intellectually compatible, he and Catherine both wrote plays during their time together. The plays she wrote should not be undervalued. Since the mid-twentieth century Catherine's works have been gaining admiration for their wit and erudition. Critics have pointed out that Catherine's "folk-inspired operas reveal a daring writer, pulling together elements of history, legend, popular song, and elevated poetry, all in the service of demonstrating Russia's legitimacy while glorifying its culture" (O'Malley, 2006). Mamonov, due to his intellectual prowess, was one of those favorites whom Catherine seemed to have been sincerely in love with.

 Mamonov would have likely remained her favorite longer than three years, but he fell in love with sixteen-year-old Princess Darja Shcherbatova. Many historians give Mamonov only pecuniary motivations for hesitating to leave Catherine for his new sweetheart, but Mamonov seems to have genuinely cared for the empress and would have been reluctant to hurt the feelings of a woman who had been so kind and generous to him. Things came to a head on Catherine's sixtieth birthday, and when she found out Mamonov loved another she reacted with her predictable kindness. When Mamonov and Shcherbatova knelt before Catherine to ask her forgiveness, she personally betrothed the couple and gifted Mamonov with an estate with 2000 serfs on it and 100,000 rubles with which to support his bride-to-be (Rounding, 2008). When the couple wed a few weeks later the empress herself placed a diamond headdress on the bride and blessed her with an icon before the ceremony.

 Catherine had already replaced Mamonov with the swarthy twenty-two year old Platon Zubov, which doubtlessly helped her sanguinity during her former favorite's marriage to his teen bride.

 It was shortly thereafter that news reached the court about the French Revolution. A profound and devout believer in the natural rule of Enlightened autocrats, Catherine was horrified and repulsed by such an event. She didn't see why the crippling taxes and economic inequality between the haves and have-nots should excuse an uprising against a monarchial government. She described the French National Assembly as a "Hydra with twelve hundred heads" and called the new leaders of France "a crowd of lawyers, fools masquerading as philosophers, rascals, young prigs destitute of common sense, puppet of a few bandits who do not even deserve the title of illustrious criminals" (Massie, 2011). It was her fear of revolution and democracy that spurred her to destroy Poland when its king, her former favorite Stanislav Poniatowski, embraced the political ideologies of democracy. The last years of her reign would reflect her terror of potential insurgency in her own lands.

Catherine began to have disagreements with Potemkin; their ideas of what was best for Russia were no longer as in sync as they had been. There is no historical evidence, except that of hindsight, that would suggest Potemkin was in any danger of being replaced as Catherine's leading friend and advisor. True, Potemkin and the new boy-toy Zubov were at loggerheads, but that didn't cause Catherine to dismiss either one of them from court. They were both too valuable and too dear to her to be cast aside, although only Potemkin was worthy of her regard.

It was only in early October of 1791 that Potemkin would finally leave Catherine's service, via the grave. When she was informed of his death she fainted, and was so insensible that doctors were summoned to her because attendants feared she had suffered a stroke (Montefiore, 2000). Her grief was profound. The loss of her best and most trusted statesman, and the paranoia the democratic revolutions in other nations had engendered in her, weakened her resolve and contracted her horizons. She was in her golden years, but her Golden Age was behind her.

Her final favorite, Zubov, took full advantage of Catherine's lessened reserves. Everyone at court could see that Zubov was a puffed-up putz who was taking advantage of the empress in ways her former favorites has not. Catherine's son and grandson, the future Paul I and Alexander I, hated the stupid and arrogant Zubov with a purple passion for this very reason. Their opinion was shared by many at court. Her infatuation with an idiot and buffoon like Zubov damaged Catherine's reputation both at home and abroad.

On November 5, 1796 she rose as usual and drank her customary cups of coffee. At 9:00 AM, she told her attendants she wished to be alone for a bit and retired to her dressing room. After a long wait, her valet hesitantly checked on Catherine. He found her on the floor of her bathroom; she had had a stroke. Her family was summoned rushed to her bedside, but she never awoke after the initial attack. Last Rites were administered and a few hours later, at 9:45 PM on November 6, the empress Catherine II of Russia passed away. There was no horse in her bedroom at the time. She was sixty-seven years old.

Her son Paul, who had become convinced that he had been sired by Peter III not Sergei Saltykov, had Peter's remains brought to lie in state at the Winter Palace with Catherine's body. He made Alexis Orlov, the man who had brought Catherine the news of Peter's death and who had headed the guards at Ropsha, walk behind Peter's coffin carrying Paul's crown on a pillow. Both Catherine and Peter were interred at the St. Peter and Paul's Cathedral near the tomb of Peter the Great.

CHAPTER TWENTY-THREE

The French Enlightenment philosopher Denis Diderot said that Catherine the Great had the "soul of Caesar with the seductions of Cleopatra" (Montefiore, 2000). She was one of the strongest and most capable rulers Russia, and the world, has ever known. She dragged Russia into its place as a modern European state. She rationalized and reformed Russian law and government. She instituted the Charters of the Nobility and the Townspeople in 1785. The Charters were significant. Although "restricted to the upper and middle classes, the Charters were the first fruit of Enlightenment though about the rights and duties of the citizen to be enacted into Russian law" (Bushkovitch, 2011).

She was profoundly concerned with child health and life expectancy among her subjects. She wrote, "If you go to a village and ask a peasant how many children he has he will say ten, twelve, and sometimes even twenty. If you ask how many of them are alive, he will say, one, two, three, rarely four. This mortality should be fought against" (Massie, 2011). To combat this problem Catherine exponentially increased the number of schools and hospitals in her country, and introduced institutional orphanages in Moscow and St. Petersburg. She founded Russia's first College of Medicine in 1763 and attempted to lure European doctors to the country by offering them lavish salaries and benefits. Furthermore, Catherine embraced the new technology of vaccination.

The empress made Russia one of the first countries in the world to inoculate its populace. To prove its safety she allowed Dr. Thomas Dimsdale to inoculate her with the smallpox vaccine in 1764. The whole of Russia waited to see what would happen, and after "two weeks of fearful waiting ... Catherine did not succumb to the dreadful disease ... special prayers of thanksgiving were offered in Russian churches" (Gorbatov, 2006). Catherine's courageous efforts to popularize inoculations against smallpox saved countless lives.

She was also an able military strategist. Her armies trounced the Ottoman Empire twice, subjugated the Cossacks, and took the Ukraine as well as huge swathes of Poland. Catherine's able minister, Potemkin, negotiated so well with Turkey that Russia was able annex the Crimea without firing a shot. There, with Catherine's blessings, Potemkin created prosperous villages and fortified cities. Although these would be mocked by his enemies as "Potemkin Villages" painted on cardboard, the settlements were very real (Massie, 2011). Russian land acquisitions gave the country easy access to the Black Sea; Catherine financed Potemkin's yen for a naval force, thereby enabling Slavic domination of the area for decades. Russian ships did well in the Gulf of Finland and the Baltic Sea as well, beating the Swedish navy like a drum. During the Russian-Swedish war, Catherine "showed the steel nerves that had brought her to the throne ... Hearing the guns of the Swedish fleet from her palace windows, she continued to work without giving them any notice" (Bushkovitch, 2011).

The empress was the "greatest collector and patron of art in the history of Europe" (Massie, 2011). She built the Hermitage Museum and multiple other public works, founded libraries, started academic journals, and won the respect of Voltaire himself. Among the works she acquired were "approximately 4,000 Old Masters, which included 225 painting offered to Catherine after Frederick the Great [of Prussia] could not afford to buy them and the eight Rembrandts, six Van Dycks, three Rubens, and one Raphael in the Pierre Crozat collection. Catherine also bought coins and medals, *objets de vertu*, applied art and porcelain, of which one of the most spectacular examples was the 944-piece Green Frog Service, 1773-1774 by Josiah Wedgwood, featuring British scenes" (Perrie et al., 2006). The empress not only supported the arts, she made them. Catherine found time to write neoclassical comedies and French dramas, all while fulfilling her role as the autocrat of Russia.

Yet what is this remarkable woman most remembered for? Her lovers.

In total, Catherine had a dozen lovers over a 44 year period:

Sergie Saltykov (1752-1755)
Stanislas Poniatowski (1755-1758)
Grigory Orlov (1760-1772)
Alexander Vasilchikov (1772-1774)
Grigory Potemkin (1774-1776)
Peter Zavadovsky (1776-1777)
Simon Zorich (1777-78)
Ivan Rimsy-Korsakov (1778)
Alexander Lanskoi (1779-1784)
Alexander Yermolov (1785-1786)
Alexander Dmitriev-Mamonov (1786-1789)
Platon Zubov (1789-1796).

That's it. An even dozen. Jennifer Aniston has been romantically linked with as many men and she is still a "good girl" in the public mind. Why, then, is the love life of Catherine the Great treated as "both a legend and a joke" (Montefiore, 2000)? If nothing else, the empress's love life has served as a "sexual Rohrschach blot" (Dawson, 2003) that can be used to display the cultural horror and fascination about women's status and sexual pleasure.

Her sexual career caused uproar during her lifetime, and certainly during the hyper-moralistic and hypocritical reign of Victorian "ethics". Prince Mikhail Shcherbatov, a former courtier of Catherine's who felt that the generous monarch was not as generous as he *deserved*, wrote a profoundly critical book about the empress entitled *On the Corruption of Morals in Russia*, while Catherine still lived. It was printed after her death, and reprinted in English during the 1850's for the delighted perturbation of the British sensibilities. In the book Shcherbatov bemoaned that Catherine "had set other women the example of the possession of a long and frequent succession of lovers … women scarcely think it a vice in themselves to copy her … although she is in her declining years, although grey hair covers her head and time has marked her brow with the indelible signs of age, yet her licentiousness still does not diminish". In short, Catherine taught other women that *they* could also have sex just for fun, and the empress continued to have lovers even after she wasn't young anymore. For Shcherbatov, Catherine was an awful woman because she did not adhere to the social convention that only men could have sex for pleasure and with younger people. Sadly, most people concurred with him then and there are still plenty of people who hold that mindset in the modern day.

Critics from the nineteenth and early twentieth centuries, most of whom were men, were particularly horrified by the way Catherine treated her lovers. They were aghast at the idea that when Catherine took a new lover the "young man never left the Palace except at the side of his illustrious mistress. From the start he was a bird in a gilded cage; the cage was beautiful but strictly guarded, Her Majesty would permit no accidents to happen the new favorite" (T.C.M., 1896). In short, she was believed to treat her lovers as if they were women. She was the one who would cloister them for their own good, as opposed to the accepted system wherein husbands and fathers restricted the movement of girls and women. She bought them presents to keep the poor dear things happy, instead of receiving gifts in exchange for her compliance. It was a reversal of the "natural order"! Catherine embodied unnatural womanhood.

    Slut shaming Catherine was also useful politically. Any criticism of Catherine's rule or foreign policy could use her lack of chastity as a tool to denigrate her abilities. In political cartoons about her Catherine's "sexuality was frequently part of the visual code of the critique" (Dawson, 2003). As the empress gained power for Russia, the cartoons lampooning her became lewd and even pornographic. There was no story of sexual excess that could not be laid at Catherine's feet. In famous works of fiction she has been depicted as "an insatiable nymphomaniac with dominatrix tendencies who regards each side in opposed national armies as a 'main of cocks'" (Jones, 2014). Stories about her sexual excesses grew cruder, more extreme, more common, and more unlikely to have actually happened:

    "This titillating humbug reached its greatest extent during the later years of the Empress when no foreigner could discuss Russia without bringing the subject round to Catherine's sexuality. When the gossipy Oxford don John Parkinson visited Russia after Potemkin's death, he picked up and popularized any tidbit he could find and linked it all to Catherine's love life, even canal building: 'A party was considering which of the canals had cost the most money; when one of them observed there was not a doubt about the matter. Catherine's Canal (that is the name of one of them) had unquestionably been the most expensive' ... The diplomats sniggered in the dispatches about 'functions' and 'duties' and coined puns that would shame a modern tabloid newspaper, but they were usually misinformed and **historians have simply repeated the lies that seem to confirm every male fantasy about the sexual voracity of powerful women**. There are few subjects in history that have been so willfully misunderstood." (Montefiore, 2000).

Hullabaloo about Catherine the Great's private use of her privates continues even into these sexually 'liberated' times. Catherine, like other powerful women before her, has become "emblematic of the imbrication of sexual voraciousness with women holding power" (Dawson, 2003). Her ravenous desires continue to "invoke anxieties about a woman in power and the power of women, represented by sexuality and female sexual appetite (Dawson, 2003). The fact she took men to bed because she had an emotional attachment to them has been downplayed, fixating instead on the physical allure of these "prodigious cocksmen" (Prioleau, 2004). Catherine the Great narratively became nothing more than a woman who really liked sex with lots and lots of men.

Visual media, such as movies and television, took up Catherine's reputation as a vamp where political cartoons had left off. *The Scarlett Empress*, a 1934 film starring Marlene Dietrich, featured the empress as a sexual man-eater. Another movie released the same year did not make Catherine look like a tramp; it made her look like a simpering idiot. *The Rise of Catherine the Great*, starring Elizabeth Bergner, depicted Catherine as a pitiful woman in love with Peter -- a virtuous woman who pretends she is adulterous simply to make him jealous – who finds the role of empress overwhelming without male assistance. Prior to the women's liberation movement, representations of "Catherine as a powerful woman [frequently blended] into those of her as a lascivious woman" (Dawson, 2003), so if Catherine is depicted as chaste she must therefore be weak. In the 1945 film *A Royal Scandal* Tallulah Bankhead's comic portrayal of Catherine as man-hungry and vain was wonderfully done, but hardly demonstrated the truth of the powerful tsarina.

The 1991 television biopic *Young Catherine* starred Julia Ormond as a proto-feminist empress who committed infidelity only out of a duty to Russia and in response to Peter's cruelty towards her. The televised version of her life is more historically accurate than the movie versions, but it whitewashes the empress into a "saintly, nearly monogamous Catherine" (Ford and Mitchell, 2010). Decades after the feminist movement, Catherine can be strong and sexual but that sexuality must still be properly moralized. *Catherine the Great*, a 1995 made for television movie, seemed as interested in featuring almost-but-not-quite-nude bits of Catherine Zeta-Jones and her costars as it was in retelling history. In this version of events Catherine can have love, or she can be powerful, but she doesn't get to have *both*. Nevertheless, it does Catherine the service of recognizing her intelligence, even if it never lets her age – she continues to be a slim twenty-something even during events during which she was a plump fifty-something.

Then there is the never-ceasing baloney about the horse. You never know where or when the obloquy about the horse will pop up in popular culture. The popular television sitcom *Big Bang Theory* trotted the slander out once more on the first episode of season five, when Amy Farrah Fowler (Mayim Bialik) tells Penny (Kelly Cuoco) that Catherine the Great engaged in "interspecies hanky-panky". The story revolved around Penny's feelings as a slut after she had sex with a friend of her ex-boyfriend's, and Catherine's sex life was used as a comforting comparison; contrasted to an empress who had sex with a horse Penny wasn't slutty at all!

Why do slurs about Catherine and the horse continue to capture attention? Partly it is because Catherine was a master equestrienne, and one of her most famous portraits is Vigilius Eriksen's depiction of her atop her horse leading her forces to victory over Peter III.

The story of her death inverts this image, demeans her, and makes her seem ridiculous rather than powerful. The story is at heart a "misogynist attempt to discredit Catherine's real achievements" (O'Malley, 2006). Moreover, the idea of Catherine having sex with a horse alludes to the myth that multiple sex partners or "too much" sex will enlarge a woman's vagina. The fact she could supposedly accommodate a horse's penis proves (and is proof) that she was a dirty skank. It also stimulates the prurient heterosexual male fantasies that "focus on the apogee of a presumed female eagerness for vivid sex ... the horse story has, to [some] male minds, insistently underscored her sexual excess" (Alexander, 1988).

There is probably another reason the tale of Catherine and her steed was invented and continues to be promulgated; it isn't easy to slut shame the empress any other way. Shame involves both social approbation and the target's acceptance of the wrongdoing. Catherine the Great could not be shamed about her lovers during her lifetime, no matter how disapproving some people were. She was doing nothing differently than any other royal in her position had done, and by appointing 'favorites' she openly acknowledged that a man was sharing her bed. Since Catherine would not demonstrate the "appropriate" shame for having human lovers, a non-human sex partner was created to shame her.

The idea of Catherine being crushed by a horse during sex may also have roots in Carl Jung's analytical psychology. According to Jung, some of the things represented by a horse are power and libido. Catherine was powerful, something more often equated with the masculine gender. To die because sex with a horse was too much for her to handle, if not vaginally then at least in terms of a large mass crashing down on her, would be her "comeuppance" for trying to trying to control sex/power she had no business trying to master.

Catherine also "deserves" a degrading death because she violated cultural norms, and miscreants must be punished. Women are to this very day still culturally constructed as being more gentle, kind, loving, and motherly than men. Men, in contrast, are idealized as forceful, aggressive, lusty, and patriarchal. Catherine flips this ideology because she dominated the men around her while at the same time retaining "feminine" qualities; she was manly without becoming masculine.

Men are also theorized to be the gender most helpless in the thrall of sexual needs; women are portrayed as "naturally" monogamous and men are portrayed as "naturally" more prone to sexual indiscretions. Again, Catherine turns this ideology on its head. She was not inherently driven to mate with only one man for life. If she became disenchanted with a lover, she replaced him with a new man who beguiled her. Women are also supposed to be *emotionally* attracted to their mates, unlike the more "shallow" male emphasis on the looks of his partner. Catherine, like male rulers, picked her lovers because they were hotties, even if she didn't like their personalities in the long run.

In the eighteenth century kings and emperors and noblemen kept mistresses, and while it was morally frowned upon it was also accepted as 'natural' and perhaps inevitable for a 'real man'. Women were held to a higher standard of chastity. Then, as now, it was common to the point of cliché for a wealthy older man to be involved with beautiful women younger than his own children, but women are thought to be deviant for the same behavior. It has long been argued by sociobiologists like E.O Wilson that young women *prefer* older men for their "maturity" or because evolution drives them to seek elderly mates. Catherine is proof that if given the option then wealthy and powerful women are just as likely to pick young and vigorous men to sleep with.

Being crushed by a horse in a humiliating sex act demonstrates "what happens" to women who break the unwritten social rules. Jezebel, Cleopatra, and Anne Boleyn all died as a result of their gendered rebellions, but Catherine the Great died only after a long full life and while still enjoying a lover who was only 1/3 her age. With no real 'evidence' illustrating the inevitable downfall of Bad Girls, evidence of Catherine's just desserts had to be spun out of thin air.

Catherine the Great has been slut shamed because in too many ways the empress acted too much like an emperor. Catherine co-opted masculine cultural privileges as well as male power when she usurped Peter's throne, and many people wanted her taught a lesson for such misbehavior. Nothing teaches women a lesson quite like the word slut. Slut shaming is the reason why all of Catherine the Great's accomplishments can be belittled or ignored due to the fact she had lovers. "Slut" is the ultimate disparagement for a woman who reigns.

Again, and sadly, it must be pointed out that the slut shaming that was so effective in rewriting history as it concerns Catherine the Great is still being used to discredit women. For example, any woman who files discrimination and sexual harassment lawsuits is frequently called upon to prove she is *not* a slut in a court of law. Defense attorneys for the organizations being sued for sexual harassment will call the plaintiff's former lovers to the witness stand to testify about the frequency of sexual intimacy during the relationship. Defense attorneys have even gone so far as to subpoena the gynecological records of the plaintiff (Tanenbaum, 2000:1) Of course, the only reason to try to introduce a the sex-life of the plaintiff in court would be to insinuate that she, as a slut, was inherently untrustworthy and probably begged for male coworkers or bosses to "flirt" with her. If she is a slut, then she could not have been harassed or discriminated against even if she weren't just making everything up like those sneaky women are prone to do.

The irony of implying that a woman is a slut, thus discriminating against her and subjecting her to verbal sexual harassment, in order to demonstrate that she was *not* treated differently because of her gender is lost on the many defense attorneys. Considering how hard it is to get a conviction in a sexual harassment case, the irony seems to be out of reach for judges and juries as well.

Janine Brookner, a respected CIA agent, was accused by a male underling she had disciplined as being, among other things, "sexually provocative"

(Kessler, 2004:148). In short, she was accused of being a slut. An investigation was launched and, despite the galling lack of evidence, Brookner was reprimanded. Oddly enough, when it got down to the he-said/she-said lack of proof that allows male rapists to walk out of a court as a free men every day, the *male* accuser's word on the matter was enough. Even though the male accuser had ample motivation to be lying in a malicious attempt to destroy the career of the woman who disciplined him, the woman was still regarded as the less likely of the two to be telling the truth. This did not sit well with Brookner. She sued the socks off the CIA for its misogynistic shenanigans, and was given a settlement of over half a million dollars (Kessler, 2004:149). Perhaps the CIA should have realized that a woman smart enough and strong enough to succeed in their ranks would not meekly accept misogynistic authority.

At least Brookner won her suit. Most other women who speak up about harassment or gender discrimination aren't so lucky.

For example, there is the case of Melissa Nelson; a dental hygienist who was fired by her boss James Knight because he had begun to find her too attractive:

"Nelson, 32, worked for Knight for 10 years, and he considered her a stellar worker. But in the final months of her employment, he complained that her tight clothing was distracting, once telling her that if his pants were bulging that was a sign her clothes were too revealing, according to the opinion. He also once allegedly remarked about her infrequent sex life by saying, "that's like having a Lamborghini in the garage and never driving it" ... He later told Nelson's husband that he worried he was getting too personally attached and feared he would eventually try to start an affair with her. " (Foley, 2012)

The fact the Nelson had no interest in Knight, who is more than 20 years older than she is, didn't matter. What counted was that *he* wanted to have sex with *her* and therefore *she* was a threat to *his* happy home. His erections were her fault. His X-rated thoughts were also her fault. He decided to fire her lest he be led into sin -- which could apparently happen without Nelson's consent or cooperation.

Ludicrous right? Not to the uniformly male justices of the Iowa Supreme Court, which "ruled 7-0 that bosses can fire employees they see as an "irresistible attraction," even if the employees have not engaged in flirtatious behavior or otherwise done anything wrong. Such firings may be unfair, but they are not unlawful discrimination under the Iowa Civil Rights Act because they are motivated by feelings and emotions, not gender". I fail to see how this could happen to a man employed by a heterosexual dentist, but maybe that is a reflection of my lack of keen legal insight.

Melissa Nelson lost her job because as a human being with a vagina she was a *potential* slut. Her sexuality could not be considered safely contained by a mere woman. If Dr. Knight experienced temptation, surely it was her 'tight clothes' and Lamborghini-like genitals that were to blame.

It gets even worse when women dare to fight back. Anita Hill, who accused Supreme Court nominee Clarence Thomas of sexual harassment, is one of the most famous examples of women being punished for daring to tell on a male superior. She was discredited, and her testimony ignored, by a campaign to portray her as "a little nutty and a little slutty" (Brock, 2003:107). The reporter who wrote that pithy phrase, David Brock, went on to write a bestselling book that was an extended character assassination entitled *The Real Anita*

Hill. The book quoted anonymous sources who insisted that Hill had a "feminist agenda", and it was clear in the book that calling Hill a feminist was just another way of saying she was a man-hating nutcracker (Brock, 1994:344). The book asserted that she routinely claimed sexual harassment as an excuse for leaving a job she was unqualified for, and maintained that she left her job in Washington, DC to accept a teaching position at Oral Roberts law school simply because she "couldn't hack it" in the competitive atmosphere of the nation's capital (Brock, 1994:337). As has been charged against women throughout recorded history, Hill was accused of being too emotional and demanding; she was described as "temperamental" and "willful" (Brock, 1994:345). Brock's book made it clear that Hill could not be trusted, and she had only testified against Clarence Thomas because she was part of a leftist conspiracy aimed at destroying all men.

Brock later regretted writing what he called "sloppy, skewed, slanderous material" about Hill (Brock, 2003:108). He lamented that he had become "famous for calling Anita Hill a slut", going so far as to call his former allegations against Hill as "inexcusable" and "disgusting" (Brock, 2003:109-110). He confessed that Anita Hill's accusations against Clarence Thomas have been corroborated by other journalists, and regrets his role in letting Thomas get away with abusing her. Brock's candor highlights the tenuous nature of the term slut. Hill had done nothing to 'earn' a reputation as a promiscuous woman. In fact, she was a rather prudish Baptist. Yet reality had no bearing on whether or not she could be called a slut, and once she had been labeled as a slut, there were no accusations too far-fetched or obscene to be leveled against her.

That's why slut shaming is such an effective tool for discrediting women or negating their accomplishments. "Slut" becomes the defining feature of the woman being targeted. Here theoretical harlotry outweighs any positive thing she might do. It also minimizes women because it downplays any of their negative actions as well. Catherine the Great is neither lauded for her charities nor castigated for the usurpation of her husband's throne to the extent that she is talked about for her active sex life. More than three decades of exemplary rule have been reduced to a rumor about a horse.

CHAPTER TWENTY-FOUR

Before women can be slut shamed – either historically or in the future – the idea of a slut had to be conceptualized and imprinted into culture. Where do these beliefs about the 'correct' sexuality and behavior of women come from? Who got to decide what was and was not normal for men and women? Is it done by a single person? Is there a committee? Does this same committee judge what will and won't be considered slutty? If there isn't a committee, and thus no one to distribute an official informational packet, how come everyone thinks they know what makes someone a slut? How does this pervasive cultural consensus come into being?

Like all behavioral norms, sexual mores come from both the deliberate and *subconscious* needs of those in power and are then spread throughout the public via family, society, and popular culture. It just so happens that the most powerful members of Western societies are typically wealthy white men (Dean, 1994:272). There are exceptions, of course, and those exceptions increase in number every year, but for now the majority of those in authority are rich WASP dudes. Like the rest of human race, the people in power tend to focus on what is best for them, their families, and their group. What's good for them is often instinctively translated into being good in general and therefore good for everyone. This is a very human thing to do and it doesn't make them evil or The Enemy. However, it does mean that social norms are usually biased in favor of well-heeled people in general and affluent white heterosexual adult males in particular.

Not all men benefit equally from this system, of course. Men who aren't moneyed enough, or who physically lack the desired amount of "manliness", or who are disabled, or who are homosexual – those guys typically don't have the same sweet deal as the Big Shots. Think of the men who lose their jobs when a multinational company moves a factory to a country with a more easily exploited workforce. The fact the move put the hurt on his fellow men didn't make the rich white male CEO of the company so much as blink. The men affected by it weren't Fat Cats, so they didn't *really* matter, penis owners or not.

There are some things almost all men can count on, however, simply because of their gender. One of most obvious rewards is that men are almost never pejoratively called sluts. They can get laid more than eggs in a chicken coop and the worst thing they are going to get called is a "player". A promiscuous man is a stud, not a slut. No one wonders if he'll ever be able to find Ms. Right; instead people wonder when he will ever settle down after sowing his wild oats. Nor is his promiscuity supposed to limit his choice of a marital partner. He will never be "used goods". There are no cultural messages assuring him that promiscuous men don't live happily ever after. Nobody ever tells him that women won't buy the bull if the horns are free or the pig if the sausage is free or any other farmyard metaphors, because his sexuality is never compared to a limited commodity or livestock.

George Clooney is a prime example of men's immunity to sluttiness. Clooney's diverse love life has been the focus of tabloids for years. When he and Stacy Keibler ended their relationship in 2013 gossip sites reported that he had "recently retired another trophy girlfriend" (Vanderberg, 2013). In spite of his being a "notorious womanizer" he was still touted as being the ultimate prize for a woman to drag to the altar, and the only concerns his engagement to Amal Alamuddin sparked was the worry he would get "cold feet" before she could bag him (Gates, 2014). People were not startled that Amal Alamuddin would be willing to marry a man with a playboy past. No one asked Amal Alamuddin how she felt about her fiancé's past sex life, as they did to director Guy Ritchie when he became engaged to Madonna.

One of the best things about being exempt from sluttiness is that a man's sexual history is not used as an indicator of his *worth* as a human being. For girls and women it is a different story. They are taught that their devout adherence to the sexual guidelines is their only hope of being thought of as a decent person. Jessica Valenti writes that, "boys are taught that the things that make them men – good men – are universally accepted ethical ideals, woman are led to believe that our moral compass lies somewhere between our legs" (2010). Therefore, to be considered a good person a man must be brave, noble, honorable, trustworthy, and hardworking; to be considered a good person the main thing a woman must do is to keep her knees together -- except when culture tells her she must spread them apart.

The cultural rules about correct behavior (especially when it comes to sex) are much stricter for women than for men, and the social demands that women follow these rules are more stringently enforced. The penalties for breaking the rules are also unequal. When men ignore moral sanctions they are sowing their wild oats. When women do the same thing, they are harlots. Female fields don't need wild oats; they are to remain unplowed. Thus, while unsanctioned behavior can get anyone labeled a bad boy or a bad girl, only the bad girls get called sluts. Bad boys don't have this problem. Bad boys have cool clothes, attitude, and lots of sex.

James Bond is a prime example of how bad boys are lionized in popular media for doing the same things that get trollops demonized. James Bond has been inside more women than a gynecologist yet he's a hero, the ultimate "good guy" bad boy. In books and on television, male protagonists actively seek and receive sex yet they go on to save the day and/or live happily ever after. Virginity or sexual restraint is never used to indicate that the hero is worthy of the heroine's affections. There are instances in mass media that counteract or resist gender ideologies, but they are still the exception and are often couched as humor. How funny to see the sexually aggressive girl! How funny to see the boy burdened with virginity!

Inasmuch as men, even if they are very bad boys indeed, aren't called cheap tramps if they digress from sexual mores they are also spared the uniquely feminine phenomenon of slut shaming. Slut shaming is harmful to all women, not just the tarts getting shamed. Slut shaming serves to ensure the social compliance of all women even if they are one of the so-called good girls. The good girls constrain their lives and careers in an attempt to *avoid* being called a slut and suffering the fallout thereof. Furthermore, because men are mostly exempt from slut shaming they are unlikely to understand other gendered issues, like the majority of workplace sexual harassment.

For example, the California Supreme Court unanimously threw out the workplace sexual harassment lawsuit lodged against the writing staff of the popular television sitcom *Friends* by former assistant Amaani Lyle. According to Lyle, the sexual language and graphic behavior on the part of the writers rose to level of harassment, even though it was not aimed at her personally.

> "Her suit claims she was forced to listen to her bosses discuss oral sex, ideal breast size and their desire to turn the character played by Matt LeBlanc into a serial rapist. In a formal declaration, which became fodder for writers' room banter after it was posted on the Web site thesmokinggun.com, Ms. Lyle said that one writer passed around a "dirty little coloring book that would allow a person to make the pictures anatomically correct," and another enjoyed blacking out letters on scripts to change the word "Friends" to the word "penis." Ms. Lyle conceded that none of the remarks were directed at her but said that the constant banter was both an offense and an imposition: "I can recall sitting around waiting to go home while writers were sitting around pretending to masturbate" and continually talking about their penises." … A "Friends" writer named in Ms. Lyle's suit entertained co-workers with a story of having oral sex with a prostitute who turned out to be a man; according to legal filings, this anecdote formed the basis of a story in which a character unwittingly kisses a man in a wig in a poorly lighted bar. (Noxon, 2004)

This toxic atmosphere was not harassment in the opinion of the California Supreme Court. They determined that "the plaintiff's suit was without merit for two reasons. First, none of the three writers' offensive conduct was aimed at the plaintiff. Second, due to the nature of the writers' work, the pervasive sexual atmosphere was necessary for the creative process of writing an "adult" themed show" (Funaro, 2009). In essence, it is considered normal to expect a female employee to endure "jokes" about serial rape or to watch grown men pretend to masturbate provided that they don't say it would be funny if she *personally* was raped and as long as it is deemed necessary for creativity *in the opinion of those harassing her*. A group of men decided that another group of men had the right to determine whether or not a woman was allowed to feel harassed by a fuselage of gender-based slurs.

Although men are largely immune from slut shaming, they are not its most active carriers. The gender that indulges in the most slut shaming is also the gender who suffers the most from its effects. The women and girls surrounding the so-called slut, often including her own mother, can be much harsher to her than any men or boys she encounters (Tanenbaum, 2000). For example, Jennifer Aniston and Taylor Swift have both slut shamed the hell out of other women. Aniston and her friends have famously been slinging mud on Angelina Jolie ever since Jolie "stole" Aniston's former husband, Brad Pitt. Taylor Swift slut shamed an actress for "stealing" Swift's boyfriend in the song "Better Than Revenge". The lyrics state that the unnamed thespian, speculated to be Camilla Belle, is "better known for the things she does on the mattress". In Swift's music video to "You Belong With Me", the singer is the nice girl being ignored in favor of a woman wearing more scanty attire who is locking lips with the object of Swift's affection; a woman who is clearly the doxy unfairly using her sluttiness to get the attention of the man that non-slut Swift has a crush on. The good news about Swift is that as she has come into her own as a feminist her slut shaming of other women has dropped off dramatically. Feminism appears to be the cure for slut shaming.

Why do women slut shame other women in the first place, though? Why does it take feminism to make them aware of the negative fallout as a gender? Why do women do it when it only reinforces a cultural narrative that can hurt them as well? As it so happens, women do it for many of the same reasons men do it. Women have been taught since birth that slut is the worst accusation that can be leveled against a girl or woman. When you are rejected or cheated on, the hurt and anger drives you to seek the strongest negative expression you can find. I know how tempting it is to go after the other woman in a love triangle. One of my early fiancés (long story) dumped me for another woman. This woman happened to have had multiple sex partners in her past. I, however, had been a good girl and had relinquished my invaluable-for-a-Southern-Baptist-woman virginity only when an engagement ring had been proffered. Both my ex and his new fiancée had broken the implied social contract; men were supposed to always pick the nice girl and sluts were always supposed to be punished!

Did I take this as a life lesson, realizing that a previously uninhabited vagina is not relationship magic and that I was too young to be settling down anyway? No, I did not. I slut shamed, viciously and without mercy, the living daylights out of the woman he left me for. Some of it was from the rage that level of personal betrayal can generate. I have to admit that to this day I'm happy about the fact she cheated on him and left him after a couple of years of marriage. It's petty of me, but there it is. However, a significant part of my anger toward the ex and his new lover was because, having been raised in the no-hymen-no-diamond school of thought, I believed I had been permanently denied my happily ever after by their shenanigans. I had also been lead to believe being single was a Fate Worse Than Death, so I was livid that his change of heart might doom me to being an Old Maid. I wish I were joking about it, but I promise Old Maid was more than just a card game when I was lass.

This brings up the second reason women will slut shame other women. Slut shaming emerges from the female-female competition for what they have been acculturated to believe is an absolute necessity for a happy life: a man. Women are repeatedly shown in popular media that only good girls get the guy and live Happily Ever After. In order to keep their own status as good girls intact, other women will gleefully roast a floozy and feast on her bones. The context -- the unfairness of it and the sexism underlying the whole thing -- doesn't matter as much as proving to everyone else that they, unlike hussies, know how to act. As non-sluts, they have been not-so-subtly promised that they will be rewarded with true love, a house in the suburbs, and 2.5 children--the things culture promises whores will be denied. Non-sluts aren't going to risk losing out on the potential reward. The women who indulge in slut shaming don't care about the collective struggle for gender equality as much as they are interested in feathering their own emotional and material nest.

Moreover, there are some real benefits to be reaped if a woman succeeds in being a good girl. The same culture that punishes those who defy its norms also rewards those who maintain the party line. Ironically, this means that women who adhere to sociocultural presentations of the correct women's sexuality can be rewarded with the lack of a slut label even if they are having as much sex as any of the purported strumpets. Jennifer Aniston, who is forevermore linked in the public mind with her quintessentially nice character of

Rachel Green from the sitcom *Friends,* has been romantically involved with multiple men. Nevertheless, she maintains her distinction of being a good girl. Other serial daters who have seldom been the active targets for public slut shaming, despite the fact they are obviously sexually active, are Cameron Diaz, Diane Keaton, Drew Barrymore, Taylor Swift, and Kate Hudson. Why? It is because the sex lives of these women can be framed (true or not) as being emotionally motivated rather than physically driven for sexual satisfaction. This backs up the current gender ideology that women are less swayed by the lusts of the flesh. It doesn't explicitly challenge the belief that women only "give it up" in exchange for the promise of romantic attachment. That's why these women are more often described as 'unlucky in love' than as jezebels.

Women can also be invested in the status quo because they benefit from the current mode. Wealthy women who have been rewarded by the system with a nice husband and a big house usually don't see anything all that bad with the way things are, slut shaming be damned. Men aren't the only ones who can enjoy perks from the behavioral norms rich white guys set up. As an illustration, let's look again at the hypothetical factory move from the US to an area where the workforce is 'cheaper'. Even if the new non-American workers suffer from unsafe conditions and work 18 hour shifts, the economic and/or political elite of the host nation won't do anything that might make their people 'costlier'. The ruling class will keep those wages low and prevent unionization like the incoming multinational company wants. Why would they sell out their own people like that? It is because they know they will *personally* gain from it. Likewise, women and minorities can be content within a system stacked against their gender and ethnicity because they *personally* gain something from their compliance.

A girl or woman is considered to be utterly compliant to normative authority may escape slut shaming altogether, even though she will still be the bull's-eye for sexist barbs. Former First Lady of the United States, Laura Bush, has earned the sobriquet of The Perfect Wife (Gerhart, 2005). The term is a compliment from her admirers and a sneer from those who mock her as a Stepford Wife. Laura Bush has been quoted as saying that "the most important part of my job" is being the wife of George W. Bush "whether my husband is president or not" (Gerhart, 2005). She has given no overt challenges to the ideal of femininity and although she is far from a feminist icon, she has managed to avoid almost all slut shaming.

However, few women can manage the aplomb and outward acquiesce to sociocultural gender norms that Laura Bush commands. Even Jessa Duggar Seewald, a reality show semi-celebrity famous being one of 19 children raised in a strict conservative home and for her promotion of abstinence and female modesty, has recently fallen victim to slut shaming. Her crime? She has been accused of consummating her marriage too soon after the wedding vows. While Jessa Duggar famously never kissed or hugged her fiancé prior to being legally wed (and even abstained from kissing during the service), she was theoretically "busted" in an act of "lust" at her wedding reception (Elliot, 2014). Even though Jessa and Ben Seewald were in private and no one actually saw the supposed lusty act, gleeful titters of slut shaming have zipping through the blogosphere and tabloid papers.

A woman can do everything "right" according to the strictest and demanding moral codes, and still get slut shamed.

Slut shaming matters. It undermines all women because it is still being used to punish women who enact male privileges. It also does immense harm to the so-called loose woman. Being labeled a slut does a lot of social and emotional damage. It implies many things about a woman when someone uses it, and none of those things are good. According to the Whorf-Sapir hypothesis, how we see and think about the world is dependent on the words we use to describe it (Holtgraves, 2001:153). Words can literally determine how we see or think about a person. It isn't just about how other people will view the harlot, either. If a woman, especially a young woman, is told she is a skank then she will subconsciously begin to devalue herself. The perceived minx can start to see herself as worthless, which often leads to depression, risky behavior, and even self-harm.

Once a woman is labeled a slut, there are real consequences that she'll be forced to deal with. It could just be a very painful social shunning, or she could be punished even more severely. A scarlet woman may lose her job, custody of her kids, relationships with her family, her spouse, and some cases even her life. Worse, the slut label is one that sticks like hell-based glue and will follow a woman from one community to another, especially with today's social media, so she may have to pay for her perceived trashiness for the rest of her life.

CHAPTER TWENTY-FIVE

Neither does slut shaming merely affect women as individuals; it is systemic. In the legal system women who are victimized, particularly from sexual assault, are "declared to be "whores" and "sluts" by the men who abuse them [and] then confront a legal system which pits the same issue in the form of a question: was she in fact a slut who deserved it, as the perpetrator claims, or not-a-slut, deserving of some redress?" (Weisburg, 1996:261). Slut shaming allows rape culture to flourish because in cases of rape the burden is on the victim to prove she wasn't a slut who deserved to be raped. Did she do anything slutty to provoke the sexual assault? Was she drunk, dressed alluringly, or "putting out the wrong signals" by flirting? If she has committed any of these sins, often the legal system and/or jury will decided she deserved to be violated; her slutty behavior made the misguided rapist assume he could have her. Slut shaming is an important part of the reason rapes are frequently explained away with "boys will be boys" rationalizations.

Recently Eckerd College president Donald Eastman III claimed that sexual assaults on college campuses were caused by the drinking and promiscuity of both sexes. He was bewildered by the negative response, saying that the comments "kind of don't tell us this is the fault of the victim, don't blame sexual assault on alcohol, don't blame sexual assault on casual sex ... "But so far," Eastman said, "they haven't told me what you really ought to blame it on." The idea that rape is solely the fault of the rapist and that responsibility for rape lies only on the rapist was beyond Eastman. Apparently alcohol and voluntary intercourse confuses men, and they will then sort of accidently rape another person because they never know when it is totally okay to have sex with someone's unconscious body. (The answer to that conundrum is: never.) Eastman must not think his gender is very bright.

In 2010 a twenty-four year old woman from Liverpool went on a date and had sex with a man she met online, and she reported to the police that she was subsequently gang raped by her date and four other men: Kelvin Chinakwe, Olatunji Owolabi, Afolabi Sanyaolu, Senthil Venkatachalam, and Funsho Bello. The case made it to trial, but presiding Judge Robert Brown ordered the jury to return not guilty verdicts. Why? Because prosecutor Michael Leeming, the man responsible for bring the victims attackers to justice, discovered and submitted to court the fact that the rape victim had written about sexual fantasies involving group sex. Judge Brown told the jury, ""It is right to say that there is material in the chatlogs from the complainant, who is prepared to entertain ideas of group sex with strangers, where to use her words 'her morals go out of the window' … This material does paint a wholly different light as far as this case is concerned … We take the view that it would not be appropriate to offer any evidence … This case depended on the complainant's credibility. Not to put too fine a point on it, her credibility was shot to pieces" (BBC, 2010).

The reasoning appears to that if a woman had fantasies about group sex and was then gang raped, her attackers may have thought they were doing her a favor. Her telling them "no" or "stop" wasn't as real as her admission of fantasies. Her fantasies negated her rights to determine with whom she would voluntarily have sex. Following this line of argument, Brad Pitt and George Clooney could rape almost any heterosexual woman in the developed world and the jury would be instructed to return not guilty verdicts against them because the victim had once admitted she had fantasies about having sex with them. Women can be slut shamed and raped with impunity because of the thoughts they had dared to entertain about sex. It is okay to rape a woman if she failed to keep her ladybrain in line with socially acceptable female sexuality.

When comedian Bill Cosby was accused of sexual assault by more than a dozen women (the number of accusers would continue to climb into the second dozen and into the low thirties by the time of this book's release) many of his alleged victims were slut shamed and blamed for their own assaults. When Fredricka Whitfield interviewed alleged Cosby victim Janice Dickinson, she asked Dickinson questions that clearly suggested that Dickinson had been stupid for doing such unladylike things as trusting Bill Cosby, agreeing to be alone with him, and taking a pill he offered her. Whitfield's interview was also shown in conjunction with photos of Dickinson, one of the first supermodels, posing in provocative and sultry ways. The implicit message was that if Dickinson hadn't been an easy, drug-addicted attention-whore who wanted a career in acting then maybe Cosby wouldn't have *assumed* she would be fine with a little involuntary sex. Richard Stellar wrote an opinion piece for online entertainment magazine *The Wrap* about the "allegations of sexual misadventure and impropriety" surrounding Cosby, wherein he shrieked that there was only a tempest in this teapot because of the "scurrilous environment where media outlets and journalists lie in wait, like aging corpulent prostitutes, their hair dyed flame red and their nails like elongated daggers — waiting to blow any John who dares to topple those who may be kings" while accusing the victims of being "aging actresses who have one eye on the CNN camera, and the other on a book or reality show deal" (Stellar, 2014). Stellar later wrote an apology to the victims for his attempts to humiliate them and defend Cosby.

Notwithstanding the slut shaming attempts, the weight of the combined testimony of so many women made it hard to pass the whole thing off as bitter vamps having morning after regrets. However, the desire to blame victims for their own sexual assault will lead people into complex conspiracy theories when the evidence seems too much to be easily dismissed with run of the mill sexism. Rush Limbaugh, for example, suggested that Cosby's conservative political views might be behind the rape allegations:

"I had to stop and remember, Bill Cosby has numerous times in the recent past given public lectures in which he has said to one degree or another that black families and communities had better step up and get hold of themselves and not fall prey to the forces of destruction that rip them apart. And basically he started demanding that people start accepting responsibility. And the next thing you know he is the nation's biggest rapist as far as CNN is concerned." (Rowe, 2014)

Slut-shaming is not reserved for those women who report the sexual assaults of conservative darlings, by any means. A woman who reports that she was raped by a liberal hero will find that her progressive allies, male and female, will also dump a bucket full of slut shaming down on her head.

The women who accused Julian Assange of rape were also victims of slut-shaming and slander. Their names were given as "Sarah" and "Jessica", ostensibly for their privacy as victims, but their pictures being plastered all over YouTube quickly rendered their privacy a farce. Progressive icons accused the women of lying about the rape, and having set the encounters up as a means of discrediting Assange. Wikileaks supporters declared that "Sweden is tailor-made for sending a young man into a honey trap." (Harding, 2010). Furthermore, the usual accusations of vengeful, man-hating feminism were leveled against them:

"An attractive blonde, Sarah was already a well-known 'radical feminist'. In her 30s, she had traveled the world following various fashionable causes. While a research assistant at a local university she had not only been the protégée of a militant feminist academic, but held the post of 'campus sexual equity officer'. Fighting male discrimination in all forms, including sexual harassment, was her forte." (Pendlebury, 2010)

Any possibility that a rape might have occurred was explained away. It quickly made rounds on the internet that the only charge against Assange was "sex by surprise", the mythical Swedish charge of having consensual sex with a broken condom (Valenti, 2010). Prominent liberals, such as Michael Moore and Naomi Wolf, cast aspersions on the victims and blithely promoted the lie. (Michael Moore later apologized and admitted that the victim blaming he had engaged in was repellent (Marcotte, 2010)) Furthermore, because one of the victims had had consensual sex with Assange the evening before, her refusal to have sex with him the next morning didn't *really* count, according to progressive slut shamers.

"[Jessica] had snagged perhaps the world's most famous activist, and after they arrived at her apartment they had sex. According to her testimony to police, Assange wore a condom. The following morning they made love again. This time he used no protection.

Jessica reportedly said later that she was upset that he had refused when she asked him to wear a condom. Again there is scant evidence — in the public domain at least — of rape, sexual molestation or unlawful coercion." (Pendlebury, 2010)

How nice that there is a common ground for both sides of the political spectrum: the belief that women are filthy harlots who will lie about sex crimes to besmirch honorable men. Throw those silly slappers to the wolves!

Even being the child victim of a horrendous sex crime does not provide protection from slut shaming after rape. *The New York Times* published an article about an 11 year old girl who suffered a brutal gang rape by 18 men and boys, and it contained such slut shaming gems as (emphasis mine):

> The case has rocked this East Texas community to its core and left many residents in the working-class neighborhood where the attack took place with unanswered questions. Among them is, if the allegations are proved, how could their young men **have been drawn into such an act**? ..."It's just destroyed our community," said Sheila Harrison, 48, a hospital worker who says she knows several of the defendants. **"These boys have to live with this the rest of their lives."** ... Residents in the neighborhood where the abandoned trailer stands — known as the Quarters — said the victim had been visiting various friends there for months. **They said she dressed older than her age, wearing makeup and fashions more appropriate to a woman in her 20s.** She would hang out with teenage boys at a playground, some said. (McKinley, 2011)

If the reporter had not asked how the attackers had been "drawn in", and if he had included a few simple statements about victim blaming in sex crimes after the quotations about what Harrison and other "residents" were saying, the article would have not have been such a masterpiece of slut shaming. As it stands, the article implies that the victim, in spite of being 11 years old, possibly inspired her rapists to assault her in some way. The reporter made no comment about the fact that someone had expressed concern over how the *attackers* would recover from this terrible event. Additionally, the reporter did not point out in the article that the residents' accusation against the victim, that she seemed older than she really was, could not actually be considered an extenuating circumstance for gang rape. If the girl had been in her 20s, it would have still been a gang rape. With his silent compliance, the reporter tacitly agreed that the victim, by wearing make-up and seeming to be older than 11, had perhaps colluded in her sexual assault and mitigated the travesty of the crime.

Slut shaming after having been a rape victim also happened to a Missouri teen named Daisy Coleman. Daisy was only fourteen when she snuck out of her home Maryville with her thirteen year old friend to meet with a high school senior on the football team named Matthew Barnett:

"Daisy and her friend slipped out a window and went to Barnett's house. Daisy drank a big glass of something. She doesn't remember what happened next. Her 13-year-old friend went into a bedroom with a 15-year-old boy, who later told the police that "although the girl said 'no' multiple times, he undressed her, put a condom on and had sex with her." Daisy was carried out of a bedroom where she'd been with Barnett "unable to speak coherently." The boys drove the girls home. The 13-year-old and three of the boys told the police Daisy was crying when she was carried to the car. Her mother found her scratching at the front door in the early morning. The boys had told the 13-year-old to go inside, saying they'd wait with Daisy until she sobered up. They left her outside in a T-shirt and sweatpants. She'd been out for about three hours, in 22-degree weather. Melinda Coleman, a veterinarian whose husband, a doctor, had died in a car accident six years earlier, sounds like she did everything right. She gave her daughter a warm bath, noticed signs of rape or sex, called 911, and took Daisy to the hospital." (Bazelon, 2013)

    The police officers who investigated the rape, including Sheriff Darren White, did a thorough and competent investigation, after which he "felt confident the office had put together a case that would 'absolutely' result in prosecutions … Within four hours, we had obtained a search warrant for the house and executed that … We had all of the suspects in custody and had audio/video confessions" (Bazelon, 2013). With the confessions of the rapists, surely this sexual assault was beyond contestation and slut shaming could not be employed to excuse it? Sadly, no.

    Matthew Barnett, the grandson of a local political figure, and his family were popular in Maryville and the town rallied around the rapist. They didn't want this poor boy's life ruined just because some trollop snuck out of her house and got herself raped. In spite of the evidence, in March of 2012 Nodaway County prosecutor Robert Rice did not charge Matthew Barnett with a crime of any kind (Green, 2014). Daisy Coleman was slut shamed and bullied so viciously that she tried to commit suicide. The whole Coleman family was targeted so brutally by the good townsfolk of Maryville that Daisy's widowed mother had to flee the area with her children. The Coleman house then burned down in "mysterious" circumstances. The only thing Maryville failed to do while driving the family out on a rail was to tar and feather them.

The case was only reopened when it came to national attention following an article in the *Kansas City Star* by reporter Dugan Arnett and the scrutiny of the hacker activists group Anonymous. Due to international outcry, a special prosecutor named Jean Peters Baker was assigned to investigate the rape in October of 2013. After a few months of searching, Baker "did not file sexual assault charges due to there being a lack of evidence to pursue the charge" and because "she also took into account the large amount of unrest the case has caused in Maryville" (Green, 2014). Did the audio/video confessions evaporate? One can only assume.

In January of 2014, Matthew Barnett – who was a student at the University of Central Missouri and had gotten to have a nice, normal life after raping Daisy and destroying the Coleman family before the world found out about his vile actions – plead guilty to the misdemeanor charge of endangering the welfare of a child. He is on probation for two years for his crime. Daisy Coleman continues to endure a harsher sentence; "Melinda Coleman said her daughter Daisy Coleman tried to take her own life on Sunday. Melinda said Daisy attempted suicide after being "terrorized" on social media by teenagers after she attended a party over the weekend" (Green, 2014). If you go by the punishment received, Daisy's "crime" of telling the cops she was raped is worse than the rape itself. Is it any wonder so many rape victims are reluctant to report their assaults?

Sadly, young girls are often caught in the cultural crossfire; their childhood makes them de facto pure yet they can be coaxed into performing adult social behaviors that fulfill the cultural expectations of a coquette. The eleven year old rape victim probably didn't understand the twisted nature of the attention she was getting when she wore lipstick. Daisy Coleman seems to have had a crush on a big football hero and thought he liked her back; she didn't look at him as a potential rapist. In their desire to be 'liked' or gain approval they mimic the behaviors culture tells them will make them attractive and popular, but they are then slut shamed when someone uses their performance of gender as an excuse to sexually assault them.

One of the clearest examples of this woman/child demand is the not-very-subtle sexualization of 1930s child star, Shirley Temple. The studio bosses cast her in several films where she had to act in ways that mimicked the femme fatales of the era, like Mae West and Marlene Dietrich. This included sexually suggestive postures, facial expressions, dance moves, and costumes. One of the most blatant examples is the short film "War Babies", a so-called spoof of *What Price Glory?,* which featured Temple at the tender age of three reprising Dolores Del Rio's role of Charmaine, the seductive love interest of two competing marines. The young star was also given roles in films such as *Heidi* that etched her indelibly in the minds of the public as a faultless cherub. Together the dichotomy implies that little women, no matter how chaste they seemed, are sex on legs right from the cradle and it is okay to think of them as such. As academic film theorist Ara Osterweil pointed out:

This displacement of adult sexuality onto the body of a child involved an industry wide fetishization in which Temple's infantile sexuality was both deliberately manufactured and scrupulously preserved. As Twentieth Century Fox executive Darryl Zanuck commanded, "Keep her skirts high. Have co-stars lift her up whenever possible to create the illusion now selling so well. Preserve babyhood." It is clear that Temple's innocence —and those signature shots of her underpants — were crucial to her erotic appeal. (2009)

Despite the fact that the child actress's eroticism was obviously crafted by the studio who owned her contract, it was Temple herself that got the blame for her sexualization. Silent film actress Louise Brooks once accused Temple of being "a swaggering, tough little slut" (Spratley, 1990). In 1937 novelist Graham Greene wrote a review of the film *Wee Willie Winkie* in which he decried Shirley Temple's adult eroticism (emphasis mine):

> The owners of a child star are like leaseholders—their property diminishes in value every year. ... Miss Shirley Temple's case, though, has peculiar interest: **Infancy is her disguise, her appeal is more secret and more adult.** Already two years ago she was a fancy little piece (real childhood, I think, went out after *The Littlest Rebel*). In *Captain January* she wore trousers with the mature suggestiveness of a Dietrich: **her neat and well-developed rump twisted in the tap-dance: her eyes had a sidelong searching coquetry**. Now in *Wee Willie Winkie*, wearing short kilts, she is completely totsy. Watch her swaggering stride across the Indian barrack-square: hear the gasp of excited expectation from her antique audience when the sergeant's palm is raised: **watch the way she measures a man with agile studio eyes, with dimpled depravity. Adult emotions of love and grief glissade across the mask of childhood, a childhood skin-deep.** It is

clever, but it cannot last. **Her admirers—middle-aged men and clergymen—respond to her dubious coquetry, to the sight of her well-shaped and desirable little body,** packed with enormous vitality, only because the safety curtain of story and dialogue drops between their intelligence and their desire. … (Greene, 1994)

As vile as the implicit sexualization of children is, it is mild compared to travesty that can occur when it is done explicitly. In several parts of the world the local culture still practices the repellent tradition of marrying girls to adult men. I am sad to say the problem has grown exponentially in the last decade because of "opium brides". Opium farmers will sell their daughters, even those who are 12 years old or younger, to an adult man in order to repay a monetary debt (Hoonsuwan, 2012). Child brides often die during or after giving birth because their malnourished bodies are too young and weak to withstand the strain of pregnancy and labor. However, sometimes these brides die as a result of being raped by their new husbands on their wedding night. The death of an 8 year old girl in Yemen recently made international headlines when she died of internal bleeding after her husband insisted on consummating his marriage with her (Wellham, 2013).

Although girls are more likely to be sexually assaulted, all children are prospective victims. Boys, as well as girls, are largely powerless as individuals. They are therefore are equated with women in terms of their place in the social hierarchy of value and are vulnerable to predation. The worse the standing of women in a culture, the more vulnerable boys are. When a society is militaristic, considers men to be inherently superior to women, and practices has extreme sex-segregation, adult male sexual abuse of children is sometimes even culturally condoned.

In the Kandahar region of Afghanistan, Pashtun tribal members frequently take boys, roughly 9 to 15 years old, as lovers (Brinkley, 2010). The boys are kept as sex partners even by married men. The Afghan term for an older man with a boy lover is *bacha baz,* which can be translated as "boy player." Not only is it tolerated, men brag about their status as *bacha baz*.

The *bacha baz* claim they take little boys as lovers because women are "unclean". Women are so low on the social totem pole they are literally considered to be garbage capable of polluting men. Sex with women is therefore something that must be endured for the sake of begetting children. There is an Afghan expression saying that: "Women are for children, boys are for pleasure." (Brinkley, 2010). Islamic law condemns homosexuality, but *bacha baz* rationalize that they are not violating this prohibition "because they aren't in love with their boys" (Brinkley, 2010). In a twisted way, the *bacha baz* are correct; they are not homosexuals. Most adult sexual encounters by the men who molest boys have are with women, and homosexuality should not be conflated with pederasty.

Deeply-held misogynistic beliefs about the lower worth of women also created widespread pederasty in ancient Greece and Rome (Percy, 1996). This was especially true in Sparta. Brides had to shave their heads on their wedding night, theoretically to look more boyish, in order to help their grooms adjust to the idea of having sex with a woman. It makes it strange to watch a movie like *The 300* when you know King Leonidas would have been a pederast, and would have consented to his young son's sexual relationship with one of the king's adult peers.

Although pederasty is not openly condoned in the United States, it is frequently allowed to thrive if the adult male has enough sociopolitical clout and is discrete in his crimes. The conviction of Penn State University football coach Jerry Sandusky illustrates this perfectly. Sandusky was allowed to prey on boys from impoverished backgrounds, and was shielded by the other hegemonic males even when he was caught more than once actively raping a child (Chappell, 2012). Joe "JoePa" Paterno, the head football coach who wielded more power at Penn State than the Pope does in the Vatican, knew about the rapes. Nonetheless, he chose to shield his friend and fellow coach at the expense of the children (Wojciechowski, 2012). University president Graham Spanier, athletic director Tim Curley, and a vice president, Gary Schultz also stepped up to the plate to prevent, as long as possible, any consequences befalling Jerry Sandusky for his predilection of raping little boys (Chappell, 2012). Any of these men could have reported Sandusky to the police for his crimes, or at least used their social power to crush him like a bug. Instead, they chose to protect the Good Old Boy network first and foremost.

Moreover, while men are axiomatically impervious to slut shaming, *boys* are not -- so long as their attacker is an adult male. Dottie Sandusky defended her husband by calling his victims things like "clingy" or "a charmer", and has implied more than once that the boys who accused Jerry Sandusky were gold-digging liars (Lohr, 2012). Dottie wasn't alone in blaming and slut shaming the victims. The mother of the first victim to come forward had to withdraw her son from Central Mountain High School because of the actions of the school's vice principal, Steve Turchetta. Not only did Turchetta casually "out" the teen as Sandusky's accuser, he told the parents of other football players that the charges against Sandusky would "never stick", and Sandusky would be able to "walk away" (Buell, 2011). Turchetta also actively humiliated the teen in response to the Sandusky allegations, insinuating the teen's friendship with a volunteer coach was *another* attempt by the teen to lure an older man into his slutty clutches.

"Mother One claims her son developed a close bond with a 28-year-old volunteer coach, which Turchetta abruptly ended. One day, she recalled, her son told her that Turchetta was in his face, yelling at him: "With what you've done already, no 28-year-old man needs to be around you." "I think he was accusing my son of having some kind of relationship with him," she said. "That's how my son took it, too." (Buell, 2011)

The slut shaming that targeted Sandusky's first accuser is a twin of slut shaming that frequently happens when a girl or woman has been a victim of rape. People excused Sandusky by accusing the male rape victims of being liar and/or slut who "asked for it", or had somehow coerced Sandusky into assaulting them. As it is with women and female rape victims, other men and boys slut shamed the victims so that the violation was distanced from their own experiences. This is a way they can, erroneously, assure themselves that *they* will never be raped, because they don't act like a "slut". Slut shaming further lessens the chances of a victim demanding justice, since it takes away almost all of the support of his social circle and community.

CHAPTER TWENTY-SIX

Often resistance to social change is a function of fear. The unknown is a dangerous place. Feminism demands that we all march together into a future where men and women are treated as equals, regardless of ethnicity, disability, sexual orientation, or gender performance. That is why the idea of a woman's power cause such fear that she has to be slut shamed to keep her 'in her place' or 'in line'; if women get out of place they change things. Worse, people who are less familiar with feminism's goals assume that there will be an inversion of the current cultural system, wherein able-bodied white heterosexual men make less money at the same job and hold only a tiny under-represented fraction of the authoritarian positions in politics and society. For the people who are currently benefitting from the cultural norms -- or who feel that their gender will be stripped from them – feminists and the feminist agenda of equality are terrifying. The idea of female empowerment is also a dire concept to misogynists.

Slut shaming, at its core, is enacted misogyny. David Gilmore, in his 2011 book *Misogyny: The Male Malady*, explains that men who hate women are actually *afraid* of women, and that the fear of women is actually born from the fear that a woman will emasculate him. It's Freud's castration anxiety writ large. For this reason a "common theme in most cultures is a metaphorical and semantic linkage between the concept-phonemes "woman" and "danger" … Woman is depravity itself: if she fails to drown you in vice, pollute you with poison, or sicken you through her insatiable sex drive, she will burn you like fire" (Gilmore, 2011). Women are scary and a slut is one of the scariest women of all because she has not followed the social rules that symbolically keep women from breaking free and devouring men. A man who does not fear women or women's sexuality is therefore a man who is secure in his own manhood. Men who have a deeper knowledge of their intrinsic value as humans don't feel compelled to slut shame women because they are not afraid of losing their masculinity.

The perceived danger of emasculation is apparent in the words used to describe the sexuality of women who are presumed to be sexually deviant from the norm. Terms to describe women's libido are more often than not relatable to either eating or emasculation or both. Women who are sexually active are said to have a voracious sexual appetite, they are rapacious, they are ravenous, they devour men, they are uncontrolled, and they are insatiable. Their avid interest in sex makes them appear greedy for love or to be grasping hungrily for affection. They are said to be demanding and it is claimed that their desires are unquenchable. They are *man-eaters*. But how is eating related to emasculation? What does either eating or emasculation have to do with a woman's sluttiness?

It has been convincingly argued by philosophers, anthropologists, and social scientists that the consumption of food is implicitly and subconsciously equated with sex or the desire for sex. When women are "depicted as sensuously voracious about food (almost never in commercials, and only very rarely in movies and novels), their hunger for food is employed solely as a metaphor for their sexual appetites" (Bordo, 1993). In commercials, the act of a woman eating is frequently rendered an orgasmic experience. Music videos often show a woman eating ice-cream or a Popsicle or licking food off her fingers to suggest her sexual interest, *particularly* her willingness/desire to engage in fellatio.

In contrast, if a woman is seen "pigging out" on high calorie food in popular culture, she is almost always rendered comic or unattractive or gross. Why? It is because she is transgressing against the cultural perceptions of femininity. Woman who are good, women who are seen as healthy and attractive, are all in *control* of themselves (Bordo, 1993). They must control their appetites or they are bad girls. This is one of the reasons why thin women are perceived of as more attractive in Western culture; their lack of body fat displays their mastery of their appetites. If they can control their urge to eat, their sexual urges are also assumed to be subjugated to their willpower. Women can be willing to eat ice-cream or have sex, but they must eat only *moderate* proportions and only have sex in a socially sanctioned relationship. Otherwise, they are gluttonous trollops.

A fat woman's body not only represents her loss of control – as physical marker denoting her immoderate consumption of food/sex -- it can represent a fear of emasculation. In movies or television fat women are frequently used as a comic trope. One of the most common representations of a fat women is the Brawn Hilda, a hefty woman who is "strong" and "mannish" who "usually (purposefully or not) emasculates the hero by beating him up or outdoing him in "manly" activities (such as arm wrestling, boxing, hot dog eating, pretty much anything unfeminine really) … a gag character whose humor stems from being the opposite of a hot exotic chick" (tvtropes.org). The message the media delivers is that fat women are dangerous to masculinity because they might be as masculine or even more masculine than some men.

This fear of emasculation by fat women becomes more explicit when a frighteningly large woman physically dwarfs or crushes a smaller male for the comic delight of the audience. For example, in the 2004 movie *Dodgeball*, Justin Long's character is required to lift a very large girl during cheerleader tryouts; he succeeds briefly but then is crushed beneath the weight of the heavy girl. This not only knocks him out of the competition, it renders him ridiculous in front of the thin girl he wishes to date. The fat woman in this context didn't have to be manlier than the protagonist. Just the size of her body was enough to make him less manly when he was near her.

The slut is the Brawn Hilda of sex. Their demanding, voracious appetite for sex might make them manlier than the men around them. Women's sexuality is culturally constructed as "passive" and male sexuality as "active" (Wheedon, 1987). Men are supposed to seek out sex, and women are supposed to be pursued and then relent if the suitor is successful. A slut, like Brawn Hilda, is too mannish. The fear of the mannish trollop has ancient roots, with "the Roman word virago (literally man-woman), suggesting a threatening, voracious female sexuality" (Garton, 2004). A floozy has an active sexuality, and is suspected of pursuing men and thus making them passive prey. A harlot might make demands that one many cannot physiologically meet; inasmuch as sexual activity and gender are linked a failure to satisfy the sexual expectations of a woman would humiliate a man and emasculate him. A slut could *eat him alive*.

The subliminal connection between sluts/food/sex and emasculation is a longstanding one, and the ways that cultures perpetuates this message are not always subtle. For example, myriad cultures have folktales and myths of the *vagina dentata* – the toothed vagina.

There are "local variations, [but] the myth generally states that women are terrifying because they have teeth in their vaginas and that the women must be tamed or the teeth somehow removed or softened –usually by the hero figure –before intercourse can safely take place" (Creed, 2012). The risk men face when encountering *vagina dentata* is obvious: they can be castrated if they place their penis into a vagina whose voracious sexuality can literally chew off their manhood. They have been unmanned by the ultimate symbol of the woman and by a woman's unrestrained appetite. A man can be emasculated when his penis is *turned into food* and *consumed* by an untamed vagina. See? Not subtle.

The slut and Brawn Hilda are both threats to masculinity, but a fat woman can be visibly identified and avoided. She is an easy target for stigma, and often spares culture the effort of shaming her by constantly shaming herself to the point of neurosis (Bordo, 1993). Sluts are harder to see. A woman may dress "like a slut" but not actually "be" one and a modestly dressed woman may be a slut in disguise. No one can tell. Contrary to myth there is no way to easily discern a woman's number of sex partners after the loss of virginity; she won't be physically changed enough to mark her as separate from the Good Girls. A woman can have had one hundred lovers yet the one hundred and first man may be none the wiser.

However, this Crouching Nice Girl, Hidden Bimbo aspect of women's sexuality can be used against all women. Because sluts look no different from anyone else, *any* woman may be accused of being a slut. Once she is accused, unless she possesses a remarkably tough hymen that made it to adulthood and can prove she has never been penetrated vaginally, it is almost impossible to offer *evidence* that she is a Good Girl. If she had had even one sexual partner or had sex only one time, her vagina is no different that the slutty vagina. The obsession with female virginity exists in part because it is the only way a man can be 'reassured' that he has not married or is not having intercourse with a jezebel. Since sexually experienced women can emasculate him, non-virginal women are inherently risky because they might be Secret Man-eating Sluts.

Fallen women are not merely women who have "too" much sex. Sluts, regardless of the lack or abundance of sexual partners, are women who act like men. Manly behaviors -- accruing power, asserting dominance, earning or independently controlling wealth, or other masculine cultural attributes – are transgressive when done by women, and those women who transgress are often punished for their lack of femininity. One of the most common forms of sociocultural punishment is name-calling and the attendant snubbing that can occur. Calling a thin woman "fat" to indicate she is a Bad Girl due to her unrestrained appetite won't work, because she is visibly NOT fat. Calling her a slut, in contrast, will label her a Bad Girl because she can never be visibly NOT a cheap tramp. The term slut is a cultural code word denoting those unnatural female creatures that behave in a masculine fashion and are thus a threat to men, gender ideologies, and the inherent social order.

Women slut shame women as frequently as men. Are women afraid of women too? Yes, no, and maybe. Yes, in that women also receive the messages about how vicious women are and are therefore leery of their own gender. Some woman may have had first-hand experience with the social power and damaging effects of Mean Girls. No, in that women will slut shame other women with an eye toward earning male approval rather than out of maliciousness aimed at women in general. Culturally, woman are often informed that the true measure of their worth is the how much they are valued by men. This not only drives women's efforts to look pretty, it drives their efforts to act "pretty" too. Nothing says, "I'm not a bitch! I'm on your team! You should like me!" as much as attacking women who might be engaged in threateningly masculine behavior. Maybe, in that many women are more afraid of men's anger than they are interested in feminist solidarity. Slut shaming other women may be a way of deflecting social wrath onto others in an effort to shield themselves.

But why does the slut shaming of women who have been dead for hundreds -- or even thousands -- of years still matter? It's not like they are affected anymore. Academic history marches on regardless of public perceptions. Who cares if a handful of queens are remembers as sluts?

It matters because the slut shaming of famous women is a strong cultural message to girls and women alive *today*. They learn that no matter what you do or what you achieve or how strong you are, the only thing that really matters is whether or not you are a jezebel.

Cultural norms are often learned "indirectly, as a consequence of [people's] observation of, and participation in, social relations" (Spiro et al., 1987). If we want to change slut shaming, we need to change the social importance of whether or not a woman is a slut. To change the social importance of a woman's sex life, we have to change the way we talk about it. We have to stop using loaded words – words charged with some underlying cultural implication – to communicate about women's sexuality and we can start at the top. Jezebel was not a "harlot" as we understand it. Cleopatra was not a "seductress". Anne Boleyn was not a "home-wrecker". Katheryn Howard was not a "whore". Catherine the Great's sexuality was not "voracious".

Those words are loaded with bias and should be ditched by biographers, especially academic and/or serious historians. If nothing else, it would promote accuracy.

In order to be portrayed as slutty, the sex lives of all these women had to be wildly exaggerated or made up whole cloth. If they were really bawdy tarts, wouldn't the truth about their sexuality suffice? If they aren't harlots for *who* they did, they must be strumpets for *what* they did. It wasn't that they had sex with men; it's that they acted as if they were men. They had power and autonomy and effected their sociocultural environment. That's the crime for which they are slut shamed as punishment.

It would nice if we could all learn about women who made significant contributions to history and the world without having so much emphasis placed on their theoretical degree of sluttiness. Think of the way perceptions of Jezebel would change if she were known as the devout (or even radically devout) adherent to her natal religion and loyal matriarch instead of a harlot. Imagine a world where it was understood that Cleopatra formed a political alliance with Julius Caesar and then with Mark Antony and used her body to seal the deal for the good of her people. Anne Boleyn should be known as the woman who was futile in her attempt to escape Henry VIII's interest but then tried to make the best of a bad situation, rather than a lewd temptress who busted up a twenty year marriage. Katheryn Howard should be remembered as a young girl who was murdered in a medieval honor killing, not as a prostitute. Catherine the Great should be honored more for her leadership and intelligence than her "voracious sexual appetite".

These women deserve more from history than the perpetual obsession with their genitalia. All women deserve more than being the sum of their private parts.

Slut shaming is a long standing social behavior that needs to end for the strong queens in the past, the accomplished women leaders in the present, and the as yet unborn women who will act as heads of state the future.

BIBLIOGRAPHY

Abramson, Mitch. 2012. "Suspensions of Staten Island HS Football Stars Ban Possibly Tied to Probe of Bullied Classmate's Suicide." *NY Daily News*, November 17. http://www.nydailynews.com/new-york/staten-island-hs-football-stars-ban-related-bullied-teen-suicide-article-1.1203903.

Ackerman, Susan. 1993. "Ackerman, Susan. 'The Queen Mother and the Cult in Ancient Israel.' Journal of Biblical Literature (1993): 385-401." *Journal of Biblical Literature*, 385–401.

———. 1998. "The Queen Mother and the Cult in Ancient Israel." In *Women in the Hebrew Bible: A Reader*, edited by Alice Bach, 179–94. Routledge.

Adams, David. 2007. *Why Do They Kill?: Men Who Murder Their Intimate Partners*. Nashville: Vanderbilt University Press.

Ajuan Maria Mance. 2006. "Jezebel." In *Writing African American Women*, edited by Elizabeth Ann Beaulieu, 474–76. Greenwood Publishing Group.

Alexander, John T. 1988. *Catherine the Great: Life and Legend*. Oxford University Press.

Allen, Prudence. 2005. *The Concept of Woman: The Early Humanist Reformation, 1250-1500, Part 1*. Wm. B. Eerdmans Publishing.

Anglim, Simon. 2003. *Fighting Techniques of the Ancient World (3000 B.C. to 500 A.D.): Equipment, Combat Skills, and Tactics*. Macmillan.

Anisimov, Evgeniĭ Viktorovich. 2004. *Five Empresses: Court Life in Eighteenth-Century Russia*. Greenwood Publishing Group.

Ashton, Sally-Ann. 2009. *Cleopatra and Egypt*. John Wiley & Sons.

Attwood, Tony. 2006. *The Complete Guide to Asperger's Syndrome*. Jessica Kingsley Publishers.

Aubet, Maria Eugenia. 2001. *The Phoenicians and the West: Politics, Colonies and Trade*. Cambridge University Press.

Bain, Robert Nisbet. 1899. *The Daughter of Peter the Great: A History of Russian Diplomacy and of the Russian Court Under the Empress Elizabeth Petrovna, 1741-1762*. A. Constable & Company.

Baskin, Judith Reesa. 2002. *Midrashic Women: Formations of the Feminine in Rabbinic Literature*. UPNE.

Bassett, Laura, and Jennifer Bendery. 2012. "Rush Limbaugh: I'll Buy Georgetown Women 'As Much Aspirin To Put Between Their Knees As They Want.'" *Huffington Post*, March 1. http://www.huffingtonpost.com/2012/03/01/rush-limbaugh-sandra-fluke_n_1313891.html.

Bazelon, Emily. 2013. *Sticks and Stones: Defeating the Culture of Bullying and Rediscovering the Power of Character and Empathy*. Random House.

Benson, Vicky. 2010. *Recognizing the Spirit's of Jezebel and It's Attributes*. Xulon Press.

Bergner, Daniel. 2013. *What Do Women Want?: Adventures in the Science of Female Desire*. Reprint edition. Ecco.

Bernard, G. W. 2010. *Anne Boleyn: Fatal Attractions*. Yale University Press.

Birke, Lynda. 1999. "Bodies and Biology." In *Feminist Theory and the Body: A Reader*, edited by Janet Price and Margrit Shildrick. Taylor & Francis.

Blackaby, Susan. 2009. *Cleopatra: Egypt's Last and Greatest Queen*. Sterling Publishing Company, Inc.

Bleaney, Rob. 2012. "Amanda Todd: Suicide Girl's Mum Reveals More Harrowing Details of Shocking Cyber Bullying Campaign That Drove Her Daughter to Death." *Mirror*, October 15. http://www.mirror.co.uk/news/world-news/amanda-todd-youtube-teens-mum-1379909.

Bokhari, Farhan. 201AD. "Pakistan Woman Survives Attempted 'Honor Killing' in Punjab Province." *CBSnews*, June 5. http://www.cbsnews.com/news/pakistan-woman-survives-attempted-honor-killing-in-punjab-province/.

Bordo, Susan. 1993. *Unbearable Weight: Feminism, Western Culture, and the Body*. University of California Press.

———. 2013. *The Creation of Anne Boleyn: A New Look at England's Most Notorious Queen*. Houghton Mifflin Harcourt.

Bostock, John. 2014. Accessed June 30. http://www.perseus.tufts.edu/hopper/text?doc=Perseus%3Atext%3A1999.02.0137%3Abook%3D9%3Achapter%3D58.

Braidotti, Rosi. 1999. "Signs of Wonder and Traces of Doubt: On Teratology and Embodied Differences." In *Feminist Theory and the Body: A Reader*, edited by Janet Price and Margrit Shildrick, 290–301. Taylor & Francis.

———. 2013. *Nomadic Subjects: Embodiment and Sexual Difference in Contemporary Feminist Theory*. Columbia University Press.

Bramley, Peter. 2014. *Henry VIII and His Six Wives: A Guide to Historic Tudor Sites*. The History Press.

Brenoff, Ann. 2011. "Girls Are Good At Math, New Study Claims." *Huffington Post*, December 13.

http://www.huffingtonpost.com/ann-brenoff/girls-good-at-math-study_b_1146191.html.

Brinkley, Joel. 2010. "Afghanistan's Dirty Little Secret." *http://articles.sfgate.com/2010-08-29/opinion/22949948_1_karzai-Family-Afghan-Men-President-Hamid-Karzai*, August 29.

Brock, David. 1994. *The Real Anita Hill: The Untold Story*. Simon and Schuster.

———. 2003. *Blinded by the Right: The Conscience of an Ex-Conservative*. Random House, Inc.

Buell, Ryan D. 2011. "Penn State Scandal: Mother Of Alleged Jerry Sandusky Victim Claims Mistreatment By Son's School." *Huffington Post*. November 22. http://www.huffingtonpost.com/2011/11/22/penn-state-scandal-jerry-sandusky-victim-mother_n_1108979.html?page=2.

Bull, Marcus Graham, and Catherine Léglu. 2005. *The World of Eleanor of Aquitaine: Literature and Society in Southern France between the Eleventh and Thirteenth Centuries*. Boydell Press.

Burgan, Michael. 2009. *Empire of Ancient Rome*. Infobase Publishing.

Burleigh, Nina. 2013. "Sexting, Shame and Suicide." *Rolling Stone*, September 17. http://www.rollingstone.com/culture/news/sexting-shame-and-suicide-20130917.

Burns, Jasper. 2006. *Great Women of Imperial Rome: Mothers and Wives of the Caesars*. Routledge.

Burstein, Stanley Mayer. 2007. *The Reign of Cleopatra*. University of Oklahoma Press.

Bushkovitch, Paul. 2011. *A Concise History of Russia*. Cambridge University Press.

Buss, David M., and Cindy M. Meston. 2009. *Why Women Have Sex: Understanding Sexual Motivations from Adventure to Revenge (and Everything in Between)*. Macmillan.

Callahan, Maureen. 2013. "Author Uncovers Surprising Secrets of Female Sexuality, Including Monogamy and Fantasies." *New York Post*, May 12. http://nypost.com/2013/05/12/author-uncovers-surprising-secrets-of-female-sexuality-including-monogamy-and-fantasies/.

Canfora, Luciano. 2007. *Julius Caesar: The Life and Times of the People's Dictator*. University of California Press.

Carol P. Christ. 2002. "Feminist Theology and a Post-Traditional Thealogy." In *The Cambridge Companion to Feminist Theology*, edited by Susan Frank Parsons, 78–96. Cambridge University Press.

Carter, Koby A. 2010. *Overthrowing Jezebel: Ask Me How I Know!*. AuthorHouse.

Cartledge, Paul. 1992. "The Politics of Spartan Pederasty." In *Homosexuality in the Ancient World*, 75–94. Routledge.

———. 2003. *Spartan Reflections*. University of California Press.

Casanova, Giacomo. 2007. *History of My Life*. A.A. Knopf.

Catherine the Great. 2007. *The Memoirs of Catherine the Great*. Random House Publishing Group.

Chapman, Ben, Joe Kemp, Corky Siemaszko, and Justin Tasch / NEW YORK DAILY NEWS. 2012. "Tormented 15-Year-Old Felicia Garcia Jumped to Death in Front of Train after Bullying over Sex with Football Players." *NY Daily News*. October 25. http://www.nydailynews.com/new-york/15-year-old-throws-front-train-staten-island-article-1.1191808.

Chappell, Bill. 2014. "Penn State Abuse Scandal: A Guide And Timeline." *NPR.org*. Accessed January 26.

http://www.npr.org/2011/11/08/142111804/penn-state-abuse-scandal-a-guide-and-timeline.

Chauveau, Michel. 2004. *Cleopatra: Beyond the Myth*. Cornell University Press.

Cholakian, Patricia Francis, and Rouben Charles Cholakian. 2013. *Marguerite de Navarre: Mother of the Renaissance*. Columbia University Press.

Claire Ridgway. 2011. "Mary Boleyn -- Was She Really the Mistress of Francis I?" *The Anne Boleyn Files*. October 30. http://www.theanneboleynfiles.com/mary-boleyn-was-she-really-the-mistress-of-francis-i/.

Cohen, Daniel. 2010. "Asherah: Hidden Goddess of the Bible." In *Goddesses in World Culture*, edited by Patricia Monaghan, 39–54. ABC-CLIO.

Coogan, Michael David, and Mark S. Smith. 2012. *Stories from Ancient Canaan*. Presbyterian Publishing Corp.

Creed, Barbara. 2012. *The Monstrous-Feminine: Film, Feminism, Psychoanalysis*. Routledge.

Cressy, David. 1997. *Birth, Marriage, and Death : Ritual, Religion, and the Life-Cycle in Tudor and Stuart England: Ritual, Religion, and the Life-Cycle in Tudor and Stuart England*. Oxford University Press.

Dawson, Ruth. 2003. In *Women in German Yearbook*. U of Nebraska Press.

Dean, Carolyn J. 1994. "The Productive Hypothesis: Foucault, Gender and the History of Sexuality." *History and Theory* 33 (3): 271–96.

"Death Threats | Fat, Ugly or Slutty." 2014. Accessed November 19. http://fatuglyorslutty.com/category/death-threats/.

Delahunty, Mary. 2013. "Liars, Witches and Trolls: On the Political Battlefield." In *Griffith REVIEW 40: Women & Power*, edited by Julianne Schultz. Text Publishing.

Denny, Joanna. 2007. *Anne Boleyn: A New Life of England's Tragic Queen*. Da Capo Press.

Dever, William G. 2005. *Did God Have a Wife?: Archaeology and Folk Religion in Ancient Israel*. Wm. B. Eerdmans Publishing.

———. 2012. *The Lives of Ordinary People in Ancient Israel: Where Archaeology and the Bible Intersect*. Wm. B. Eerdmans Publishing.

Dewhurst, John. 1984. "The Alleged Miscarriages of Catherine of Aragon and Anne Boleyn." *Medical History* 28 (01): 49–56. doi:10.1017/S0025727300035316.

Dio, Cassius. 1987. *The Roman History: The Reign of Augustus*. Translated by Ian Scott-Kilvert. Penguin Books Limited.

Dixon, Professor Simon. 2010. *Catherine the Great*. Profile Books.

Domini, Daniel. 2010. *Fight Back and Conquer the Spirit of Jezebel*. Xulon Press.

Dukhia, Monita. 2007. *Out of the Miry Clay*. Xulon Press.

Dunn, Jane. 2007. *Elizabeth and Mary: Cousins, Rivals, Queens*. Knopf Doubleday Publishing Group.

Elliott, Annabel Fenwick. 2014. "Did Jessa Duggar and Ben Consummate Their Marriage at the RECEPTION?" *Mail Online*, November 6. http://www.dailymail.co.uk/femail/article-2824486/Did-Jessa-Duggar-Ben-Seewald-busted-consummating-marriage-RECEPTION.html.

Ellis, Simon P. 1992. *Graeco-Roman Egypt*. Osprey Publishing.

Erickson, Carolly. 1980. *Great Harry*. Macmillan.

Everitt, Anthony. 2007. *Augustus: The Life of Rome's First Emperor*. Random House LLC.

Fagan, Peter J. 2004. *Sexual Disorders: Perspectives on Diagnosis and Treatment*. JHU Press.

Farquhar, Michael. 2001. *A Treasury of Royal Scandals: The Shocking True Stories History's Wickedest Weirdest Most Wanton Kings Queens*. Penguin.

———. 2014. *Secret Lives of the Tsars: Three Centuries of Autocracy, Debauchery, Betrayal, Murder, and Madness from Romanov Russia*. Random House Publishing Group.

Fausto-Sterling, Anne. 2008. *Myths of Gender: Biological Theories about Women and Men, Revised Edition*. Basic Books.

Fine, Cordelia. 2011. *Delusions of Gender: How Our Minds, Society, and Neurosexism Create Difference*. W. W. Norton & Company.

Fischer, Mindy. 2014. "The Internet Teaches Ann Coulter A Much Needed Lesson.... -." May 12. http://samuel-warde.com/2014/05/internet-teaches-ann-coulter-much-needed-lesson/.

Ford, Elizabeth A., and Deborah C. Mitchell. 2010. *Royal Portraits in Hollywood: Filming the Lives of Queens*. University Press of Kentucky.

Fox, Julia. 2009. *Jane Boleyn: The True Story of the Infamous Lady Rochford*. Random House LLC.

Fraser, Antonia. 1992. *The Wives of Henry VIII*. Knopf Doubleday Publishing Group.

Frauenfelder, Mark. 2012. "Conservative Media's Response to Sandra Fluke Testimony." *Boing Boing*. March 8. http://boingboing.net/2012/03/08/conservative-medias-response.html.

Freed, Sandie. 2012. *The Jezebel Yoke: Breaking Free from Bondage and Deception*. Baker Books.

Frick, Anders. 2012. "Video: Dietisten som blev programmerare." *IDG.se*, November 19. http://www.idg.se/2.1085/1.477569/video--dietisten-som-blev-programmerare.

Friedmann, Paul. 1884. *Anne Boleyn: A Chapter of English History, 1527-1536*. Macmillan.

Fuentes, Agustín. 2012. *Race, Monogamy, and Other Lies They Told You: Busting Myths about Human Nature*. University of California Press.

Gabillet, Annie. 2014. "Now That George's Engaged, Let's Look Back at His Many Loves." *POPSUGAR Celebrity*. Accessed November 6. http://www.popsugar.com/Who-Has-George-Clooney-Dated-17990733.

Gaines, Janet Howe. 1999. *Music in the Old Bones: Jezebel Through the Ages*. SIU Press.

———. 2013. "How Bad Was Jezebel?" *Biblical Archaeology Society*, May. http://www.biblicalarchaeology.org/daily/people-cultures-in-the-bible/people-in-the-bible/how-bad-was-jezebel/.

Galarneau, Lisa. 2014. "2014 Global Gaming Stats: Who's Playing What, and Why? | Big Fish Blog." *Big Fish Games*. January 16. http://www.bigfishgames.com/blog/2014-global-gaming-stats-whos-playing-what-and-why/.

Garton, Stephen. 2004. *Histories of Sexuality: Antiquity to Sexual Revolution*. Routledge.

Gąsiovowski, Wacław, and Busancy (Viscount de.). 1908. *Tragic Russia*. Cassell and company, limited.

Gates, Daniel. 2014. "George Clooney 'Freaking Out' About 'Forced' Marriage to Amal Alamuddin?." *Gossip Cop*. July 2. http://www.gossipcop.com/george-clooney-cold-feet-marrying-amal-alamuddin/.

Gerhart, Ann. 2005. *The Perfect Wife: The Life and Choices of Laura Bush*. Simon and Schuster.

Gilies, Rob. 2013. "2 Charged in Deadly Canada Cyberbullying Case." *Yahoo News*, August 19. http://news.yahoo.com/2-charged-deadly-canada-cyberbullying-case-053506130.html.

Gilmore, David D. 2011a. *Misogyny: The Male Malady*. University of Pennsylvania Press.

———. 2011b. *Misogyny: The Male Malady*. University of Pennsylvania Press.

Goldenberg, Suzanne. 2005. "Why Women Are Poor at Science, by Harvard President." *The Guardian*. January 18. http://www.theguardian.com/science/2005/jan/18/educationsgendergap.genderissues.

Goldsworthy, Adrian. 2010. *Antony and Cleopatra*. Yale University Press.

Gorbatov, Inna. 2006. *Catherine the Great and the French Philosophers of the Enlightenment: Montesquieu, Voltaire, Rousseau, Diderot and Grim*. Academica Press, LLC.

Graham, Professor Timothy, and Dr Anne Van Arsdall. 2012. *Herbs and Healers from the Ancient Mediterranean through the Medieval West: Essays in Honor of John M. Riddle*. Ashgate Publishing, Ltd.

Greene, Graham. 1994. *The Graham Greene Film Reader: Reviews, Essays, Interviews & Film Stories*. Hal Leonard Corporation.

Grenoble, Ryan. 2012. "Amanda Todd: Bullied Canadian Teen Commits Suicide After Prolonged Battle Online And In School." *Huffington Post*, October 11. http://www.huffingtonpost.com/2012/10/11/amanda-todd-suicide-bullying_n_1959909.html.

Gress, David. 1998. *From Plato to NATO: The Idea of the West and Its Opponents*. Simon and Schuster.

Griffiths, Morwenna. 1988. "Feminism, Feelings, and Philosophy." In *Feminist Perspectives in Philosophy*, edited by Morwenna Griffiths and Margaret Whitford. Indiana University Press.

Grimbly, Shona. 2013. *Encyclopedia of the Ancient World*. Routledge.

Gruen, Erich. 2003. "Cleopatra in Rome: Facts and Fantasies." In *Myth, History and Culture in Republican Rome: Studies in Honour of T.P. Wiseman*, edited by David Braund and Christopher Gill, 257–74. University of Exeter Press.

Gruen, Erich S. 1996. *Studies in Greek Culture and Roman Policy*. University of California Press.

Gwyn, Peter J. 2011. *The King's Cardinal: The Rise and Fall of Thomas Wolsey*. Random House.

Hadley, Judith M. 2000. *The Cult of Asherah in Ancient Israel and Judah: Evidence for a Hebrew Goddess*. Cambridge University Press.

Hannah, Barbara. 2006. *The Archetypal Symbolism of Animals: Lectures Given at the C. G. Jung Institute, Zurich, 1954-1958*. Chiron Publications.

Harding, Kate. n.d. "The Rush to Smear Assange's Rape Accuser." *Salon*.

Harmsworth, Andrei. 2014. "Beyonce's Risqué Performance Slammed by Parents." *Metro*, January 27. http://metro.co.uk/2014/01/27/grammys-2014-beyonces-risque-performance-slammed-by-shocked-parents-4278835/.

Hart, Kelly. 2009. *The Mistresses of Henry VIII*. History Press.

Hartwell-Walker, Marie. 2014. "Friends with Benefits: Can Women Handle It?" *Psych Central.com*. Accessed November 24. http://psychcentral.com/lib/friends-with-benefits-can-women-handle-it/0002860.

Hassler, Christine. 2013. "Can Women Have Casual Sex Without a Post-Hookup Hangover?" *Huffington Post*, October 8. http://www.huffingtonpost.com/christine-hassler/can-women-have-casual-sex_b_4055428.html.

Hazleton, Lesley. 2009. *Jezebel: The Untold Story of the Bible's Harlot Queen*. Random House LLC.

Hendrickx, Sarah, and Matthew Tinsley. 2008. *Asperger Syndrome and Alcohol: Drinking to Cope?*. Jessica Kingsley Publishers.

Hennessy, Rosemary. 2012a. *Materialist Feminism and the Politics of Discourse (RLE Feminist Theory)*. Routledge.

———. 2012b. *Materialist Feminism and the Politics of Discourse (RLE Feminist Theory)*. Routledge.

Henson, Mr S. V., SV. 2009. *The Pride The Rebellion and Jezebel*. NCA Equal Opportunity Books.

Higgs, Liz Curtis. 2004. *Bad Girls of the Bible: And What We Can Learn From Them*. Random House LLC.

Hodgetts, Edward Arthur Brayley. 1914. *The Life of Catherine the Great of Russia*. Brentano's.

Hölbl, Günther. 2001. *A History of the Ptolemaic Empire*. Psychology Press.

Holtgraves, Thomas M. 2001. *Language As Social Action: Social Psychology and Language Use*. Psychology Press.

Hoonsuwan, Monsicha. 2012. "Afghanistan's Opium Child Brides." *The Atlantic*. February 9. http://www.theatlantic.com/international/archive/2012/02/afghanistans-opium-child-brides/252638/.

House, Paul R. 1998. *Old Testament Theology*. InterVarsity Press.

Hrdy, Sarah Blaffer. 1999. *THE WOMAN THAT NEVER EVOLVED*. Harvard University Press.

Huffington Post. 2008. "Air America Host Randi Rhodes Suspended For Calling Hillary A 'Big F*cking Whore,'" April 11. http://www.huffingtonpost.com/2008/04/03/air-america-host-randi-rh_n_94863.html.

———. 2014. "Teens Assaulted Audrie Pott Before Her Suicide," January 16.

http://www.huffingtonpost.com/2014/01/16/audrie-pott-suicide_n_4608720.html.

Hughes, Lindsey. 2008. *The Romanovs: Ruling Russia, 1613-1917*. Hambledon Continuum.

Hull, Liz. 2010. "Anne Boleyn DID Have an Affair with Her Brother: The Poem That 'Proves' the Adultery of Henry VIII's Queen." *Mail Online*, February 23. http://www.dailymail.co.uk/news/article-1252993/Poem-backs-claims-Anne-Boleyn-lovers--brother.html.

"Husband Guilty of 'Honour Killing.'" 2014. *BBC News*. June 4. http://www.bbc.com/news/uk-england-manchester-27662204.

Ives, Eric. 2005. *The Life and Death of Anne Boleyn: "The Most Happy."* Wiley.

Ives, Eric. 2009. *Lady Jane Grey, A Tudor Mystery*. Wiley-Blackwell.

James C. McKinley Jr. 2011. "Gang Rape of Schoolgirl, and Arrests, Shake Texas Town." *The New York Times*, March 8, sec. U.S. http://www.nytimes.com/2011/03/09/us/09assault.html.

James, Susan. 2000. "Feminism in Philosophy of Mind: The Question of Personal Identity." In *The Cambridge Companion to Feminism in Philosophy*, edited by Miranda Fricker and Jennifer Hornsby. Cambridge University Press.

Johnson, Allan G. 2005. *The Gender Knot: Unraveling Our Patriarchal Legacy*. Temple University Press.

Jones, David J. 2014. *Sexuality and the Gothic Magic Lantern: Desire, Eroticism and Literary Visibilities from Byron to Bram Stoker*. Palgrave Macmillan.

Jones, Prudence J. 2006. *Cleopatra: A Sourcebook*. University of Oklahoma Press.

Jung, C. G. 2014. *Collected Works of C.G. Jung, Volume 5: Symbols of Transformation*. Princeton University Press.

Kalof, Linda. 1993. "Dilemma of Femininity: Gender and the Social Construction of Sexual Imagery." *The Sociological Quarterly* 34 (4): 639–51.

Kane, Emily W., and Mimi Schippers. 1996. "Men's and Women's Beliefs about Gender and Sexuality." *Gender and Society* 10 (5): 650–65.

Kaus, Gina. 1935. *Catherine the Great*. Cassell.

Kelly, H. A. 2004. *The Matrimonial Trials of Henry VIII*. Wipf and Stock Publishers.

Kennedy, Diane M., and Rebecca S. Banks. 2011. *Bright Not Broken: Gifted Kids, ADHD, and Autism*. John Wiley & Sons.

Kessler, Ronald. 2004. *The CIA at War: Inside the Secret Campaign Against Terror*. Macmillan.

Kien, Jenny. 2000. *Reinstating the Divine Woman in Judaism*. Universal-Publishers.

Kimmell, Michael. 2010. *Misframing Men: The Politics of Contemporary Masculinities*. Rutgers University Press.

Kingkade, Tyler. 2014. "College Student Alyssa Funke Commits Suicide Following Cyberbullying Over Porn." *Huffington Post*. May 22. http://www.huffingtonpost.com/2014/05/22/alyssa-funke-suicide-porn_n_5373138.html.

Kizewski, Holly K. 2014. "Jewel of Womanhood: A Feminist Reinterpretation of Queen Katherine Howard." University of Nebraska-Lincoln. http://digitalcommons.unl.edu/cgi/viewcontent.cgi?article=1073&context=historydiss.

Klein, Isaac. 1979. *A Guide to Jewish Religious Practice*. KTAV Publishing House, Inc.

(kniāginiā), Ekaterina Romanovna Dashkova. 1995. *The Memoirs of Princess Dashkova*. Duke University Press.

Laffey, Alice L. 1988. *An Introduction to the Old Testament: A Feminist Perspective*. Fortress Press.

Lau, Andree. 2012. "B.C. Teen's Torment Ends In Suicide." *The Huffington Post*, October 11. http://www.huffingtonpost.ca/2012/10/11/amanda-todd-teen-bullying-suicide-youtube_n_1959668.html.

LeClaire, Jennifer. 2013. *The Spiritual Warrior's Guide to Defeating Jezebel: How to Overcome the Spirit of Control, Idolatry and Immorality*. Baker Books.

Leonard, Carol S. 1993. *Reform and Regicide: The Reign of Peter III of Russia*. Indiana University Press.

Licence, Amy. 2013. *In Bed with the Tudors: From Elizabeth of York to Elizabeth I*. Amberley Publishing Limited.

———. 2014. *The Six Wives and Many Mistresses of Henry VIII: The Women's Stories*. Amberley Publishing Limited.

"Limbaugh Revives 'Sex-Retary Of State' Label For Hillary Clinton." 2014. *Media Matters for America*. Accessed January 26. http://mediamatters.org/video/2011/06/23/limbaugh-revives-sex-retary-of-state-label-for/180814.

Lincoln, W. Bruce. 1981. *The Romanovs: Autocrats of All the Russias*. Dial Press.

Lindqvist, Jörgen. 2012. "Bråttom Byta Ut Den Manliga Besättningen." *Computer Sweden*, November 30. http://computersweden.idg.se/2.2683/1.479735/brattom-byta-ut-den-manliga-besattningen.

Lindsey, Karen. 1996. *Divorced, Beheaded, Survived: A Feminist Reinterpretation of the Wives of Henry VIII*. Da Capo Press.

Lipscomb, Suzannah. 2009. *1536: The Year That Changed Henry VIII*. Lion Books.

Little, Lester K. 2007. *Plague and the End of Antiquity: The Pandemic of 541-750*. Cambridge University Press.

Loades, D. M. 2009. *Tudor Queens of England*. A&C Black.

Lohr, David. 1920. "Dottie Sandusky Testifies: Wife Defends Former Penn State Coach Jerry Sandusky In Molestation Case." *Huffington Post*. June 19. http://www.huffingtonpost.com/2012/06/19/dottie-sandusky-jerry-sandusky-trial-testimony_n_1610410.html.

Loughlin, Marie H. 1997. *Hymeneutics: Interpreting Virginity on the Early Modern Stage*. Bucknell University Press.

Lovell, Stephen, Alena V. Ledeneva, and A. B. Rogachevskiĭ. 2000. *Bribery and Blat in Russia: Negotiating Reciprocity from the Middle Ages to the 1990s*. St. Martin's Press.

Mackay, Lauren. 2014. *Inside the Tudor Court: Henry VIII and His Six Wives through the Writings of the Spanish Ambassador Eustace Chapuys*. Amberley Publishing Limited.

Madariaga, Isabel de. 1991. *Catherine the Great*. Yale University Press.

Mahon, Elizabeth Kerri. 2011. *Scandalous Women: The Lives and Loves of History's Most Notorious Women*. Penguin.

"Main/Brawn Hilda - Television Tropes & Idioms." 2014. Accessed August 21. http://tvtropes.org/pmwiki/pmwiki.php/Main/BrawnHilda.

Malkin, Michelle. 2012. "Michelle Malkin - The War on Conservative Women." *National Review Online*. March 7.

http://www.nationalreview.com/articles/292791/war-conservative-women-michelle-malkin.

Marcotte, Amanda. 2010. "The Perils of Charging Rape." *Slate*, December 22. http://www.slate.com/articles/double_x/doublex/2010/12/the_perils_of_charging_rape.html.

———. 2011. "The Solution to MRA Problems? More Feminism -." *The Good Men Project*. March 8. http://goodmenproject.com/ethics-values/solution-mra-problems-more-feminism/.

Mark Joyella. 2011. "Kirsten Powers On Bill Maher: His Comments On Bachmann, Palin Are Degrading To 'All Women.'" March 29. http://www.mediaite.com/tv/kirsten-powers-takes-on-bill-maher-his-comments-on-bachmann-palin-are-degrading-to-all-women/.

Markoe, Glenn. 2000. *Phoenicians*. University of California Press.

Marr, Andrew. 2012. *A History of the World*. Pan Macmillan.

Marsella, Anthony J. 2005. "'Hegemonic' Globalization and Cultural Diversity: The Risks of Global Monoculturalism." *Austrailian Mosaic* 13 (11): 15–19.

Marsh, W. L., E. F. Schnipper, C. L. Johnson, K. A. Mueller, and S. A. Schwartz. 1983. "An Individual with McLeod Syndrome and the Kell Blood Group Antigen K(K1)." *Transfusion* 23 (4): 336–38.

Martin, Emily. 1997. "Medical Metaphors of Women's Bodies: Menstruation and Menopause." In *Writing on the Body: Female Embodiment and Feminist Theory*, edited by Katie Conboy, Nadia Medina, and Sarah Stanbury. Columbia University Press.

———. 1999. "The Egg and the Sperm: How Science Has Constructed a Romance Based on Stereotypical Male-Female Roles." In *Feminist Theory and the Body: A Reader*, edited by Janet Price and Margrit Shildrick. Taylor & Francis.

———. 2001. *The Woman in the Body: A Cultural Analysis of Reproduction*. Beacon Press.

Massie, Robert K. 2011. *Catherine the Great: Portrait of a Woman*. Random House Publishing Group.

Masson, Charles François P. 1801. *Secret Memoirs of the Court of Petersburg [by C.F.P. Masson]. Tr. [from Mémoires Secrets Sur La Russie]*.

Matt Gertz. 2012. "NRA Spokesman Ted Nugent's Top 10 Inflammatory Comments." *Media Matters for America*. February 15. http://mediamatters.org/blog/2012/02/15/nra-spokesman-ted-nugents-top-10-inflammatory-c/184266.

Matusiak, John. 2013. *Henry VIII: The Life and Rule of England's Nero*. The History Press.

Maynard, Mary. 2012. *Science and the Construction of Women (RLE Feminist Theory)*. Routledge.

McCabe, Elizabeth A. 2008. *An Examination of the Isis Cult with Preliminary Exploration Into New Testament Studies*. University Press of America.

McCabe, Janice. 2005. "What's in a Label? The Relationship between Feminist Self-Identification and 'Feminist' Attitudes among US Women And Men." *Gender and Society* 19 (4): 480–505.

McCarter, Joan. 2007. "Hillary Clinton Facing Undiscussed Sexism." *Daily Kos*, December 2. http://www.dailykos.com/story/2007/12/02/416967/-Hillary-Clinton-Facing-Undiscussed-Sexism.

McDevitt, Jill. 2014. "Slut-Shamed to Death for Saying Yes to Sex, Murdered for Saying No." *A Day in the Life of a Sexologist*. May 25. http://sexologist.tumblr.com/post/86799922779/slut-shamed-to-death-for-saying-yes-to-sex-murdered.

McGowan, Harriet. 2007. *Jezebel in Our Midst*. Xulon Press.

McKinlay, Judith E. 2004. *Reframing Her: Biblical Women in Postcolonial Focus*. Sheffield Phoenix Press.

M.D, Louann Brizendine. 2007. *The Female Brain*. Crown Publishing Group.

Meade, Marion. 1991. *Eleanor of Aquitaine: A Biography*. Penguin.

Media Matters Staff. 2011. "Limbaugh Revives 'Sex-Retary Of State' Label For Hillary Clinton." *Media Matters for America*. June 23. http://mediamatters.org/video/2011/06/23/limbaugh-revives-sex-retary-of-state-label-for/180814.

Michael Satchell. 2008. "Jezebel Was a Killer and Prostitute, but She Had Her Good Side - US News." *US News & World Report*, January 25. //www.usnews.com/news/religion/articles/2008/01/25/jezebel-was-a-killer-and-prostitute-but-she-had-her-good-side.

Millar, Fergus. 2006. *A Greek Roman Empire: Power and Belief Under Theodosius II (408-450)*. University of California Press.

Montefiore, Simon Sebag. 2005a. *Potemkin: Catherine The Great's Imperial Partner*. Vintage Books.

———. 2005b. *Potemkin: Catherine The Great's Imperial Partner*. Vintage Books.

Monter, William. 2012. *The Rise of Female Kings in Europe, 1300-1800*. Yale University Press.

Moscati, Sabatino. 2001. *The Phoenicians*. I.B.Tauris.

Moss, Walter G. 2003. *A History of Russia Volume 1: To 1917*. Anthem Press.

Muir, Hazel. 2003. "Einstein and Newton Showed Signs of Autism." *NewScientist*, April 30.

Nandy, Chandan. 2014. "Honour-Killing of 21-Year-Old Delhi College Girl Reflects Fractured Modernity." *Times Of India Blogs*. November 20. http://blogs.timesofindia.indiatimes.com/nandygram/honour-killing-of-21-year-old-delhi-college-girl-reflects-fractured-modernity/.

Neville, Peter. 2006. *A Traveller's History of Russia*. Interlink Books.

Newton, Michael. 2014. *Famous Assassinations in World History*. ABC-CLIO.

North, Joanna. 2013. *Mindful Therapeutic Care for Children: A Guide to Reflective Practice*. Jessica Kingsley Publishers.

Norton, Elizabeth. 2011. *Anne Boleyn: Henry VIII's Obsession*. Amberley Publishing Limited.

Olyan, Saul M. 1988. *Asherah and the Cult of Yahweh in Israel*. Society of Biblical Literature 34. Atlanta: Scholar's Press.

O'Malley, Lurana Donnels. 2006. *The Dramatic Works of Catherine the Great: Theatre and Politics in Eighteenth-Century Russia*. Ashgate Publishing, Ltd.

Osterweil, Ara. 2009. "Reconstructing Shirley: Pedophilia and Interracial Romance in Hollywood's Age of Innocence." *Camera Obscura* 24 (3 72): 1–39. doi:10.1215/02705346-2009-008.

Patai, Raphael. 1990. *The Hebrew Goddess*. Wayne State University Press.

Patrick, Nancy J., and Dion Betts. 2008. *Hints and Tips for Helping Children with Autism Spectrum Disorders: Useful Strategies for Home, School, and the Community*. Jessica Kingsley Publishers.

Pendlebury, Richard. n.d. "The Wikileaks Sex Files: How Two One-Night Stands Sparked a Worldwide Hunt for Julian Assange." *Mail Online*.

Percy, William Armstrong. 1996. *Pederasty and Pedagogy in Archaic Greece*. University of Illinois Press.

Perrie, Maureen, Dominic Lieven, and Ronald Grigor Suny. 2006. *The Cambridge History of Russia: Volume 2, Imperial Russia, 1689-1917*. Cambridge University Press.

Phelan, Jessica. 2012. "Greek Journalist Yiorgos Trangas Fined for Calling Angela Merkel a 'Dirty Berlin Slut.'" *GlobalPost*. February 23. http://www.globalpost.com/dispatches/globalpost-blogs/weird-wide-web/greek-journalist-yiorgos-trangas-fined-angela-merkel-dirty-berlin-slut.

Phipps, William E. 1992. *Assertive Biblical Women*. Greenwood Publishing Group.

Pleasance, Chris. 2014. "Father Stabbed Daughter to Death for Using Mobile in Honour Killing." *Mail Online*, October 10. http://www.dailymail.co.uk/news/article-2788439/father-brought-daughter-24-britain-learn-english-stabbed-death-using-mobile-honour-killing.html.

Plutarch, John Dryden, and Arthur Hugh Clough. 1875. *Plutarch's Lives: The Translation Called Dryden's*. Little, Brown,.

Porter, Linda. 2007. *The First Queen of England: The Myth of "Bloody Mary."* Macmillan.

Preston, Diana. 2009. *Cleopatra and Antony: Power, Love, and Politics in the Ancient World*. Bloomsbury Publishing USA.

Princess Michael of Kent. 2007. *Crowned in a Far Country: Portraits of Eight Royal Brides*. Simon and Schuster.

Prioleau, Elizabeth. 2004. *Seductress: Women Who Ravished the World and Their Lost Art of Love*. Penguin.

Quirk, Joe. 2006. *Sperm Are from Men, Eggs Are from Women: The Real Reason Men and Women Are Different*. Running Press.

Radzilowski, John. 2007. *A Traveller's History of Poland*. Interlink Books.

Ramet, Sabrina Petra. 2002. *Gender Reversals and Gender Cultures: Anthropological and Historical Perspectives*. Routledge.

Read, Max. 2013. "Patriotic American Ted Nugent Shit His Pants to Avoid the Draft." *Gawker*. February 13. http://gawker.com/5983634/patriotic-american-ted-nugent-shit-his-pants-to-avoid-the-draft.

Reeve, Elspeth. 2012. "Rush Scrubs 'Slut' Comment, Demand for Fluke Sex Tapes." *The Wire*. March 8. http://www.theatlanticwire.com/politics/2012/03/rush-scrubs-demand-for-fluke-sex-tapes/49643/.

Reuter, Karen L., and John P. McGahan. 2013. *Obstetric and Gynecologic Ultrasound: Case Review Series: Case Review Series*. Elsevier Health Sciences.

Richter, Don. 2005. *Overcoming the Attack of the Jezebel Spirit*. Xulon Press.

Ripley, George, and Charles Anderson Dana. 1883. *The American Cyclopaedia: A Popular Dictionary of General Knowledge*. D. Appleton.

Robinson, Adlen. 2014. "FCN Series on the Payette Bibles Continues." *Forsyth County News*, August 17. http://www.forsythnews.com/section/20/article/25224/.

Rogers, Lesley. 2001. *Sexing the Brain*. Columbia University Press.

Roller, Duane W. 2004. *The World of Juba II and Kleopatra Selene: Royal Scholarship on Rome's African Frontier*. Routledge.

Rosario, Frank. 2012. "Bullied SI Teen Who Killed Self 'tortured' by Classmates after Sex at Party: Sources." *New York Post*. October 25.

http://nypost.com/2012/10/25/bullied-si-teen-who-killed-self-tortured-by-classmates-after-sex-at-party-sources/.

Rounding, Virginia. 2008. *Catherine the Great: Love, Sex, and Power*. Macmillan.

Routledge, Robin. 2012. *Old Testament Theology: A Thematic Approach*. InterVarsity Press.

Saltus, Edgar. 1920. *The Imperial Orgy: An Account of the Tsars from the First to the Last*. Boni & Liveright (Incorporated).

Scarisbrick, J. J. 2011. *Henry VIII*. Yale University Press.

Schiff, Stacy. 2010. *Cleopatra: A Life*. Hachette Digital, Inc.

Schutte, Kimberly. 2014. *Women, Rank, and Marriage in the British Aristocracy, 1485-2000: An Open Elite?*. Palgrave Macmillan.

ScienceDaily. 2014. "'Women Worse at Math than Men' Explanation Scientifically Incorrect, Experts Say." Accessed November 18. http://www.sciencedaily.com/releases/2012/01/120118123141.htm.

Scott-Kilvert, Ian. 1987. *Cassius Dio: The Roman History: The Reign of Augustus*. Penguin.

Sergeant, Philip Walsingham. 1905. *The Courtships of Catherine the Great*. Lippincott.

Sex and Society. 2010. Marshall Cavendish.

Sharps, Linda. 2012. "Facebook's 'Bikini Jailbait' and 'I Hate Teen Moms' Pages Are OK, Breastfeeding Still Not." *The Stir*. October 29. http://thestir.cafemom.com/technology/145882/facebooks_bikini_jailbait_and_i.

Shcherbatov, M. M. 2009. *On the Corruption of Morals in Russia*. Cambridge University Press.

Shecter, Vicky Alvear. 2010. "When Historical 'Facts' Aren't So Factual." *A Dead Man Fell From the*

Sky ... September 29. http://www.garycorby.com/2010/09/when-historical-facts-arent-so-factual.html.

Sherwood, Harriet. 2011. "Death in the West Bank: The Story of an 'Honour' Killing." *The Guardian*. June 30. http://www.theguardian.com/world/2011/jun/30/honour-killing-west-bank-palestine.

"Shirley Temple Scandal Was Real Reason Graham Greene Fled to Mexico." 2014. *The Independent*. Accessed February 13. http://www.independent.co.uk/news/uk/home-news/shirley-temple-scandal-was-real-reason-graham-greene-fled-to-mexico-400856.html.

Silver, Morris. 1995. *Economic Structures of Antiquity*. Greenwood Publishing Group.

Sim, Alison. 2011. *The Tudor Housewife*. The History Press.

Slattery, Juli. 2009. "Your Husband's Sex Drive Is God's Gift to You." *Focus on the Family*. http://www.focusonthefamily.com/marriage/sex_and_intimacy/understanding-your-husbands-sexual-needs/your-husbands-sex-drive-is-gods-gift-to-you.aspx.

Slote, Michael. 2011. *The Impossibility of Perfection: Aristotle, Feminism, and the Complexities of Ethics*. Oxford University Press.

Smallwood, E. Mary. 2001. *The Jews Under Roman Rule: From Pompey to Diocletian : A Study in Political Relations*. BRILL.

Smith, Lacey Baldwin. 2013. *Anne Boleyn: The Queen of Controversy*. Amberley Publishing Limited.

Smith, Mark S. 2002. *The Early History of God: Yahweh and the Other Deities in Ancient Israel*. Wm. B. Eerdmans Publishing.

Snyder, Josey Bridges. 2012. "Jezebel and Her Interpreters." In *Women's Bible Commentary*, edited by Carol Ann Newsom, Sharon H. Ringe, and Jacqueline E. Lapsley, 180–83. Westminster John Knox Press.

Solomon, Jon. 2001. *The Ancient World in the Cinema*. Yale University Press.

Southern, Patricia. 2012a. *Ancient Rome: The Republic 753BC-30BC*. Amberley Publishing Limited.

———. 2012b. *Mark Antony: A Life*. Amberley Publishing Limited.

Spelman, Elizabeth V. 1999. "Woman as Body: Ancient and Contemporary Views." In *Feminist Theory and the Body: A Reader*, edited by Janet Price and Margrit Shildrick, 32–41. Taylor & Francis.

Spielvogel, Jackson. 2014. *Western Civilization*. Cengage Learning.

Spiro, Melford Elliott, Benjamin Killborne, and L. Lewis L. Langness. 1987. *Culture and Human Nature*. Transaction Publishers.

Spratley, Lois. 1990. "Journalist Delves Into Steamy Story Of Louise Brooks." *Daily Press*, September 23. http://articles.dailypress.com/1990-09-23/news/9009220339_1_barry-paris-louise-brooks-pandora-s-box.

Staff, NewsOne. 2014. "Grammy Fallout: UK Newspaper Runs Shocking, Disrespectful Beyoncé Headline [VIDEO]." *News One*, January 28. http://newsone.com/2854302/what-uk-newspaper-calls-beyonce-a-whore-after-grammy-performance-video/.

———. 2014. "Grammy Fallout: UK Newspaper Runs Shocking, Disrespectful Beyoncé Headline [VIDEO]." *News One*. Accessed March 29. http://newsone.com/2854302/what-uk-newspaper-calls-beyonce-a-whore-after-grammy-performance-video/.

Starkey, David. 2003. *Six Wives*. HarperCollins.

Steve Doughty. 2012. "Men Who Murder Their Cheating Partners CAN Use 'Loss of Control' as a Defence." *Mail Online*, January 18. http://www.dailymail.co.uk/news/article-2087868/Men-murder-cheating-partners-CAN-use-loss-control-defence.html.

Strasser, Annie-Rose. 2012. "Female Journalist Attacked By Limbaugh Yesterday Responds: He 'Just Doesn't Think Women Count'." March 7. http://thinkprogress.org/media/2012/03/07/439527/tracie-mcmillan-responds/.

Streeter, Michael. 2007. *Catherine the Great*. Haus Publishing.

Streissguth, Thomas. 1999. *Queen Cleopatra*. Twenty-First Century Books.

Stuart, Keith. 2013. "Gamer Communities: The Positive Side." *The Guardian*, July 31. http://www.theguardian.com/technology/gamesblog/2013/jul/31/gamer-communities-positive-side-twitter.

Suetonius. 2004. *Lives of the Caesars*. Translated by John C. Rolfe. Barnes & Noble Publishing.

Tanenbaum, Leora. 2000. *Slut!: Growing up Female with a Bad Reputation*. HarperCollins.

Tang-Matrinez, Zuleyma. 1997. "The Curious Courtship of Sociobiology and Feminism: A Case of Irreconcilable Differences." In *Feminism and Evolutionary Biology: Boundaries, Intersections, and Frontiers*, edited by Patricia Gowaty. Springer Science & Business Media.

T.C.M. 1896. "Parisian Medical Chit Chat." Edited by J. C. Culbertson. *Cincinnati Lancet and Clinic: A Weekly Journal of Medicine and Surgery* 37 (December): 685–88.

The Washington Post. 2011. "Ed Schultz Suspended from MSNBC after Calling Laura Ingraham a 'right Wing Slut,'" May 26.

http://www.washingtonpost.com/lifestyle/style/ed-schultz-suspended-from-msnbc-after-calling-laura-ingraham-a-right-wing-slut/2011/05/26/AGOcV2BH_story.html.

Thomas. 2010. "Lubricated Holes and Mangina Attack Dogs: A Glimpse At The MRA Abyss." *Yes Means Yes*. September 20. http://yesmeansyesblog.wordpress.com/2010/09/28/lubricated-holes-and-mangina-attack-dogs-a-glimpse-at-the-mra-abyss/.

Thompson, Jason. 2011. *A History of Egypt: From Earliest Times to the Present*. Random House LLC.

Thu, Mark Frauenfelder at 8:21 am, Mar 8, and 2012. 2014. "Conservative Media's Response to Sandra Fluke Testimony." *Boing Boing.* Accessed November 5. http://boingboing.net/2012/03/08/conservative-medias-response.html.

Tigay, Jeffrey H. 1986. *You Shall Have No Other Gods: Israelite Religion in the Light of Hebrew Inscriptions*. Scholars Press.

Torre, Miguel A. De La. 2014. *Doing Christian Ethics from the Margins: Second Edition Revised and Expanded*. Orbis Books.

Trow, M. J. 2013. *Cleopatra: Last Pharaoh of Egypt*. Constable & Robinson.

Troyat, Henri. 1980. *Catherine the Great*.

Tyldesley, Joyce. 2011. *Cleopatra: Last Queen of Egypt*. Profile Books.

UPI. 2013. "Parents: RCMP Knew of Blackmailer before Amanda Todd Committed Suicide," November 15. http://www.upi.com/Top_News/World-News/2013/11/15/Parents-say-police-knew-of-abuse-in-Amanda-Todd-case-before-suicide/UPI-44961384556483/.

Vagi, David L. 2000. *Coinage and History of the Roman Empire, C. 82 B.C.--A.D. 480: History*. Taylor & Francis.

Valenti, Jessica. 2009. *He's a Stud, She's a Slut, and 49 Other Double Standards Every Woman Should Know*. Seal Press.

———. 2010a. *The Purity Myth: How America's Obsession with Virginity Is Hurting Young Women*. ReadHowYouWant.com.

———. 2010b. "What the Assange Case Reveals about Rape in America." December 11. http://www.washingtonpost.com/wp-dyn/content/article/2010/12/10/AR2010121002571.html.

Vanderberg, Madison. 2013. "What Are George Clooney's Exes Up To?" *Hollyscoop*. July 18. http://www.hollyscoop.com/george-clooney/what-are-george-clooneys-exes.html.

Villalva, Brittney R. 2012. "Amanda Todd: 15-Year-Old Tells Story of Bullying and Suicide Before Death (VIDEO)." *Christian Post*. October 14. http://global.christianpost.com/news/amanda-todd-15-year-old-tells-story-of-bullying-and-suicide-before-death-video-83253/.

Waliszewski, Kazimierz. 1895. *The Story of a Throne (Catherine II. of Russia)*. W. Heinemann.

———. 1913. *Paul the First of Russia: The Son of Catherine the Great*. W. Heinemann.

Wallace, Irving, Amy Wallace, David Wallechinsky, and Sylvia Wallace. 2008. *The Intimate Sex Lives of Famous People*. Feral House.

Warnicke, Retha M. 1991. *The Rise and Fall of Anne Boleyn: Family Politics at the Court of Henry VIII*. Cambridge University Press.

Waterhouse, Lynn. 2013. *Rethinking Autism: Variation and Complexity*. Academic Press.

Weedon, Chris. 1987. *Feminist Practice and Poststructuralist Theory*. B. Blackwell.

Weir, Alison. 2007. *The Six Wives of Henry VIII*. Grove Press.

———. 2010. *Captive Queen: A Novel of Eleanor of Aquitaine*. Random House, Inc.

———. 2011. *Mary Boleyn: The Mistress of Kings*. Random House Publishing Group.

Weisberg, D. Kelly. 1996. *Applications of Feminist Legal Theory to Women's Lives: Sex, Violence, Work, and Reproduction*. Temple University Press.

Weiss, Stefanie Iris. 2012. "Monogamy Is a Patriarchal Myth and Other Things Your Parents Probably Never Taught You: Part 1." *Huffington Post*, October 1. http://www.huffingtonpost.com/stefanie-iris-weiss/monogamy_b_1925862.html.

Wellham, Melissa. 2013. "8-Year-Old Child Bride Dies after Forced Marriage." *Mamamia*. September 12. http://www.mamamia.com.au/news/8-year-old-child-bride-dies-after-forced-marriage/.

White, Ellen T. 2007. *Simply Irresistible: Unleash Your Inner Siren and Mesmerize Any Man, with Help from the Most Famous--And Infamous--Women in History*. Running Press.

Whitley, Catrina Banks, and Kyra Kramer. 2010. "A NEW EXPLANATION FOR THE REPRODUCTIVE WOES AND MIDLIFE DECLINE OF HENRY VIII." *The Historical Journal* 53 (04): 827–48. doi:10.1017/S0018246X10000452.

Wilkinson, Josephine. 2011. *Mary Boleyn: The True Story of Henry VIII's Favourite Mistress*. Amberley Publishing Limited.

Wilson, Derek. 2003. *In the Lion's Court: Power, Ambition, and Sudden Death in the Reign of Henry VIII*. Macmillan.

Wojciechowski, Gene. 2012. "Joe Lied." *ESPN.com*. July 12. http://espn.go.com/college-football/story/_/id/8160430/college-football-joe-paterno-enabled-jerry-sandusky-lying-remaining-silent.

Yee, Gale A. 2003. *Poor Banished Children of Eve: Woman as Evil in the Hebrew Bible*. Fortress Press.

n.d.

ABOUT THE AUTHOR

Kyra Cornelius Kramer holds degrees in Biology and Anthropology from the University of Kentucky, as well as a M.S. in Medical Anthropology from SMU. She is the author of the Amazon Bestseller Blood Will Tell: A Medical Explanation of the Tyranny of Henry VIII, and she currently lives with her husband and three children in Bloomington, IN.

BLOOD WILL TELL

A Medical Explanation of the Tyranny of Henry VIII

Kyra Cornelius Kramer

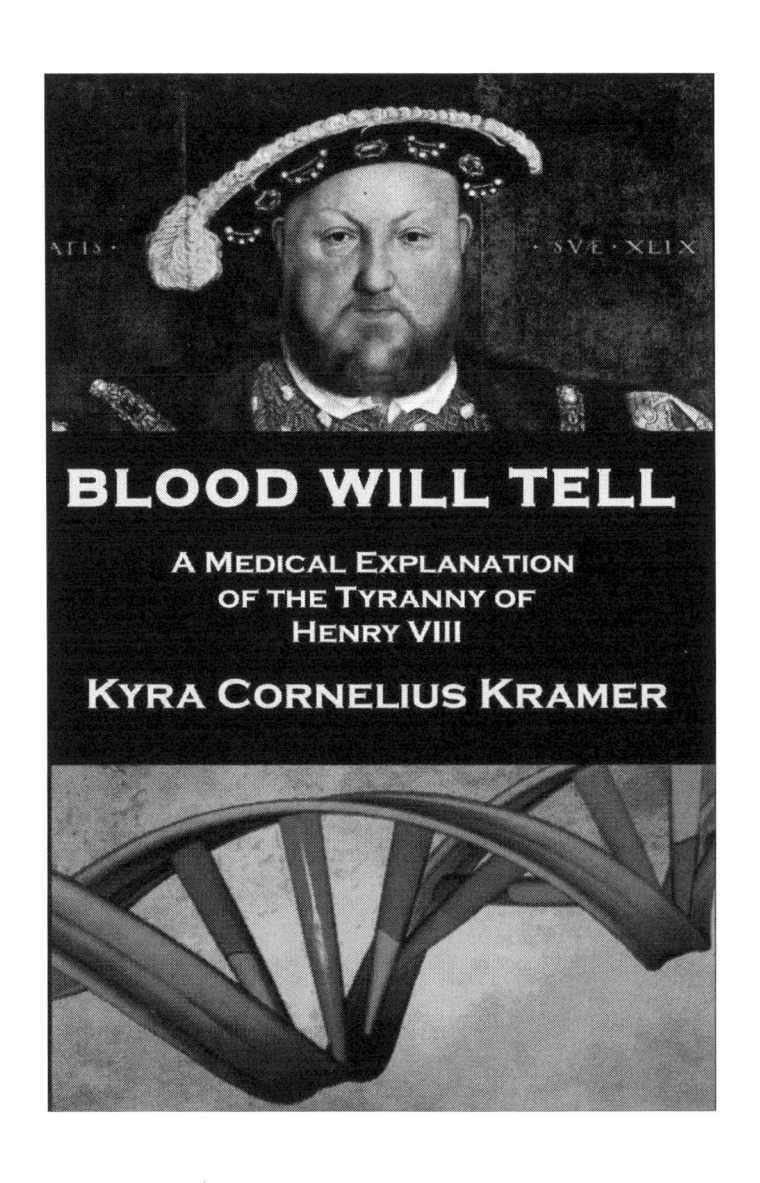

TAKE A LOOK INSIDE:

Chapter One
King Henry VIII:
The Man, the Monarch, and the Myth

Henry VIII did *not* have syphilis.

The belief that this incredibly famous English king had syphilis is one of the most enduring myths circulated about him. It was first postulated by a Victorian physician in 1888 as an explanation for Henry's checkered reproductive record and his nightmarish tyrannical behavior (Keynes, 2007:179). Since the King was renowned for indulging his lusts this hypothesis seemed to fit the facts like a glove, and was more or less accepted as an enjoyably scandalous certainty for the next few decades. Even after the theory was soundly and conclusively debunked in 1931 by Frederik Chamberlin, the premise that Henry was riddled with syphilis continued to be promulgated. Today, in spite of the fact that syphilis has been ruled out as the cause of Henry's troubles *for almost 100 years*, the idea that the King had this particular sexually transmitted disease keeps resurfacing. Regardless of the fact that it is untrue, it continues to be taught in history classes, included in non-fiction works, and is now discussed ardently on the internet. It shows up in books that are in all other respects well researched, where it has been quoted from an otherwise reputable source. Scholars have insisted for decades that neither Henry, nor any of his wives, showed symptoms of syphilis, but the popular conviction that the King was syphilitic has nevertheless persisted unchecked. Reality has been no match for this everlasting scandal. Why?

Although the myth that Henry had syphilis is still being mistakenly given as a "fact," the scientific evidence that Henry was *not* infected with syphilis is incontrovertible. For syphilis to have affected Henry's first wife's pregnancies, the King would already have had to be infected by 1509, at the latest. He died in 1547. This means he would have had syphilis for more than 30 years. Symptoms of the tertiary, or late stage, of syphilis present themselves between 15-30 years after contracting the disease (Gross, 2011). The signs of syphilis that has reached this point are hard to miss. Moreover, it is not as though the physicians of that time were unaware of syphilis. It has often been assumed that Columbus and his crew brought this venereal disease back from the New World, but a body has been exhumed from a graveyard in London by archaeologists which proves that the English were already suffering, and dying, of syphilis years before that famous voyage took place (Glass, 2001). Columbus was probably linked with syphilis simply because of an unfortunate coincidence: shortly after his ships returned from North America, a syphilis epidemic began to affect troops fighting in Italy and rapidly expanded outward into the populations of Germany, Switzerland, and France, eventually spreading all the way into England by 1496 (Lancaster, 1990:188). The most common treatment for syphilis in the Tudor period involved dosing patients with massive quantities of mercury "salts", yet there is no record of Henry ever having been prescribed mercury for any medicinal reason, nor of any of his wives, mistresses, or children having taken them (Keynes, 2007:180). In contrast, Henry's contemporary, King Francis I of France, who was diagnosed with syphilis (although modern medical experts suspect he may have had gonorrhea instead), is known to have been dosed with "Chinese wood" and mercury by his court physicians.

Had it been suspected that Henry had syphilis, word of his condition would doubtlessly have circulated in European courts. The fact that he was the English monarch would not have stopped the doctors from reporting his disease, any more than it stopped royal physicians from making the King of France's condition common knowledge. Doctors would not have been the only ones able to see that Henry had syphilis. The symptomatic lesions common in syphilitic patients would have been difficult to conceal from the courtiers who attended him in his bath and even helped him with toilet hygiene. Royalty suffering from a sexually transmitted disease would have been too juicy a tidbit of malicious news to have been kept quiet. Additionally, passing on such gossip was an ambassador's supreme duty; if Henry had been syphilitic, all the crowned heads of Europe would have heard about it from their representatives at the English court.

Furthermore, none of Henry's surviving offspring showed signs of congenital or tertiary syphilis, which, as has been noted in several scholarly works, is not exactly a subtle physical condition (Whitley and Kramer, 2010). Since three of his surviving children were the firstborn offspring of their respective mothers, it could be argued those infants survived because the women had not yet contracted syphilis from the King, but that could not account for the health of Henry's daughter, Mary, who was the result of his first wife's fifth (or possibly sixth) pregnancy. If her father had been syphilitic, then Mary would undoubtedly have been infected, especially if the disease was to blame for all of the miscarriages which ended the Queen's earlier pregnancies. Mary, who lived into middle age, never showed any of the characteristics of congenital syphilis.

Without a doubt, Henry did *not* have syphilis. So why does the belief that he was syphilitic persist? What is it about this particular king that makes people want to believe he had a sexually transmitted disease? Come to think of it, what is it about Henry VIII that captures the imagination and spurs investigation into every lurid detail of his life?

Henry, unlike most of England's other Kings, is still vividly remembered more than 500 years after he ascended the throne and he remains an abiding topic of interest, not only for scholars but also for the public at large. He is the focus of academic study and popular entertainment, including books, documentaries, dramas, and blockbuster films. In contrast, think of Edward III. Few people other than historians know much about him, even though Edward III was an extremely important monarch who reigned for fifty years during a particularly eventful time in English history. Why is Henry VIII engraved on people's minds when so many other rulers, even strong ones such as Edward III, have faded from the public imagination? Perhaps it is due to his infamous reputation as a wife-killing tyrant and his ruthless quest for a male heir. Certainly most people find his marital exploits to be a fascinating story, full of intrigue, lust, murder, and power. From an academic standpoint, Henry's legacy centers mostly around his break with the Catholic Church, which laid the foundations for the Church of England. Considering that Henry's split with Rome was so momentous, it is ironic that he is probably more well-known for his connubial exploits and his obsession with fathering a son than for helping to change the religious climate of Europe.

The most famous of Henry's romances was his pursuit of, and eventual marriage to, Anne Boleyn. His passionate attachment to Anne began while he was still married to his first Queen, usually referred to as Catherine of Aragon, but who signed her name "Katherina", which will be the spelling used in this book. The public, and even many historians, have therefore viewed Anne as a home-wrecker who induced Henry to cast aside his first wife. She is often depicted as a calculating Jezebel who led Henry by the nose and encouraged his cruelty toward rivals, politicians, priests, the Catholic Church, Katherina, and even his daughter, Mary. Anne is frequently depicted as a schemer who destroyed a family, and the traditional forms of English worship, in order to get a crown. However, the fact her husband executed her on what appear to be false charges has also rendered her sympathetic. Even if she had seduced the King, did she deserve her gruesome fate? Curiosity about Henry and his relationship with his most famous ladylove has spawned hundreds of books, both serious historical accounts and titillating historical fiction. It is arguably one of the most famous love-triangles in the English-speaking world, and serves to keep Henry's life story at the forefront of popular culture.

Another part of Henry's allure may lie in the numerous unanswered questions about his extraordinary life. One of the most significant mysteries is his difficulty in obtaining a male heir. His six marriages produced only three living children. In fairness, there were some extenuating circumstances in his reproductive history with his later Queens. Jane

Seymour, his third wife, died before they could try for a second child. He never consummated his fourth marriage, and there is a strong possibility that he couldn't have sex with his sixth wife either. In spite of these explanations for the lack of offspring in his later marriages, it is notable that his reproductive attempts outside of wedlock were no more successful. Although Henry had few mistresses, compared to other kings of his era, there were still a number of young women he was sexually intimate with for an extended period of time, yet only one of his amours is definitely known to have given birth to a child he fathered. It is also suspicious that his first two Queens, Katherina of Aragon and Anne Boleyn, had such similar obstetric histories. Both women endured myriad stillbirths, miscarriages and neonatal deaths. Could this be attributed to living in an era without sufficient medical care, or to a physiological flaw in *both* of the women? It seems unlikely that the two women's experiences could mirror each other so closely simply due to chance. It seems more plausible that something about Henry VIII himself was actually the reason there were so few children in the royal nurseries. After all, he was the common factor in every single pregnancy.

A further cause of the persistent interest in Henry VIII is his dynamic image. Most people have seen the famous painting of the bloated, middle-aged King, standing with his fists anchored pugnaciously to his hips, wearing sumptuous clothes covered in embroidery and jewels. The force of his personality can still be felt, even from a two-dimensional depiction in oil. He appears to stare out of the portrait with his cold disdain for the viewer, secure in the knowledge that he holds the power of life or death over everyone around him. His appearance thoroughly matches his reputation as a brutal thug who murdered women when he tired of them.

    The celebrated portrayal of Henry as a philandering beast is the reason syphilis is so readily connected to his name. The acquisition of a sexually transmitted disease is, erroneously, culturally conceptualized as the end result of promiscuity, rather than of the bad luck of having one infected sex partner. There is a fixed social ideology about illnesses that are transmitted through sexual activity; there is an assumption that they are indicators of wanton lasciviousness on the part of the infected person, as opposed to being the unfortunate consequences of sex with a single infected partner. Sexually transmitted diseases are also socially imbued with a feeling of "punishment", a sort of retribution for an impure life, so the idea that the King could not easily have the son he wanted because he was infected with syphilis further reinforces this narrative. Henry is associated with a dissolute lifestyle, and was unable to beget a male heir until his third marriage, so *of course* he must have had syphilis. It provides a neat tie-in between the cultural trope about 'the kind of person' who gets sexually transmitted diseases and the King's characterization as a skirt-chasing monster. Nevertheless, beliefs about who *ought* to get sexually transmitted disease have no basis in reality, and the King did not have syphilis. Nor was he the immoral swine folklore has made him seem.

    Henry is popularly remembered as a fat, covetous, and womanizing lout, but this image is less than half the story. The aged King, with his cruel disdain for others and his harsh authoritarianism, is very different from his younger self. When Henry first ascended the throne he strove to bring harmony and chivalry to his court; he was not the contentious and brutal man he was to become. It was not until he was in his forties that the Henry of the popular myth emerges, the caricature of a corpulent, rancorous King with a disturbing habit of executing his subjects for little or no reason. By the time Henry was fifty, he had indeed turned into the savage behemoth of legend. The kind-hearted and loving monarch transformed into someone who could routinely behead friends, family, and wives without remorse. No one was safe; he was utterly merciless. When faced with the multiple atrocities he committed, it is hard for most people to imagine what a true Renaissance man Henry was when he was younger.

Why did Henry's personality alter so significantly after his fortieth birthday? What made him change from a reasonable and affable, albeit overly pampered and selfish, young monarch into a tyrannical madman? Furthermore, why did his health deteriorate so dramatically during the last fifteen or so years of his life? Was it a lack of proper nutrition and exercise, or some larger medical issue? Could either his personality change or his health problems be connected to his difficulties in fathering heirs?

Academics and non-academics alike have offered multiple theories to explain these mysteries. There are even questions and debates *about* the questions and debates. For example, there is a dispute about whether the first two children of his former mistress, Mary Boleyn, who was the older sister of his future wife, Anne Boleyn, were actually his progeny. If Mary Boleyn's children are really his, could he have had more illegitimate children that simply were not acknowledged at court? Did he actually have reproductive problems, or was he simply unfortunate enough to marry several women who all had compromised fertility? There is also serious disagreement about the nature of Henry's personality change. Some ask whether his personality really changed at all, and if it *did* change, when this change first took place (Starkey, 2008). Many historians argue that there was no sudden and abrupt change in the King's personality, maintaining that Henry simply grew older and more aware of his power, or that his failing health made him irritable, and that was the real cause of his tyranny (Scarisbrick, 1970; Smith, 1982). Alternatively, they argue that it was a change in circumstances and threats to his rule which pushed him into becoming a more ruthless monarch (Lipscomb, 2009). There is a further assertion that Henry had always been a narcissistic bully, but before his attempt to end his marriage to Katherina of Aragon no one had ever really challenged his will on anything important, and thus his true malevolence had lain dormant (Lindsey, 1995). Nevertheless, it is practically indisputable that his moodiness, paranoia, and erratic behavior became more extreme, and therefore more noticeable, after he turned forty.

Many people, from many different fields of study, have offered explanations for the enigmas which surround Henry VIII. There is conjecture about the effects of his diet, possible diseases, and the potential rhesus incompatibility of his wives, to name but a few. Does a combination of several factors account for all of his problems? Or is there a simpler answer? Could there be a medical reason to account for the high rate of miscarriage and stillbirths experienced by Henry and his unfortunate wives, as well as for his emotional instability and physical decline after midlife? Interestingly enough, there is something that could provide an answer all these questions -- and it involves Henry's blood.

Henry VIII hoped to be the legendary center of a new Camelot, and desired "to create such a fine opinion about his valor among all men that they could understand that his ambition was not merely to equal but to excel the glorious deeds of his ancestors" (Erickson, 1980:73). Sadly, it seems that the blood type he inherited from some of those ancestors had predestined him for distinction, but not in the manner he hoped. It is very plausible that the King's blood type was Kell positive (Whitley and Kramer, 2010). A person whose blood is Kell positive has an additional antigen on the surface of their red blood cells. Often being Kell positive does not cause an individual any significant trouble. However, sometimes a Kell blood type can have serious consequences, just like the problems that plagued Henry.

The Kell blood type, which the King would have inherited from his mother, was probably the cause of the troubles that have made him so prominent in the public imagination. For one thing, having a Kell positive blood type would explain why he had such difficulty siring heirs. Henry is seldom identified as the possible reason for the obstetrical losses of his first two wives, primarily because of the socio-cultural conditioning that makes most people, even medical professionals, assume that obstetrical issues are a 'female problem'. Henry might have been identified as the source of the trouble if none of his wives had become pregnant, but so few people are cognizant of the fact that the father can still cause negative reproductive outcomes even *after* conception that no one connected Henry with the miscarriages, stillbirths and newborn infant deaths. The myth that factors related to the father cannot affect a pregnancy after conception is so ingrained that even when people did speculate that the problem may have been caused by

Henry, they usually ascribed it to impotence or sterility. Considering the fact that the King's first two wives had at least eleven, and possibly thirteen or more, pregnancies, and the fact that he impregnated his third wife and one of his mistresses, it is obvious that *fertility* was not Henry's problem. Fetal and newborn mortality were the crux of his reproductive troubles, not an inability to get women pregnant.

The obstetrical losses suffered by Henry's first two Queens are similar to documented cases of Kell affected pregnancies (Whitley and Kramer, 2010), which only occur when the father of the fetus has a Kell positive blood type but the mother has the more common Kell negative blood type. When a Kell negative woman conceives a baby with a Kell positive man, she experiences Kell sensitization, wherein her body becomes "allergic" to any fetus that is Kell positive like the father. Although the first pregnancy is usually safe, since the mother's body needs at least one Kell positive pregnancy to become sensitised, any subsequent Kell positive fetus will almost always die. This means that a Kell negative woman whose partner is a Kell positive man has an increased risk of suffering from repeated late term miscarriages, stillbirths, and the death of her newborns shortly after they are delivered (Santiago, et al. 2008). This is exactly what happened to any woman who had more than one pregnancy with Henry VIII. If the King was Kell positive, there is nothing whatsoever that his Queens could have done to prevent the deaths of their babies, and they have therefore been mistakenly blamed for their tragic losses for centuries.

Since most people with the Kell positive blood type can pass either a Kell positive or a Kell negative gene on to their children, every pregnancy fathered by Henry had a chance of being Kell negative. A Kell negative fetus would not be attacked by the mother's antibodies and would have as much chance of survival as any other healthy baby born during this era. This explains why at least one of his children, Mary, survived even though she was not the first-born of Katherina of Aragon. If Mary, the fifth baby born to Henry's first Queen, did not get the Kell positive gene from her father then she would have been safe in the womb, unlike her Kell positive siblings. The pregnancies of Henry's second Queen, Anne Boleyn, were a textbook example of a healthy first child and subsequent late-term miscarriages; any of Anne's pregnancies conceived after the birth of her daughter, Elizabeth, had unsuccessful outcomes. Henry's third Queen, Jane Seymour, had only one child before her death, but a healthy firstborn is normal with a Kell positive father. The only mistress formally acknowledged to have given Henry a child was Bessie Blount, who produced a healthy firstborn son, but then had no more children by the King.

    A miserable history of lost babies is not the only thing Kell positive blood could have given Henry. If the King was Kell positive, then it is also possible that he developed a rare disease called McLeod syndrome, which occurs when a person has the "McLeod phenotype" of the Kell blood group (Miranda, et al., 2007). If you've never heard of McLeod syndrome before, you are not alone. It isn't well known except to a few doctors who are specialists in this kind of blood-antigen linked illness. Usually the symptoms of McLeod syndrome begin around a patient's fortieth birthday, and increase with time. McLeod syndrome has both physical and psychological symptoms that would explain why Henry became physically weaker and more mentally unstable after he turned forty in 1531, and why his condition continued to deteriorate until his death in 1547. McLeod syndrome explains why such a dashing young King who wanted to be the flower of English chivalry in his youth made such bad political decisions and had so many of his wives, friends and family executed in his middle age.

There is extreme difficulty in proving, beyond doubt, that Henry suffered from McLeod syndrome. For one thing, historical records may not have noted many of the symptoms needed to diagnose his condition. Additionally, symptoms may have been recorded in a manner which makes them difficult to correlate to modern diagnostic criteria. As a result, it is difficult to confirm exactly how *many* of the physical symptoms consistent with McLeod syndrome the King actually displayed. Moreover, he had other aliments which also affected his health. This problem of "co-morbidity" makes it very difficult to be sure precisely which aspects of his ill-health were caused by McLeod syndrome.

Take, for example, the well-known fact that Henry found it increasingly difficult to walk as he grew older. He had the "worst legs in the world" and was often wheeled around in a "tram", or traveling chair (Erickson, 1980:360). This could have been a result of McLeod syndrome, since a patient with this illness will often experience muscle weakness and nerve deterioration, especially in his lower limbs (Wada et al., 2003). However, taking this as conclusive evidence on which to base a diagnosis of McLeod syndrome would be problematic because he had other health problems that could have affected his ability to walk. It has been convincingly argued that the King had osteomyelitis, a chronic bone infection that makes it very painful to walk (Keynes, 2005:180). Furthermore he was, without question, vastly overweight by the time he entered his fifties. His lack of mobility may have been as much a consequence of his excessive bulk, coupled with his agonizing leg ulcers, as it was a result of McLeod syndrome. For obvious reasons the passage of time makes it impossible to figure out *exactly* which malady was causing which problem for the King. To further complicate the issue, there is extreme inconsistency in the severity of symptoms associated with McLeod syndrome. It is normal for McLeod sufferers to exhibit symptoms to differing degrees, so that one patient may have noticeable facial tics while another patient displays no facial tics at all.

Obviously the physical problems the King suffered were varied and are hard to pin on just one cause, but Henry's mental and emotional symptoms provide stronger evidence for the McLeod theory. The psychological symptoms experienced by patients with McLeod syndrome include erosion of memory and executive functions, paranoia, depression, socially inappropriate conduct, irrational personality alterations, and even schizophrenia-like behaviors (Whitley and Kramer, 2010; Jung and Haker, 2004). In some severe cases the schizophrenia-like symptoms and personality changes are the key to diagnosing McLeod syndrome (Jung and Haker, 2004:723). There is certainly strong evidence to suggest that Henry underwent a significant personality change after his fortieth birthday, in a manner consistent with the mental problems that are often linked to McLeod syndrome.

As a young man, Henry was a handsome, genial, and rational ruler. The youthful King was described, in the private letters of more than one foreign ambassador or other court contemporary, as having incredible physical beauty. His hair was red, he had very fair skin, and his face was considered as lovely as that of "a pretty woman" (Scarisbrick, 1970:13). Even in 1531, when the King was middle-aged and had lost the golden glow of youth, the Venetian ambassador to England, Ludovico Falieri, found reasons to heap praise on England's monarch, writing that:

> "In the 8th Henry such beauty of mind and body is combined as to surprise and astonish. Grand stature, suited to his exalted position, showing the superiority of mind and character; a face like an angel's, so fair is it; his head bald like Caesar's, and he wears a beard, which is not the English custom. He is accomplished in every manly exercise, sits his horse well, tilts with his lance, throws the quoit, shoots with his bow excellent well; he is a fine tennis player, and he practices all these gifts with the greatest industry. Such a prince could not fail to have cultivated also his character and his intellect. He has been a student since his childhood; he knows literature, philosophy, and theology; speaks and writes Spanish, French, and Italian, besides Latin and English. He is kind, gracious, courteous, liberal, especially to men of learning, whom he is always ready to help. He appears religious also, generally hears two masses a day, and on holy days High Mass besides. He is very charitable, giving away ten thousand gold ducats annually among orphans, widows and cripples." (Froude, 32-33:1891)

Henry was also uncommonly tall for his time, well over six feet, with the chiseled physique of a champion athlete. The fact he was an excellent dancer and a model of chivalry further added to his attractiveness. He was a master horseman, able to ride for more than thirty miles without needing a break. He also excelled at jousting, consistently outperforming any of his court contemporaries. Since jousting was a dangerous and demanding sport with the potential to cause severe injuries, or even death, the King's skill and athleticism was no small matter. He hunted almost every day, ignoring bad weather to pursue his prey for hours at a time. Henry also played an excellent game of tennis, a sport that was more like modern squash than tennis as we know it in modern times, which required a lot of physical exertion. This kind of active lifestyle meant that the King remained a gorgeous court luminary until he was in his forties, when he had to stop, or at least restrict the amount of his participation in, most forms of exercise because of his chronic pain.

    In addition to his physical accomplishments, the King had a brilliant mind. Henry's intellect impressed many of the most famous thinkers of his day. Although Henry would one day set England down the path to a complete separation from the Church of Rome, he was a devout Catholic until his midlife, and he even wrote a book in 1521 defending Catholicism from the criticisms of Martin Luther, entitled *Assertio Septem Sacramentorum*, which when translated from Latin means "The Defense of the Seven Sacraments". Notwithstanding his devotion to his religion, when he was young the King was not the implacable zealot he became in his later life. Early in his reign Henry enjoyed theological debates and would listen to opinions which differed from his own with remarkable calm. Erasmus, the famed Dutch scholar and priest who was one of the most renowned humanists of the Renaissance, praised Henry highly. Erasmus called the young King a "universal genius", and wrote that Henry "never neglected his studies; and whenever he has leisure from his political occupations, he reads, or disputes -- of which he is very fond -- with remarkable courtesy and unruffled temper" (Pollard, 1919:123). The King was not just well-mannered and gracious in matters of religion: he was lauded for his easy-going and cheerful nature in general. He also had an almost insatiable curiosity and interest in mental pursuits. He was taught mathematics, engineering, and astronomy by the most learned men in his kingdom. He spoke several languages, and was as fluent in Latin and French as he was in his native tongue. Moreover, he respected the pursuit of knowledge, establishing the Royal College of Physicians in 1518 and endowing two Regius Professorships in medicine at Oxford and Cambridge in 1540 (Furdell, 2001:9).

Adding to the bounty of accomplishments with which he was gifted, Henry was musically adept. He was an amazing musician who could play several instruments. Moreover, he could sing beautifully and certainly appreciated the vocal talents of others. The King employed almost sixty musicians for his entertainment and accepted only the very best singers in England for his Chapel Royal; the music of the Chapel was so good it was described as "more divine than human" by a visitor to his court (Roden et al., 2009:278). His interest in music was not just limited to playing and singing what others had written; he also composed his own melodies. The King's musical interests serve to illustrate his keen intellect, since modern research shows that the brains of people who are musically talented are highly developed, making musicians more broadminded and curious about learning new things (Travis et al., 2011).

It is hard for the modern reader to understand just how spectacular Henry must have seemed to those around him. To get a comparison, you would need to envision a man so athletically superb that he could win Olympic medals in several sports, make him as beautiful as any male supermodel, have him be fluent in three languages, then give him the ability to compose critically-acclaimed classical music, and finally have him earn a Ph.D in both engineering and Latin. Now, think of him as heir to the English crown as well. Only then would you have a good idea of how impressive Henry appeared to his contemporaries.

In spite of all his talents, the King was not an intense killjoy devoted to practicing his many skills. Far from it. When he was younger the King also enjoyed more relaxed pursuits, such as card games and other kinds of friendly gambling. He obviously didn't value winning enough to cheat, because he frequently lost huge sums during games of cards or dice (Loades, 1992:96). He must have been, contrary to his popular image, a very good loser, since there was never any retaliation against those who won large amounts of money from him. This did not mean he gambled foolishly. He quickly figured out when he was being scammed at cards by a group of French con men, and had them dismissed from his court (Scarisbrick, 1968:19). Not only did the King love games of chance, he was not snobbish or elitist about his gaming partners; between 1527 and 1539 he often played with his sergeant of the cellar, Robert Hill, who was a upper-level member of the kitchen staff. Hill would have been in charge of keeping track of the beer, wine, and ale consumed by Henry's household, a position far removed from the court luminaries the King could summon for games if he wanted to (Sim, 1997:33). The easy-going, cheerful, and gregarious nature of the King is a far cry from the monstrous bully that most people believe him to have been.

Although he clearly had his virtues, Henry was not a saint. Even during his youth it can be argued he was egocentric, with a propensity to show off. These qualities should probably be expected in such a talented young man, considering that athletic and musical talent were no less appreciated in the Tudor period than they are today. When such abilities are combined in a man who had been taught to believe that he was God's chosen leader of the English people, "and by the very logic of his office could do no wrong" (Smith, 1982:25), he could hardly fail to develop a swollen ego. Henry was considered the embodiment of England, and was the most important man in his Kingdom. He was so relentlessly flattered and feted by those who wished to profit from his favors that it would have been nothing short of miraculous if he had not been conceited and spoiled. Certainly the young King was vain about his looks, as he had every reason to be.

Henry was also something of a slave to the concept of romance. He loved to woo and flatter the ladies of his court, but this does not mean he was a lecherous womanizer. He formed amours for various women, and often overestimated his appeal to all members of the fairer sex, but he was so devoted to the concept of chivalry that he was never a coarse libertine. He wrote poems and sent women presents and needed to believe that the heart was always present in the bedroom; he was neither a lecher nor a rapist.

One cannot help but wonder how this man, who gave every indication of being a magnanimous and progressive sovereign, could have become the hidebound and reactionary dictator of his later rule. How did a man so devoted to the chivalrous ideal go on to legally murder his wives? The change seems so preposterous that it almost *requires* a medical explanation for the difference. What else could have affected him so strongly, in such a short time?

Even those historians who do not believe Henry experienced a radical alteration in character cannot help but recognize that the King behaved very differently in his old age than he did in his youth. Lacey Baldwin Smith, a well-respected biographer of Henry VIII, observes that in his youth Henry was "a man of honour, a warrior knight and a noble gentleman" (1982: 25), but in his later years he "became the most dangerous kind of tyrant, secretive, neurotic and unpredictable" (1982: 268). Moreover, Smith noted that since the day of the King's death, "apologists and critics have been struggling to penetrate the ambivalence of Henry's personality. Two images keep merging and reappearing: the angelic-faced athlete who inherited a brimming treasury, a stable throne, and boundless good health, and the Henry of later years who ... [died] degenerate in body and soul" (2009:123). Another distinguished historian, David Starkey, acknowledges that "Henry's is a life which naturally falls in halves" (2008:7), meaning that the Henry who was crowned in 1509 "is not the same as the man who revises [the coronation oath] . . twenty-odd years later" (2008:7). Other scholars are more willing to concede that Henry's personality did change abruptly. Recently, historian Susannah Lipscomb argued that a distinct difference in Henry's personality emerged in 1536, and that many of "the flaws in his character were fashioned or catalyzed by the events of this one year" (Lipscomb, 2009:205). There is also speculation that Henry sustained brain damage when he fell from his horse while jousting, in 1536, explaining a rapid and radical switch in his behavior (Lipscomb, 2009:205). A brain injury in 1536 is not, however, a satisfactory answer for the King's personality change, since he showed signs of the transformation several years earlier (Whitley and Kramer, 2010:839). What is certain is that Henry's moodiness, paranoia, and erratic behavior progressively became worse, and he became "markedly more distrustful and despotic" (Lipscomb, 2009:184) during the last 15 years of his life .

    The theory that Henry had a Kell positive blood type and McLeod syndrome is the result of extrapolating from historical clues. As any historian will attest, piecing together the facts from the bits of information which survived for centuries is very difficult. Often information is gleaned from letters written about court gossip and relaying only second-hand knowledge. Additionally, the writers of those letters were not impartial. The court teemed with intrigue and factional jockeying for power. Those who were in the favor of certain ministers, or wives, of the King could view the same event very differently. For example, those who favored unchanged Catholicism, and Henry's first Queen, were naturally hostile toward Anne Boleyn and wrote scathing reports of both her and the King. Those who favored religious reform and were sympathetic towards Henry's need for a male heir wrote much kinder assessments of Anne.
    A great deal of what we know about Henry's court and scandals during the time of his relationship with Anne comes from the letters of Eustace Chapuys, one of Queen Katherina's most ardent supporters and the ambassador of her nephew, Charles V of Spain. They are well written, descriptive, and detailed. However, are they as accurate as they are plentiful? It was in Chapuys' interest to portray Katherina as favorably as possible, and to describe Anne as a wanton, vicious, dangerous harpy. He clearly wanted Charles V to invade England and remove Henry, who had hurt Katherina and was openly rebelling against Papal authority, from his throne, thus allowing Katherina's only daughter, Mary, to rule in Henry's place. Chapuys was far from unbiased, and he was skilled in political

maneuvering. Lord Paget described Chapuys as "without respect of honesty or truth ... He is a great practicer, with which honest term we cover tale-telling, lying, dissimulating, and flattering" (Froude, 112:1891). This is probably unfair, but it does show that not everyone agreed with Chapuys' version of events. Yet historians frequently use his letters to ascertain the "truth" of Henry's situation and actions. Often this is from necessity. There is only scanty evidence left after the passage of 500 years, and Chapuys is frequently the closest scholars can come to an eyewitness account of life at Henry's court.

Considering the challenges that face historians in their attempts to ascertain the truth, imagine, if you will, how difficult it has been to make a medical diagnosis just by using information gleaned from those same slanted historical records. How can there ever be certainty about whether or not Henry was in the Kell positive blood group and suffered from McLeod syndrome? Fortunately, there are genetic markers for the suspected conditions, and new techniques for extracting DNA from very old remains. Thus, if Henry's body were exhumed for analysis, a DNA test could prove, beyond doubt, if the King had Kell positive blood and McLeod syndrome. However, until such analysis is allowed, historical clues will have to suffice.

The idea that Henry had McLeod syndrome is an important one. If the King's brain functions were compromised because of McLeod syndrome, his successively more paranoid and violent behavior would have been a result of his illness, rather than because he was a psychopathic murderer. One of the biggest tragedies about Henry VIII is that few people remember the fair and caring monarch he was when he first ascended the throne; most simply remember the vile despot he became. It is a shame that Henry is remembered not for the lives he spared before he was thirty-nine, but rather for the lives he took after he reached his forties. If the King had McLeod syndrome then he was as much a victim of his own illness as the people that his condition compelled him to execute. Whatever he became, the young idealist who took the throne in the spring of 1509, who was so warmly praised by Erasmus as a "lover of justice and goodness" (Erickson, 1980:62), deserves to be remembered just as much as the bloodthirsty tyrant he was when he died more than four decades later. It would be appalling were Henry to remain condemned for behavior he could not control.

CHECK OUT THE COMPLETE WORK, AVAILABLE IN BOTH EBOOK AND PAPERBACK THROUGH AMAZON.COM.

Printed in Great Britain
by Amazon